The African American Christian Man: Reclaiming the Village

Eddie B. Lane

The African American Christian Man:
Reclaiming the Village

Copyright © 1997 by Eddie B. Lane

Unless otherwise indicated, Scripture is taken from the *Holy Bible, New International Version* © 1973, 1978, 1984, the International Bible Society, used by permission of Zondervan Bible Publishers.

Publisher:

Black Family Press
1810 Park Row
Dallas, TX 75215
(214) 428-3761

Published in the United States of America

Cover Design: Fame Publishing, Inc.

DEDICATION

This volume is dedicated to

my son,

Eddie B. Lane II,

who has developed

into a man

with his own distinct personality and identity

and yet reflects so much

of my own character and personality.

My prayer is

that God will use him

in ways that bring glory

to Himself

through His church.

TABLE OF CONTENTS

TABLE OF CONTENTS

PART 3

THE PROCESS OF DEVELOPING
UNFRAGMENTED AFRICAN AMERICAN MEN

PART 4

THE CHALLENGE IN DEVELOPING
UNFRAGMENTED AFRICAN AMERICAN MEN

ACKNOWLEDGMENTS

I must thank a number of people who so graciously gave of their time and money to the production of this book. These people include Mary Helen Crossland, Don and Charlotte Test, Dr. Willie O. Peterson, Dr. Nathaniel Craft Jr., Frank Tan and the membership of Bibleway Church. Above all, my deepest thanks to my wife Betty, my companion now for almost four decades.

PREFACE

As I watched the coming together of black men in Washington D.C. on October 16, 1995 in what was to become one of the largest and most significant gatherings of black men in the history of African American men (the million man march), it occurred to me that these men were not mere representatives of the Black community, or what one would call "The Village." They were the Black community.

Two strong premonitions consumed me as I played out the role of an observer to this gathering of black men. The first thought was that the media would surely put a spin on this gathering that would seriously underrepresent the actual number of men who attended the march. My second strong impression was that the African American clergy to which I belong would seek to discredit the gathering by labeling it as something other than what it really was.

Unfortunately my instincts were right on both counts. On the one hand, the media moguls proved unwilling to acknowledge the evident bond that existed between black men of all socioeconomic status. In addition this gathering of black men presented before the world a different image of African American men which vastly contrasts with the negative stereotypes that are seen around the world everyday on both national and international media outlets.

On the other hand, the Black church clergy for the first time found itself on the margins of a major movement in the Black community, one of which they were not in charge of. In the minds of most African American clergymen the million man march was not a good thing. But their problem in labeling the march as something less than good was compounded by the fact that so many who participated in the march were themselves clergy and lay leaders hailing from the church.

The Black clergy's difficulty stems from their reluctance to admit that while being the leaders of the strongest institution in the Black community, namely, the Black church, they lacked the power and ability to gather a million black men together in any city in this country. The Black church can at best rally a million or more *women* in one gathering but unfortunately at this point in our history not a million men.

This inability of the church to summon together a million men for a march is symptomatic of the crisis we face in reclaiming "The Village," the African American community. The church has forfeited in recent years much of its influence among black men in the Black community. It is my contention that unless we first reclaim the men of the Village it will not be possible to reclaim the Village itself.

In thinking through the concept of *Reclaiming the Village* I have reflected time and again on the biblical account of Nehemiah's life. Nehemiah in my mind was one of, if not, the greatest urbanologist the world has ever known. At a time when the city of Jerusalem was in ruins and the prospects of the Jewish people were in serious decline Nehemiah responded to the challenge of *reclaiming the Village*, in his case the Jewish community. He did it not by giving away funds or suggesting various social programs to help his people's welfare. Instead Nehemiah relocated from his acquired upper middle class status, taking leave of his executive position in the king's cabinet, and moved into urban Jerusalem which had become little more than a slum settlement. Nehemiah moved back among his people.

After setting up residence in the city among his own people, Nehemiah took his first step towards reclaiming the village by acquiring for himself a firsthand knowledge of the social and economic conditions in the city. Then, before attempting to do anything at all by way of improvement, he first gathered all the men together and called attention to the dire conditions in the city which they had otherwise learned to live with. To reclaim the Village *Nehemiah began with the men* who lived in the community.

In order to reclaim the Village of the African American community the first order of business in my view must be to obtain a perspective on the need for leadership and role models in the Village. To this end I observed in the past history of the Black community that the men and women who have emerged as models and leaders in the Village were for the most part from the Black middle-class. I therefore suggest that we should also look to the Black middle-class for models and leadership for the Village of today.

In the Jewish community context of Nehemiah's day and as in ours the process of urban renewal is best led by one who has the abilities, the burden and the resources with which to start and finish the job. It is also well to remember that the urban renewal program that Nehemiah led was never simply about the slum community; it was equally concerned with the mentality of the people who lived in the community.

It is my contention that we raise up people, men and women, who not only have the burden for *Reclaiming the Village* but are equipped with the necessary resources by which they can renew the minds and the spirit of the people. Thus this book attempts to focus on what in my mind is the most essential task of our mission to *Reclaim the Village* which is to deliver a generation of unfragmented men, an increasingly-scarce resource today.

One final remark, unapologetically of a theological tenor, is of crucial importance. At the center of the Village of which I speak lies the family, itself an analogy of Trinitarian, Christological, ecclesiological and sacramental communal life. This family, in accord with the biblical record, is the micro interpersonal dynamic of the male-female relationship with children, if present, being parasitic to that primordial relationship. It does not necessarily follow from the argument herein expressed about male leadership on this micro level that the macro socio-cultural relational structures follow a similar pattern. Concretely, it does not follow from the argument of male leadership in the micro interpersonal male-female relationship that political, corporate or ecclesial leadership be male also. On the contrary, my argument is that macro socio-cultural leadership, whether female or male, functions optimally only insofar as it is grounded on the interpersonal micro dynamic.

Admittedly, the social ontology presumed, not argued, throughout this study follow from a certain theological reading of the biblical narratives. Nonetheless, I am not willing to jettison the theological "meta-narrative" herein employed in the face of "postmodern" calls to do so. Due to the nature of theological inquiry, I am willing, however, to test it. This book is a first installment on the test. My next book—concerning the African American Christian woman—will be the second.

PART 1

THE NEED TO DEVELOP UNFRAGMENTED AFRICAN AMERICAN MEN

INTRODUCTION

A HISTORICAL REFLECTION

The African American male possesses a unique history that is both distinct and distinguishable from all other men in North America. That history began a few hundred years ago on the continent of Africa, in general, and West Africa, in particular. A young African prince simply stepped outside of his father's hut to relieve himself as he had previously done on so many other occasions. This one time, instead of returning to his family, he found himself stuffed in the bowels of a ship on his way to slavery in North America, along with thousands of other young Black African men who had similarly fallen victims to the same fate.

To the horror of these young Black African men, especially those who proved to be fit and survived the long journey, they eventually disembarked and were quickly herded on to a farm in one of the slave states in the United States of America.

These young men who were probably guilty of nothing more than having relieved themselves in the bush never bargained for those trips across the Atlantic. Even less did they expect to be stripped of all their humanity, personhood and culture. In American they were mere chattel.

Standing on the threshold of the twenty first century, it is well to reflect on African American history in North America and remind ourselves that we are only a half-step away from the nightmare of slavery that officially ended around 1860 but unofficially still exists throughout America today in the forms of racial prejudice and discrimination.

Bringing up the subject of slavery evokes even today a sense of guilt for many White Americans. They seem more willing to focus on Post-Emancipation African American history. The African American is no less uncomfortable with the subject of slavery than their White counterparts. We tend to glean from the topic of slavery a sense of shame. African Americans, too, are well-content to abandon the subject altogether and move on to other matters as if slavery never happened.

The subject of slavery must never be allowed to pass away from the minds of North Americans, regardless of race or generation, because slavery, more than any other factor or historical event, shaped permanently the racial, religious, political, social and economic context of North America today. The imprint of slavery remains fresh in America's race relations and the effects of that imprint is felt still throughout the world. It truly can be said of America, "Race matters." Today, as the twentieth century ends and the twenty-first century dawns, racial divisions and nationalistic pride are pushing America to the brink of a catastrophic race war. It can be said today of America, "Race matters."

Writing this book on *African American Christian Men: Reclaiming the Village,* I am mindful of the fact that as a father I have a son who stands on the brink of adult manhood. This young man, my son, has genetic ties and, to some extent, cultural cords intertwined in the very fiber of his being both internally and externally that stretch all the way back through several generations in this country to the African continent. It is with this implication in mind that I begin reflections on the historical roots of the African American male.

My historical reflection begins with the initial arrival in North America of the ancestors of the modern day African American male. With few exceptions a North American Black male arrived as a slave. The Black Africans forced into slavery were snatched from the region of West Africa in the seventeenth century, beginning around 1619. The setting of West Africa at that time was one of a civilized people with their own religion, economic base, language, government and family structure.

According to sociologists such as Andrew Billingsly, the West African family structure in the seventieth century was not structured around the specific couples who married, i.e. the husband and the wife, but rather marriage was treated as an extended family and tribal connection. The idea of a couple getting married by themselves was basically unheard of in that extended family situation. In the West African village of the 1600s marriage was a family or tribal event in which brides and grooms were chosen by their respective tribes and the marriage became a tribal or village affair.

The family blood line of the Africans taken as slaves was traced sometimes through the family of the bride and at other times through the family of the groom. On occasion the blood line of the children was traced through both the families of the bride and the groom. Children born into the West African family context belonged to the village not just the birth parents.

But by the time the African men arrived in America they were stripped of their humanity that they were classified as subhumans at best with no sense of family. American history has rarely noted the fact that the West African ancestors of African Americans taken as slaves in the seventeenth century were men of noble African stock with strong family ties. The general consensus assumed by many is that those ancestors of African Americans who were slaves in America were male subhumanlike creatures with no sense of family.

But that first generation of young men taken from West Africa was skilled in farming such crops as cotton, rice, tobacco and a host of other profitable crops. In addition they were proficient in caring for cattle and other domesticated animals. Thus they proved to be productive farmers in North America because they brought with them skills in growing crops for the plantations in the agrarian South that was not unlike the crops they grew in West Africa.

There is an old notion suggesting that black-skinned West Africans were better fitted for plantation life as slaves because they could endure the heat and the hard labor better than either Anglo or Native Americans could. The truth is that African men survived plantation life as slaves where others did not because they had developed immunity to malaria that was carried by mosquitoes that bred prolifically on wetlands. Whites and Native Americans did not have such immunity to the fever. In addition just having survived the trans-Atlantic trip from West Africa to America while crammed in overcrowded filthy vessels evidenced a superior physical condition. Only the most physically fit of the young men, oftentimes of noble heritage, on these vessels survived the long journey.

The slave trade merchandised the packaging, advertising, buying and selling of black flesh, a human commodity. Human cargo was commonly referred to as "Black gold." These valuable African men were captured like wild animals and herded together in holding pens up and down the coast of West Africa until ships came to carry them to the Americas. A profitable business, the head count of the young men stripped and shipped from Africa swelled into the millions.

Unfortunately, the young age at which the men were

brought as slaves to America combined with years of intensive De-Africanization meant that little of their native language, religion, culture or traditions survived. However, the farming skill these men possessed was preserved. Thus an African who was snatched from his village as a young cultured man, perhaps of Nobel birth, arrived in North America on a plantation essentially as a person without culture, tradition, family relation, native language or any speck of dignity. In North America there was no village, and he was mere property in the hands of a cruel taskmaster. Regardless of the previous status of the young African male back home in his West African village, in North America he was mere chattel without the dignity of humanity.

I often hear middle class Blacks and young Whites say that it is time to put the whole subject of slavery behind us and move on. Young Whites claim slavery was not their doing and the Blacks say slavery was not their experience. Yet for the African American male psyche as a whole, slavery was the most horrific and psychologically and emotionally destructive experience that could ever be imagined. Its detrimental effect still echoes across centuries.

To suggest that African American males can put slavery behind them, ignore this part of their history and move on is tantamount to suggesting that the Jews put the Holocaust behind them and move on. Accordingly, slavery's legacy remains to this day a significant part of the psychological and emotional baggage of the contemporary African American.

As a slave the black man was stripped of his personhood and with it went his manhood and all that is involved in being a husband and a father. For the most part the slave system disregarded the role of the male as it pertained to family. In fact, legally speaking in most of the American states, there was no such thing as a slave's family. The slave master could at his/her discretion sell off the members of a slave family to whomever he/she wished.

For the purpose of psychologically oppressing and permanently brainwashing the Black male slave, the slave industry created and promoted a demeaning personality identified as "Black Sambo." In this profile black men in general were characterized as lazy but loyal, dishonest, deceitful, irresponsible, childish, dependent and a host of other unmanly traits. This Sambo personality in short order became the standard personality and character profile of all black men both slave and free.

Rosemary Reuther notes that the contemporary cords of evil as they are configured in modern day racism, has as its goal the eradication of the image of God in Black males. She wrote the following observations:

> The characteristics of racism is that it puts the category "man" below the category of a particular racial group. The species becomes the mode for defining the authentic nature of the genus, so that everyone outside the group is defined as not truly "a man" . . . The rejected group is always pictured as passive, dependent, unstable, emotional, potentially vicious, subject to unrestrained passions, lacking in true intelligence and reasoning powers. All this is summed up in the conclusion that the group is not full or truly "human."
>
> The oppressed group internalizes this image and look with contempt upon itself. Even its forms of sabotage of the power of the dominant society tends to be self-weakening, taking the form of that "laziness" that attempts to survive under the lash by appearing in contempt. The oppressor also is dehumanized by this false relationship, for he receives no authentic communication from the oppressive role, but receives back only a mask donned by the oppressed to reflect the demands of those in power. Revolt against this oppressive relationship then is really a demand for the truth and order in an unlawful and disorderly universe. The "law and order" of the oppressor is a false order. The rebel against oppression is demanding a true order based on the common nature of all men.[1]

This stereotype of black men persists even today, in spite of the fact that there never was a flesh and blood "Black Sambo." The Sambo personality was conceived, incubated, born and developed in the White community and imported into the Black community solely in and out of the evil imaginations of the human heart.

It is interesting to note that in the case of the Black female, the image of "Aunt Jemima" became the predominant characterization. This personality profile was designed to prevent any possibility of black women detracting from the beauty of White women, the idea being that real female beauty was exclusively a White female quality. It tried to preclude the possibility of a White man being attracted to a black woman. However, while the Aunt Jemima stereotype of black women faded away the Black Sambo image of black men has remained to this day.

---

[1] Rosemary Reuther, *Liberation Theology: Human Hope Confronts Christian History and American Power* (New York: Paulist Press, 1972), p.129.

A CONTEMPORARY VIEW:
TROUBLE IN THE VILLAGE

It is obvious that the history of the African American male in North America has always been a struggle. From the southern agrarian plantations to the urban concrete factories in America's major metropolitan cities the Black male has consistently struggled to find his worth and see himself as an equal with other men.

Few people dispute the fact that today's African American male have what often seems like more than their share of difficulties in the urban inner city. However, the urban Black youth are showing progress in the realm of education in spite of their social and economic difficulties. In the last four years the number of college graduates among young black men has increased significantly. This increase in Black college graduates is largely coming from African American colleges.

Although educational progress appears to be on the rise in the "Village," the Black community, there are also present signs of serious problems. In 1987 it was reported that 39% of all youth held in police custody were Black. Black male juveniles are four times more likely to be imprisoned for a violent crime than are White male juveniles.

This judicial bias is most evident in the distinction made between a man arrested for the possession, selling or use of crack cocaine and the possession, selling and/or use of powdered cocaine. The penalty for crack cocaine is much heavier than the penalty for use of powdered cocaine. I submit that the difference in punishment is not reflective of the difference in the nature of the crime but of the race and culture of the offenders. Crack cocaine is a poor man's drug sold mostly on urban streets while powder cocaine is the favorite drug of the white-collar middle class White man.

In a *New York Times* column entitled "The Myth of Black Violence" written by Evan Stark in July 18, 1990, evidence was presented to refute the notion that black youth are more "violent-prone" than are White youth.

Citing statistics from FBI crime reports, Stark tentatively surmised that homicide is the major cause of death for younger Black males, as well as for black women under 40. Inner city blacks appear to be particularly violent-prone. The homicide rate for young black males living in standard metropolitan areas is twice that for young blacks living in other locations. The figures on black teenagers seem more ominous still. From 1977 to 1982 more than half of juvenile arrests for the most violent crimes were among black teenagers, and the relative rate of incarceration for black as against white youth was an astounding 44 to 1.

However, following the argument made by Ryan and Parenti, that data of the kind just cited is more indicative of police (as well as average White American) attitudes and behavior than of racial differences. Stark states that the alternative view is supported by national surveys of crime victims as a far more accurate source of information about crime committed than arrest reports. According to the FBI, for example, the proportion of blacks arrested for aggravated assault in 1987 was more than three times greater than the proportion of Whites. But the National Crime Survey, based on victim interviews, found that the actual proportion of blacks and Whites committing aggravated assault in 1987 was virtually identical: 32 per 1,000 for blacks; 31 per 1,000 for Whites.

Similarly, the National Youth Survey involved 1,725 youths 11 to 17 years of age, whose law-violating behavior between 1976 and 1980 was determined by confidential interviews. The survey reported that, with the exception of 1976, no significant race differences were found in any of the violent or serious offense scale.

Based on the evidence Stark concluded that black youth are no more "violent-prone" than are White youth and that "race does not determine who initiates violence." However, Stark notes the disturbing fact that "fatal outcomes are far more likely when blacks are involved (in violence)."[2]

> We are piling up a human scrap heap of between 250,000 and 500,000 people a year. Blacks have outlived their usefulness. Their raison d'etre to this society has ceased to be a compelling issue. Once an economic asset, Blacks are now considered an economic drag. The wood is all hewn, the water all drawn, the cotton all picked, and the rails reach from coast to coast. The ditches are dug, the dishes put away, and only a few shoes remain to be shined.

[2] Amos N. Wilson, *Black-On-Black Violence* (New York: Afrikan World Infosys, 1990), pp. 23-24.

Thanks to old Black backs and newfangled machines, the sweat chores of the nation are done. Today's 25 million Blacks face a society that is brutally pragmatic, technologically accomplished, deeply racist, increasingly overcrowded and surly. In such a society the absence of social and economic value is a crucial factor in anyone's fight for a future.

— Samuel F. Yette, author of
The Choice: The Issue of Black Survival in America

In America today twelve states and Washington D.C. imprison Blacks ten times faster than Whites. In the "Village" one of every four black men is in some way under the watchful eye of the penal system, i.e., prison, parole, probation, etc. The United States as a whole incarcerates African Americans at a rate that is at least 7.66 times higher than the rate for Whites. The State of Texas leads the list of states where blacks are most likely to be locked up, followed by Louisiana, South Carolina, Oklahoma and Nevada.

In the "Village" it often seems as if the more things change the more they remain the same. For instance, in the context of slavery marriage between black men and black women had no recognized legal standing in a court of law. Later, in the context of urban communities following the Southern migration, black men found that it was economically more advantageous to abandon their wives and children to the welfare system than to remain with them.

Today many young blacks decide to abandon their homes because of their inability to support their families financially. Quite a few are often limited by their education. Their educational deficiencies are compounded by their parents and public school teachers who have accepted failure in education by black boys and youth as common and normal. The media also contributes by portraying them as irresponsible and immoral. The negative and biased portrayal of young African American males influences Black and White public school teachers and administrators to assume that young black men are not worth helping.

After reading my book *The African American Christian Single: Keeping a Clean Life in a Dirty World* (Black Family Press, 1996) in which I pointed out that black women outnumbered black men by five to one in terms of availability for marriage, a group of female college students asked me what right did I have to make such a statement even if it was true. I responded that it is about time that we admit to ourselves that there are real troubles in the Village.

It is highly common to find African American Christian single women asking their pastors, friends and church family to pray that God will give them a husband. As a pastor for more than thirty years I am well aware of the fact that God can do anything He wants to, including finding husbands for single black women. However, it is also time that we should recognize that in the Village we are rapidly running out of eligible black men to marry our African American daughters.

The shortage of marriageable black men constitutes a serious problem that we as a community must face because of the impact such a shortage will ultimately have on the morality of our women. I am reminded of a singles' conference I was involved in recently where a sister said, "The only thing we need from the African American brother is what is in his Calvin Kleins." The young single sister went on to point out that she, like most other African American women, had her education, career, job, car, money, home, and clothes; the only thing she lack was an African American man with whom to sleep with and have children.

Like it or not, this narrowly-defined need for the African American male is increasingly being echoed by young successful black women in the Village. Their needs dramatically suggest an urgent problem in the village that must be attended to now. Unfortunately, there are no magic buttons to push that will instantly fix this state of affairs in the Village. We must begin our task of reclaiming the village by admitting to our women the truth, namely, that we can no longer assume that there will be an African American man available for them to marry.

I propose that to reclaim the village we must find and fix the problems that negatively affect the education of black boys in public school and college. We must also find ways of keeping our sons out of prison and keeping them away from drugs and gangs.

The fastest growing industry in America today is the business of prisons. There are over a million prisons in the United States today, representing a growth of over three times the number in the 1970's. New prison constructions are a multi-billion dollar industry today. This has pushed the United States to the top of the list of countries with the most number of prisons; we are second only to Russia in the number of people being incarcerated. In 1993 the rate of incarceration of African American males reached 3,109 per 100,000 people which is six times the national average. The facts seem to suggest that throughout the justice system of arrests, pretrial hearings, convictions, sentencing, imprisonment and parole hearings the ratio of the processing of African Americans to Whites is significantly higher.

There is indeed trouble in the village but it is trouble that can be fixed.

PART 2

HOW TO
DEVELOP
UNFRAGMENTED
AFRICAN AMERICAN MEN

CHAPTER 1

WHOLE BLACK MEN ARE BUILT FROM UNFRAGMENTED BLACK BOYS

The concept of *reclaiming the village* must of necessity begin with building whole and healthy adult men from healthy and whole boys; in other words, we must create a community environment where children can grow up unfragmented in the social context. Someone has stated it well, that it is better by far to grow healthy children into healthy adults than it is to repair old men.

Building whole men begins with understanding the crucial threefold **developmental process** by which boys mature into men. This is not done at the exclusion of other areas (i.e., emotional, psychological, etc.). The threefold development involves the critical areas of the mind, the body, and the reproductive drive of the African American male. To put it another way, the maturing process of African American males involves intellectual development, physical development and the development of their reproductive drive.

While most parents give sufficient attention to the needs of their sons as it pertains to their physical development, it seems to me that too little attention is given to the development of the young Black male's intellect and the concurrent development of his reproductive drive.

Concerning the overall development of the African American male child, most parents tend to leave or surrender far too much freedom of choice to the child. This relaxed guidance of the African American male proves to be most detrimental in the area of his intellectual development and the development of his emerging sense of maleness. Thus African American males tend to grow up seriously underdeveloped intellectually and woefully undisciplined in the management of their sexuality.

This intellectual underdevelopment and lack of discipline in premature sexual activity is evident in the concentration of young black boys in athletics and other less intellectually challenging academic fields and in the number of babies sired by black boys out of wedlock, often before their twenty-first birthday.

Black boys are unchallenged intellectually at home, at school, and in the community. This neglect of the black male's intellect often leads to a serious loss of interest in careers that require strong academic credentials.

At a recent family seminar I told a mother that her fifteen year old son was at an age at which he was more of a man than he was a boy. This mother was seriously unsettled by my statement and rejected outright the idea that her little boy was just a few short years from fullblown manhood. This mother's insensitivity to her son's evolving manhood did not suggest to me that she was unaware of the boy's physical growth; what I perceived was a mother's ignorance of her son's intellectual maturity and the corresponding development in the area of his reproductive drive .

The threefold developmental process of the African American male in his intellect, physical growth and reproductive drive, brings to focus the socialization arena of the African American male, the economic context in which the African American male grows up, the family context where the African American male is parented, and the eighteen to twenty-one year period needed to grow a male child into a man.

In the area of socialization African American boys understands early that a great portion of his manliness is centered in his reproductive drive. Thus growing whole African American men involves understanding the significance that is often attached to sexuality in terms of defining genuine African American manhood. In this venue one must understand and distinguish between the black male's emphasis on sexuality and sinful immorality. In the mind of the African American Christian male to be mannish (virile) is to be manly, not immoral.

Comedian Richard Pryor, commenting on why black men can often be seen holding themselves in the seat of their pants, once said that it was because they were checking to see if they still had their private parts, seeing that the "White man" had stripped him of everything else. It is not uncommon for black men to frequently hold onto the seat of their pants. This practice is commonly understood as an expression of the maleness (virility) of the black man. It should not necessarily be seen as a tendency towards vulgarity or immorality.

It is not uncommon for young black boys today to wear their pants several inches below their waist and their underwear several inches above their pants. They are merely showing their drawers. When asked concerning this latest fad, I suggested to parents that they do not make the mistake of interpreting this current Black male style as a commentary on the moral convictions of their sons. Where and how a young man wears his pants is not a commentary on his morality. Rather, it is what he does with what he has in his pants that displays his true moral convictions.

In the parenting process the physical development is most often given exclusive and excessive attention by parents while the intellectual and the emotional development are given far too little consideration in terms of the impact each aspect will have in the overall holistic development of the boy into manhood. Therefore parents should seriously consider a holistic approach to their son's development, which means observing and responding to more than just the physical growth of the young boy. The Village, that is the African American Community, is currently deficient in the number of men who can function well intellectually but is often overstocked with men who do not manage well their sex drive.

The socialization of the African American male is undeniably wed to the economic context in which the boy is born and grows up. Economic factors impact the family structure, educational opportunities, values system and often the extent to which the young man is exposed to fragmented and or unfragmented models of manhood in a destructive community environment as opposed to exposure to constructive models of manhood in a constructive community environment.

There have been a multitude of well-documented studies over the years on the impact of economics on the nurture of children. I need not repeat it here, except to say that the general consensus exists that economics and parenting are two sides of the same coin of parenting. Economic deprivation no doubt is a significant influence in the lives of young boys who involve themselves in the use and sale of drugs and a host of other criminal activities. Thus the idea of reclaiming the village must involve a strategy to improve the economic context into which a disproportionate number of black boys are born and live.

From the window of my office I watch on a daily basis idle black boys and young men who have never held a job nor have they ever seen their father or mother work. These young men and boys spend their time acting as lookouts and drug peddlers for drug dealers. These same young men also wound and kill people for the drug dealers. Young women in poverty at an early age become involved in prostitution and drugs. In this context even children who are hardly three years of age learn to be tough in order to survive the neglect they experience from day to day. Let me hasten to add that not all young men and boys who live in a socially and deprived context end up this way.

But the fact that economics draws attention to the principle that to the extent that black male socialization is influenced by their economic context to that same extent will there be a difference in the constructive or destructive socialization of young black males depending on the economic context they live in. Thus the idea that all black males share the same values, aspirations, life goals, etc. is not true. There are serious differences among black boys and men depending on the economic context in which they were nurtured, not the least of which is the survivalist mindset of the inner city black male and the prosperity mindset of the middle class suburban black male.

John grew up in the inner city and at age twenty one had a job and his own apartment. I asked John how long had he been working. He said that he had been on his own since he was thirteen. As I listened to John it became evident to me that his primary motivation in life was to survive.

William, on the other hand, came from the suburbs and a context of middle class values. By age twenty one he had seldom held a job and was quite selective about where he would and would not work. For William, the idea of survival had never been an issue. Thus William's primary motivation was security and prosperity.

John and William are both African American men and they share a common ideology as it pertains to how they define their African American maleness. Yet in terms of their life goals and motivations they are very different. The difference is not a difference of character or integrity. The real difference is the contrast produced by economic disadvantage versus economic advantage in the areas of nurture, education, models, and such.

In the African American Village today consideration must be given to the influence of family structure on the socialization of the African American male child. In this venue we must remind ourselves that in the Village, currently 51%-plus children are parented in a context where both of their biological parents are present. In 1993, 36% of black children under the age of eighteen lived with both their parents compared to 67% in 1960.[1] It is estimated that in America 55 to 60% of children born in the 1990's will spend at least a part of their childhood in a fatherless home. In fact today the United States leads the world in fatherless homes.[2]

In the African American community a large number of fatherless children are born into single female-headed families. The role of the family in the development of children is well established as being most significant. The issue is to what extent are children impacted in terms of their nurture by the structure of their family?

Compared to children in nuclear families, children whose parents have divorced are much more likely to drop out of school, engage in premarital sex and become pregnant outside of marriage. These effects hold even after controlling for parental and marital characteristics before divorce.[3]

About 40 percent of children living in fatherless households have not seen their father in at least a year. Of the remaining only 60% sleep in their father's home at least one night a month. Only one in six sees their father an average of once or more a week.[4]

Family context is the most significant influence in the socialization of any child, regardless of gender or race. Attention must therefore be given to providing an adequate family structure for parenting children. Fatherless children are deprived of a significant model and character-shaping influence. The Black male child who has no in-resident father will of necessity

[1]   *Survey on Child Health* (Washington, D.C.: U.S. Department of Human Services—National Center for Health Statistics, 1993).
[2]   Alisa Burns, "Mother-Headed Families: an International Perspective in the Case of Australia" in *Social Policy Report* (6 Spring 1992).
[3]   Frank F. Fursterburg Jr. & Julien O. Feitler, " Reconsidering the Effects Of Marital Disruption" in *The Journal of Family Issues* (#15 1994), p. 173.
[4]   Frank F. Fursterburg Jr. & Christine Winquist Nord, "Parenting Apart" in *The Journal Of Marriage & the Family* (Nov. 1995), p. 896.

glean what he can from the community in defining what it means to be a man.

Consider the following statistics on the impact of fatherless families in the United States. Seventy percent of juveniles in state reform institutions grew up in single or no-parent situations.[5] Sixty percent of America's rapists grew up in homes without fathers.[6] Seventy-two percent of adolescent murderers grew up without fathers.[7] Eighty percent of adolescents in psychiatric hospitals come from broken homes.[8]

It is my contention that fragmented boys grow into fragmented men. We can conclude that inasmuch as it takes a minimum of twenty one years to grow a whole adult male from infancy, children who are not privy to a nurturing environment and are pushed into adulthood prematurely will most likely be fragmented by the experience.

In the case of John and William, John's premature induction into adult manhood produced in him significant fragmentation in terms of his holistic development. This fragmentation will limit to some extent his function as a whole man in the Village. William, on the other hand, though less experienced at surviving on his own is in fact more equipped for long-term survival and success. The difference in probable outcomes results from the different nurturing each experienced and the context in which that nurturing took place.

Reclaiming the Village begins with growing boys into unfragmented men. To this end much attention must be given to the critical threefold developmental process of male children. This threefold development emphasizes the boy's physical growth, intellectual development and reproductive drive. Also important are family and community socialization, the economic context into which the boy is born and grows up and the number of years parents spend growing the boy into a man.

A few weeks ago a sixteen year old young man announced in a public setting that he did not expect to be alive long enough to reach the age of twenty one. In fact he said he wanted to be like his dad who was in prison. As I listened to what the young

[5]   Nicholas Davidson, "Life Without Father" in *Policy Review* (1990).
[6]   Allen Beck, Susan Kline and Lawrence Greenfield, *Survey of Youth in Custody*, 1987 (U.S. Department of Justice: Bureau of Justice Stataistics, Sept. 1988).
[7]   Dewey Cornell, *Characteristics of Adolescents Charged With Homicide* (1987), p. 11.
[8]   Jean Bethke Elshtain, *Family Matters* (July 1993), p. 14.

man shared it occurred to me that for him life had no purpose. In growing whole men it is important to let children understand they are not conceived by chance nor are they born into a theological or sociological vacuum. Every child is a gift from God and is therefore created for a divine purpose

There is a threefold **divine purpose** to which every man is attached from the moment of conception. This threefold purpose has to do with the internal drive and heart motivation that is nurtured in the boy in the home on his way to manhood. This threefold purpose consists of the divinely ordained *will* of men to explore and conquer, combined with the internal *motivation* to rule over Gods creation and the internal *drive* to reproduce himself.

African American men know full well that their internal drive to explore and conquer is often disregarded and frequently significantly restricted by the larger society. Yet this spirit of adventure and conquest is evident in most boys beginning in early childhood. Pre K–3 boys are risk-takers who exhibit an eager, inquiring thirst to explore, examine, manipulate, and create. They are filled with *Whys*, *Hows*, *Whens*, *Whos*, and *Whats*. Another vivid example of this spirit of exploration and conquest can be seen in a young man's willingness to compete and achieve his goals by using his adventurous and creative skills. When the environment of young boys are devoid of opportunities in which their creative skills are stimulated, challenged and positively channeled, by the time they become men they will essentially be dead men walking, fit only to be numbered among the idle men on the corner.

As I read the first chapter of the book of Genesis concerning the creation of the first man it became evident to me that attached to the very existence of mankind was the command to explore and conquer.

"Then God said, 'Let Us make man in Our image, according to Our likeness; let them have dominion over the fish of the sea, over the birds of the air, and over the cattle, over all the earth and over every creeping thing that creeps on the earth.' So God created man in his own image, in the image of God he created him; male and female he created them" (Gen. 1:26-27). A note from the *Nelson Study Bible* may be helpful at this point, "We may not make images of God for He has already done so! We are His images; it is we who are in His likeness. This is the reason God values people so much: We are made to reflect His majesty on earth. '... have dominion': Rule as God's regent. That is, people are to rule as God would—wisely and prudently—over all that God has made."[9]

"God blessed them and said to them, 'Be fruitful and increase in number; fill the earth and *subdue* it. *Rule over* the fish of the sea and the birds of the air and over every living creature that moves on the ground" (Gen. 1:28). Again, the *Nelson Study Bible* explains it well, "The word translated subdue means 'bring into bondage.' This harsh term is used elsewhere of military conquest (Zech. 9:15) and of God subduing our iniquities (Mic. 7:19)."[10]

The Hebrew word *kawbash* in this context has the idea of bringing into subjection to mankind all that God has created. This responsibility given by God to Adam, the first man created, would of necessity require that Adam be possessed of a spirit within himself that equipped him with the abilities to carry out this responsibility to *kawbash* (subdue) the whole earth. Adam was created with just such a spirit, and that spirit remains alive today in every man, regardless of his race and place in the world. Therefore one of the reasons God created man was for the purpose of subduing creation.

Man's second purpose is that of **ruling over all of God's creation.** The Hebrew word *radah* has the idea of ruling or having dominion over all of creation. Thus God created in man a drive to strive to subjugate all things to himself. As quoted above man is to rule as God would over all of creation.

The third purpose for which God created man was that of **filling the earth with people.** The Hebrew words *parah* (be fruitful) and *rabah* (multiply) has the idea of a man being driven to reproduce himself and fill the earth with people. Thus it can be concluded that there is a spirit in all of mankind that drive him towards the goal of filling the earth with people.

It is the boy's or man's connection to God that creates wholeness and unity in the process of growing unfragmented boys into unfragmented adult men. The mind, will and emotions of boys, when working together with the developing muscles and reproductive drive, creates in time a man who reflects the image and glory of God.

To set forth the idea that boys develop in a unified

---

[9] *The Nelson Study Bible*, notes on Gen. 1:26 (Nashville: Thomas Nelson Publishers, 1997), p. 5.
[10] Ibid., p. 6.

threefold manner as they move steadily towards manhood and that this threefold physical, intellectual and reproductive development is to correspond to the threefold purpose that God has attached to all men may seem a bit strange. It seems to contrast with our contemporary society's prevailing unisexual focus. In addition there is in today's world a prevailing attitude of irreverence toward God and mankind that seems to characterize the thinking, attitudes and behavior of most young men.

One of the stars of the Chicago Bulls illustrates most vividly this attitude of irreverence. This athlete seems to revel in behavior that evidence a unisexual attitude and irreverence towards God and mankind. His actions includes cross dressing, nudity, brutality and vulgarity, all in the name of being himself. This same attitude is evident in much of the rap music of our day. The lyrics are in all too many instances totally irreverent toward God and mankind.

Given the propensity towards irreverence in the Village today manhood is increasingly being defined by such things as well-developed physique, fine clothes, expensive cars, and money. The contemporary man is supposed to be emotionally tough and relationally unattached. He is a man with few social and moral convictions though he may be religiously inclined. This contemporary ideal of manhood demands that the African American male in most instances be perceived to be at the top of his game in terms of social, economic and political accomplishments.

In addition to the contemporary view of manhood the African American male is subjected to a demeaning stereotype of his manhood that is rooted in the legacy of slavery. This negative historical stereotype of black men lives on today in the minds of both Whites and Blacks at all levels of social class. The general response by a number of middle class Blacks is to lay aside the old slate chronicling the history of oppression of Black people in this country and move on. However, when one takes a close and honest look at the modern day African American male it becomes evident that he cannot ignore his history. That he is imprinted intellectually, emotionally and economically by the legacy of slavery is a fact.

The modern day African American male is distinguished by the legacy of oppression that characterized most of his ancestors' history in this country. Oppression through slavery lasted for more than two hundred and fifty years. Following the Emancipation Proclamation in the 1860s, oppression was reintroduced in the form of Jim Crow laws in the South and de facto segregation in the North. This form of legal segregation lasted until the Civil Rights Movement of the sixties. The years following the Civil Rights Movement have been characterized by a more subtle oppression in the form of economic and political disenfranchisement.

It is hardly possible to define African American manhood today apart from an understanding of the impact of oppression on the holistic threefold development and purpose of manhood. The configuration of the legacy of oppression of black men into the contemporary social setting tends to be a source of embarrassment for the successful black male and a source of guilt for the White male population in general. Yet this legacy of oppression is a primary contributing factor to much of the chaos in the Village today and thus cannot be disregarded.

The reality of the residual effects of oppression on the psyche of today's African American men must be seen through the lens of the "cultural brainwashing" to which all African American men have been and continue to be subjected to.

"Cultural brainwashing" is a process of formal and informal, objective and subjective, teaching and reinforcing the idea that African American culture is substandard and inferior to other cultures in general and White culture in particular and therefore is not qualified to be on equal terms with other cultures in society.

When young Tiger Woods won the Masters in Augusta, Georgia in early 1997, his success elicited the following comment from Fuzzy Zoeller, himself a top flight golfer: " I hope he doesn't insist that they serve fried chicken and greens or what ever *they* eat for the dinner." Zoeller was firing a shot at Tiger Woods' African American heritage. The message Mr. Zoeller sent across the world of golf was that though the young African American Tiger Woods was good at the game of golf, his African American culture has a social dietary flavor to it that renders it not fit for primetime.

That 21-year old Tiger Woods cannot be accepted solely on the basis of his athletic prowess as are other golfers bears witness to the fact that the brainwashing of African American men is still with us. Just because he has African American blood in his genetic make up, Woods is comically referred to as one who is culturally inferior to others. I seriously doubt that an athlete from any other ethnic group would have elicited a similar comment.

The cultural brainwashing of black men has its roots in the creation and legendary historic survival of the Black Sambo stereotype created by the slave masters. They used it to exalt themselves and their culture as superior to the black male slave and their slave culture. Black Sambo in effect established White men as the exclusive model of genuine North American manhood in this country. Being Black and male disqualified one from equal manhood in North America.

Most young black men have never consciously heard of Black Sambo and cultural brainwashing and thus have no sense of the barriers in their own minds and in society in general. They do not realize that the presence of the Sambo personality lives today. To help them understand I will summarize briefly the Black Sambo personality.

Only within the context of the American slave system was the Black Sambo personality ever created and flourished. Nowhere else can this be found. There is no such personality type in African culture or society. Yet the characteristics of this imaginary "Sambo" was easily accepted as typical of the Black male plantation slave. In time the "Sambo" personality type outgrew the slave system and became the standard profile of the Black male personality for both slaves and free men. That stereotype lives even to this very day.

The Black Sambo personality is described as docile, irresponsible, loyal but lazy, humble but chronically given to lying and stealing. His conduct is described as being full of infantile silliness, and his talk is said to be inflated with childish exaggerations. His relationship with his slave master was said to be one of total dependence and childlike attachment.

This Sambo brainwashing tool was forced upon the Black male slave and strictly enforced with unwavering consistency in all aspects of the North American social, economic, religious, political, judicial and family contexts. In that historic oppressive context any hint of manhood on the part of the black male slave filled the breasts of White men with scorn and hostility.

The slave owners found the Sambo image taking root in the mind and spirit of the Black male slave, and for the White man this imposed and enforced Black Sambo personality caused the male slave to function in a manner that proved to be both exasperating and lovable to his White master. However, for the Black male the Sambo personality and performance was always demeaning and devastatingly fragmentative psychologically.

There is sufficient evidence to support the idea that even in modern time it is commonly believed that Black Sambo represented real black men and that the characteristics of "Black Sambo" were the clear products of racial inheritance. It might well be that this age old personality tool was the motivation behind Mr. Zoeller's comments about Tiger Woods.

One of the things that resulted from the cultural brainwashing of black men is what I refer to as a **"loss of world view."** By loss of world view I am referring to the tendency of African American men to have a narrow view of the world in terms of their place in the world and their potential for contributing to the good of society in general.

This narrow world view is most evident in the limited investments of time, money and wealth black men make in their community and in historical Black cultural and educational institutions. Far too few African American men show any interest in becoming a world leader in the political, economic or religious arenas. Very few aspire for postgraduate degrees. There is rarely monies forthcoming to support cultural or educational institutions. This narrow world view is rooted in the legacy of Black male brainwashing.

In thinking through the issue of *Reclaiming the Village*, it occurs to me that there are many evidences of significant social, domestic and economic "instability" among black men. It can be argued that in the general population long term tenured membership and relationships are increasingly the exception rather than the rule in most circles including church, job and marriage. There appears also to be a kind of instability among black men that significantly contributes to destabilizing the Black family, the Black church and the Black community.

Jimmie and Sue had been living together for more than a decade and yet Jimmie was not willing to enter into a lifetime commitment with Sue. Even though they have two young children, the issue of marriage for Jimmie was too binding over the long haul. Jimmie felt that retaining his freedom to leave Sue and the children is best for him given his uncertainty about the security of relationships in general. The fact is Jimmie is suffering from the legacy of instability that haunts so many young African American men today in the context of relationships.

In my conversations with Jimmie and other men like him another issue emerged, which is the issue of **"the absence of a sense of control"** over such things as the role his wife fulfills in the marriage, the economic role he must fill in the family and the role he must play as the man of his own house.

During premarital counseling Jake said it straight, "I expect to be responsible for providing half the family income, and nothing more." In Jake's mind he had no control over what his bride-to-be would do or not do as it pertained to the household income so he set forth what he saw as his role. In Jake's mind marriage was a fifty-fifty deal in every area.

This sense of "loss" of control over such things as their relationship with their wives, their income, and their own family life is for a number of men a contributing factor to their aberrant behavior in the area of domestic violence.

I have said that African American men are **victims** of a *legacy of oppression, cultural brain washing, loss of world view, lack of stability or control over the affairs of their personal and public life.* Thus with a view to *Reclaiming the Village* I suggest that the modern day African American male needs four things, **holistic spiritual renewal, a renewed sense of trust, a sense of unity in the context of a sense of belonging, and a new definition of life.**

As a seminary professor for more than two decades on the campus of a major graduate school, I am increasingly aware of the growing insensitivity of young African American men and women to the legacy of their past. Each year it seems as if the entering students know less and less about the legacy of black history in this country. The tendency is to only focus on the present while disregarding the past and giving little thought about tomorrow.

It was this kind of thinking that contributed to the negative reaction of most of the black students of theology on the seminary campus to the "million man march" on October 16,1995. Few of my students were able to articulate the cry of those men in Washington D.C. on that day as representing all African American men everywhere crying for renewal, a new sense of trust, unity and a new definition of themselves as men.

I have also found it to be more than a little bit interesting that the African American student of theology on the campus of the graduate school where I teach cannot understand why an organization like Promise Keepers cannot effectively minister to black men given their success in reaching White men. I suggested to my students that the ineffectiveness of Promise Keepers in reaching black men is due to the fact that the modern day African American man has a vacuum in his life that demands a kind of renewal that is unlike the vacuum in the lives of the other men to which Promise Keepers is effectively ministering.

There is however a common thread that ties both white and black men together, namely, both have needs that neither the White or Black church is effectively responding. The needs are very different in terms of the causes behind each but both are very real.

The issue of renewal among black men calls for a bibliocentric approach coming to grips with the legacy of slavery and oppression in this country combined with a will to confront the issue of racism and discrimination that so comfortably abides in our systematic and biblical theology, Christian literature and academic programs, conventions and churches.

Spiritual renewal that is designed to effectively minister to black men must take the form of public acknowledgment of and repentance for the silent and vocal affirmation of slavery and the legacy of slavery and oppression by the White evangelical community as a whole. The legacy of slavery and the resulting racial prejudice and discrimination had influenced the White evangelical institutions of higher education, both Bible colleges and seminaries, to exclude African American men and women from admission until the post Civil Right era. The White evangelical Christian community as a whole is partially responsible for the widespread liberal theology in the Black church today. The first step then is essentially one of confession and repentance.

Without such repentance and confession on the part of the White Evangelical community, Black Bible-believing Christians will find it difficult to forgive and begin the process of reconciliation. Apart from reconciliation and healing between black and white men who are Christians, there will not be genuine holistic spiritual renewal, trust, unity and new definition of manhood in and among black men in general and Black Christian men in particular.

I am reminded that a number of men and women, like myself, have spent more than a few decades teaching and ministering on the campuses of predominantly White theological institutions. Each of us continue to experience almost on a daily basis attitudes, ideas and behavior on the part of people in the system that suggest that black men are not quite ready for primetime. We gravitate toward one another, seeking each other out just to vent our frustrations and find some sense of renewal, unity, trust and redefinition of just who we really are as African American Christian men and women.

Clearly the need that has emerged as the most urgent among many needs in the Village is the need for *holistic spiritual renewal*. In large measure, due primarily to its historic alignment with oppressors and oppression, the process of holistic spiritual renewal for the African American male demands the involvement of the White evangelical community. To the extent that a case can be made that the African American Village in general and the African American Christian male in particular is due an apology and repentance from the White evangelical community, to that extent it can be said that *Reclaiming the Village* will welcome the involvement of the White evangelical community.

CHAPTER 2

IN SEARCH OF RENEWAL

In the context of the African American community itself there is much that points to a need for holistic spiritual renewal among black men. Holistic spiritual renewal includes spiritual issues, psychological issues and socioeconomic issues. Spiritual issues focus on the question, "Who is this Jesus whom we serve?" This is a theological question. The psychological issues focus on the question, "Who am I?" This is an identity question. The socioeconomic issues focus on the question, "Where do I fit in?" This is a life-mission question.

It is not unusual to find evangelicals interested in pursuing a ministry of spiritual renewal among black men. However, there seems to be little sensitivity to issues that are beyond that which can be defined as spiritual in the narrowest sense. Spiritual renewal for the African American man of necessity must be holistic and deal with that which is spiritual, psychological and socioeconomic. It is my contention that there is no trichotomy between the spiritual, the psychological and the socioeconomic. The spiritual focus begins with a focus on *biblical illiteracy* that is so prevalent among African American men today.

The prevailing biblical illiteracy among black men is the natural consequence that has resulted from the fact that the African American female outnumbers African American men in the church on an average of eight to one.

In the Black church Black males are too few in number from Sunday School kindergarten to the senior citizen Sunday School class. There are few Bible study groups in which black men are present in any significant numbers. This is the case even from the small local church to the mega church. The absence of black men in Christian education has a natural outcome in the absence of black men in the church congregation and a blatant biblical illiteracy among black men.

This absence of black men in the Black church is due in part to the fact that the preacher and the Black church is oftentimes not user friendly to black men. In addition the Black church fails to challenge black men in terms of what is required of them in the area of holistic accountability.

As a means of moving the church toward a more user-friendly Black male focus the scope and focus of the church must be expanded. James H. Harris in his book *Pastoral Theology: A Black-Church Perspective* writes:

> The church needs to do more than what most modern evangelicals typically do—praising God and winning souls to Jesus Christ through focusing on personal salvation and a "Praise the Lord . . . Thank you Jesus" mentality that concentrates on salvation from personal sin—because such a focus overlooks oppression, injustice, poverty, and a host of other social ills as manifestations of sinfulness.
>
> Encouraging people to accept Jesus, which is a major focus on evangelism, should also mean enabling them to become whole persons who are free and equal, no longer gripped by the awesome, yet empty hand of poverty and oppression. Freedom and equality under God are not abstract philosophical constructs as rationalism, empiricism, or Platonic idealism are. Justice, freedom, and equality are embedded in Christian faith and biblical tradition.[1]

The evangelicals need to learn from the Muslim faith which, with its strong focus on the social ills of the Black community, is experiencing great success in reaching black men. The success is due at least in part to the rigorous challenges, accountability and demands the Muslim faith places upon the African American male who expresses an interest in becoming a member of their group. A significant portion of what Muslims require of black men is direct training in the Muslim religion through study of the Koran. It is difficult to find a member of the Muslim faith who lacks a working knowledge of what their faith entails.

Spiritual renewal of the African American male is the first step towards reclaiming the Village. The African American male must be renewed in his realization of who is this God who created him and for what purpose. The bibliocentric truth is that

---

[1]   James H. Harris, *Pastoral Theology: A Black-Church Perspective* (Fortress Press, 1990) pp. 4-5.

God created all men to reflect His image and His glory.

The focus on holistic spiritual renewal must consider how manhood is defined biblically. I call it "Manhood! God's View." The Bible sets forth the idea that every man has a God-ordained purpose in life. Discovering and understanding that divine purpose for black men is accomplished by tackling the spiritual, psychological and socioeconomic issues in the context of the image and glory of God in man.

Regarding the image of God in man Dr. Allen Ross writes in a commentary on Genesis 1:27:

> Human life was created in (lit., "as," meaning "in essence as") the image of God (v. 27). This image was imparted only to humans (2:7). "Image" (*selem*) is used figuratively here, for God does not have a human form. Being in God's image means that humans share, though imperfectly and finitely, in God's nature, that is, in His communicable attributes (life, personality, truth, wisdom, love, holiness, justice), and so have the capacity for spiritual fellowship with Him.
>
> God's purpose in creating human life in His image was functional: man is to **rule** or have dominion (1:26, 28). God's dominion was presented by a "representative." (Egyptian kings later, in idolatry, did a similar kind of thing: they represented their rule or dominion by making representative statues of themselves).[2]

While it cannot be argued that oppression regardless of its scope and intensity can effectively erase from any human being the image of God that is in them, it is possible to make an argument that supports the idea that oppression of the kind that strips away the external and internal humanity of a human being can in time significantly diminish the reflection of the image of God in that human being. This diminished reflection of the image of God in any human being will essentially deny such men the opportunity to function in the spiritual, social, economic, family and political context of their world in accord with God's purpose for creating man in His image.

Professor Ross writes, "God's purpose in creating human life in His image was functional: man is to rule or have dominion (1:26, 28). God's dominion was presented by a "representative.""[3] This being the case I suggest that the history of the African American male's experience in America is one in which he was stripped of his humanity both internally and externally and ultimately denied the opportunity to function in accord with

---

[2] Allen P. Ross, "Genesis" in *The Bible Knowledge Commentary* (Wheaton: Victor Books, 1985), 1:29.
[3] Ibid.

God's functional purpose in creating him to represent His image.

To the extent that the image of God in man is defined as a functional reality, meaning to represent God's dominion over this world, the history and the legacy of slavery and oppression in North American stands as a testament to the denial of the black man's humanity, freedom and the opportunity to so function.

Humanity in general and manhood in particular demands a reflection of the image and glory of God in terms of function. This functional image of God in man stands as that which distinguishes men from all other animal life. Once this distinction is denied, stripped away or covered over by a dehumanizing oppressive environment or circumstances, men lose their sense of divine purpose and thus their will to function as a reflection of God's dominion over the earth. Such is what happened with African American men. There exists a deficit in their sense of divine purpose and a lack of focus on their call to function in the world and in the Village as representatives of God's dominion.

A primary spiritual issue facing black men today is the issue of his relationship with God. This issue was a factor in the success of the million man march. It is this issue as well that is now contributing to the success of the Nation of Islam in reaching young black men. Black men today are in search of spiritual renewal where they can be restored to a mindset that provides for them the satisfaction of knowing that they can function and be empowered to reflect the image and glory of God.

Manhood as defined in the Bible means living and functioning in a manner that represents God's dominion over the earth. A man's life-mission necessitates a search for opportunities to exercise authority, power, justice, love, and such. Thus in terms of reclaiming the Village, the current oppressive social and economic context in which black men live must change. The change must be a move away from oppression and inequality and toward a more user-friendly environment, in which it is possible for the African American male to function in accord with the image of God that is in him.

It is important to emphasize again that manhood defined biblically means reflecting the image and glory of God. It means having a relationship with God, it means having a clear perception of what your mission in this life is as a black man.

These are spiritual issues that must be faced by black men. The substance of these spiritual issues in terms of defining true manhood is a focus on "Who God is?" Out of the many spiritual issues revolving around the question of "Who God is?" emerges three issues that are related to the psychological, sociological and socioeconomic.

First, there is the *psychological* issue which demands that men be in touch with their holistic needs as a man. Second, the *sociological* issue requires a realization that they do not and cannot live in a relational vacuum. Finally the *socioeconomic* issue stipulates for most men to recognize and respond to their need for one wife in this life.

Genesis 2:18-25 provides the biblical basis for my definition of manhood. The text opens with God making two observations about the sociological and domestic context of the man Adam, namely that he is alone and that this state is not good for him. Having made these two observations, God then proposes to do something about Adam's situation, namely that He will create for the man Adam a corresponding helper (help meet). Note that Adam is unaware of the fact that he is alone and he does not know that it is not good for him to be alone. Adam does not realize that he was not created to exist in a relational vacuum.

Keeping in mind that God has made His observations about the relational vacuum that Adam was living in, that Adam was alone, that such a state was not good for Adam, that God was planning to create a companion for Adam, it is surprising to read the next thing that God did. He does not immediately create for Adam his corresponding helper. "Now the Lord God had formed out of the ground all the beasts of the field and all the birds of the air. He brought them to the man to see what he would name them; and whatever the man called each living creature, that was its name. So the man gave names to all the livestock, the birds of the air and all the beasts of the field. But for Adam no suitable helper was found" (Gen. 2:19-20).

I believe God did not immediately create for Adam a corresponding helper and solve this relational vacuum in Adam's life because Adam did not yet know that he was living in a relational vacuum and needed a corresponding helper to fill that vacuum. Adam is not in touch with his own need for a corresponding helper. God in His wisdom chooses not to give Adam what he does not know he needs, namely, a wife though Adam's mental and emotional ignorance does not diminish the reality of his need.

In order to sensitize Adam to his relational vacuum and awaken in him an awareness of his need for a mate, God brings all kind of animals and allows Adam's fully-developed intellect to name each of them. However, the point here is not simply to demonstrate the image of God in the man Adam by focusing on his fully developed intellect but more importantly this exercise is used by God to sensitize the man to his own need for a corresponding helper.

After Adam finishes the process of naming all the animals, the text adds this brief commentary to the narrative, "But for Adam no suitable helper was found." Finally Adam is on the same page as God is in terms of understanding his own sense of need for a mate. The exposure to the male and female creatures as he gave them names awakened in Adam a knowledge of the fact that he unlike the other creatures, was in a relational vacuum for none of the creatures God created corresponded to him. This discovery made him sensitive to his need for a creature who fit with how he was designed and created. There was not a single animal among those created by God and named by Adam that shared with Adam the image of God in him, thus the need for Eve was awakened in Adam.

Much more could be said about the fact that God did not give Adam a mate until he recognized his need for one. However, I will simply point out that Adam's psychological and emotional ability to relate to Eve was rooted in what Adam had discovered about himself in terms of his relational needs as a man created in the image of God.

To ensure immediate functional compatibility between Adam and Eve, God in His wisdom decided not to create Eve the same way Adam was made, with clay from the earth, choosing instead to take a rib from Adam and fashion it into a woman.

It is worthy of note at this point that when God presented Eve to Adam as his corresponding helper Adam did not ask any questions about how to relate to her. Adam's instant understanding of his need for Eve was the result of his understanding of himself in terms of his relational needs that set him apart for all the other animals God created and he named.

In the African American Village there seems to be growing evidence that black men are not in touch with their holistic needs. This insensitivity to their own needs is a contributing factor to the growing number of men who choose to try to live their lives in a relational vacuum, thus resulting in a lack of commitment to their families and the ever changing cycle of women in their lives.

The relational vacuum in which black men find themselves today may well be rooted in their estrangement from the Black church. These are days in which it often seems difficult for men to clearly distinguish themselves from some animals in terms of relational skills. In the context of slavery and racial segregation it was not uncommon for black men to be classified alongside the animals in terms of their sexual activity. In that context it was the church that provided the spiritual and psychological refuges to which they turned for survival.

It is my contention that the church must again become that place of refuge for black men. The good news is that there are signs that a growing number of black men are in the process of rediscovering the Black church as a place to find themselves. This emerging trend is evident in the move of a growing number of high profile black men in the athletic, entertainment and political arena who are returning to the Black church as active members.

These high profile believers confess to the vacuum that cannot be satisfied by their status, money, women, partying and materialism. This feeling of emptiness inside themselves, according to these men, can only be filled with a relationship with God through Jesus Christ. It is also interesting to note that an increasing number of churches are getting involved in prison ministries. This is another encouraging sign in view of the fact that there are such vast numbers of black men in prisons all across this country.

These encouraging signs of renewed life and relevance in the church must not conceal the challenge the church faces in becoming more user friendly in its ministry's scope and focus. Harris reminds the Black church thusly, "The Black church is compelled to become an extroverted institution—one that will take more risks, demand more justice, and force blacks and whites to move beyond personal conversion to community transformation. To do this it will have to change its focus on ministry. Rather than emulate the private, personal model represented by modern evangelism, it needs to hear anew the Great Commission in Luke 18:29 and Jesus' message of liberation in Luke 4:18."[3]

---
[3]   Harris, *Pastoral Theolog*, p. 350.

CHAPTER 3

BLACK MALE SOCIALIZATION

THE ROLE OF THE FAMILY

How black men socialize has long intrigued a large number of sociologists over the years. Some sociological studies have focused on the influence of Black male stereotypes (i.e., Black Sambo, Uncle Ben, Uncle Tom, the wild and savage heathen, and other negative images) on the self image of black men.

The popular and mistaken assumption often made is that the stereotypes are true; unfortunately our culture in its media and entertainment is guilty of promoting these stereotypes. Today's movies, for instance, constantly flashed on the big screen negative portrayals and stereotypes of the Black male. *Boyz N the Hood, Jungle Fever,* and *Waiting To Exhale* are but three examples. No less flattering are the images of black men expressed in the lyrics of much of today's rap music.

In this section I will set forth and discuss what I believe to be the three primary sources of black male socialization. These three sources or institutions are **the family, the church and the community.** Each of these three entities have roles to play in the socialization of black men. To the extent that any one of these three entities fails or negatively contributes to the socialization process, to that extent the Black community village is negatively impacted.

The first and most important entity in the socialization of black men is the family. As a biblicist I am convinced that in the mind of God children are to be born into a family context consisting of a man and his one wife. In this ideal family structure children born to the man and his wife are theirs. The first order of business God assigned to the man Adam and his wife Eve was to be fruitful and multiply, "God blessed them and said to them, "Be fruitful and increase in number. . .' " (Gen. 1:28). Men and women having their own children in the context of a two-parent (male and female) family structure is the divine ideal reproductive environment for all of humanity regardless of a person's race or culture.

In terms of the socialization of black men I suggest six things that the family structure must be equipped with to effectively contribute to the process. These six socializing ventures include but are not limited to, *personal identity as an African American male, examples of love, self-esteem, Black male gender identity, life values that reflect the history and traditions of African Americans, and a functional religious belief system that is Christian-based and focused.*

I am reminded of a story of a boy who placed a few duck eggs under a mother hen mixing them with chicken eggs. He timed the placing of the duck eggs so they would hatch along with the chicken eggs. Sure enough, at the appointed time the eggs hatched and the young ducklings and chicks all followed the hen around acting like they all were chickens. He watched them to see if any would swim. In time it became evident that neither the chick nor ducklings would swim. The chicks did not swim because swimming was against their nature, but the ducklings did not swim even though it was in their nature to swim because they thought they were chickens. When ducks are socialized by a mother hen to feel and think like they were chickens, they will feel and think like chickens even though they are ducks.

To some degree it is the same with black men in that much of their behavior is reflective of their socialization. In many instances the socialization of black men is such that it causes them to think and act in ways that are in direct conflict with their identity as black men.

To the majority of White Americans the words *young Black males* are virtually synonymous with the terms *sexual promiscuity* and *criminality.* Seen in this dominant White American consciousness the African male is existentially guilty, that is, he is guilty by his mere existence or for merely having the audacity to be alive. A pervasive belief among many White Americans is that their world would be safer and more secure if all young Black males were imprisoned, summarily cordoned and confined to ghettos, or kept under constant surveillance. It is not quirky coincidence that such perceptions, feelings and attitudes towards African American males occur most prevalently within the context of White American dominance. According to Wilson, ultimately criminality of the Black male regardless of its nature, truth or reality, resides in any act or attitude on the part of Black males which appear to White Americans to defy White American authority, control or dominance.[1]

The comments of Mr. Wilson are hard. They are also woefully and overly generalized. Yet there is a grain of truth in his indictments. The fact is that when the identity of Black males is often intertwined with a high level of negative and hostile stereotypes, the comments suggest and/or imply a direct connection between violence, anger, and destruction and the Black male. Therefore, the positive socialization of Black males must take place in this negative and often oppressive context.

The Black family's role in the socialization of black men begins with *equipping them with a Black male identity*. Black male identity is a sense of Black male personhood that is inclusive of the mind, muscles and heart, combined with a cultural orientation that is consistent with the history and culture of the North American Black male.

Concerning culture H. Richard Niebuhr writes:

Culture is the "artificial, secondary environment" which man superimposes on the natural. It comprises language, habits, ideas, beliefs, customs, social organizations, inherited artifacts, technical processes, and values. This "social heritage"—this "reality sui generis" which the New Testament writers frequently had in mind when they spoke of "the world"—which is represented in many forms but to which Christians like other men are inevitably subject, is what we mean when we speak of culture.
Though we cannot venture to define the "essence" of this culture, we can describe some of it's chief characteristics. For one thing, it is inextricably bound up with man's life in society; it is always social.[2]

Niebuhr goes on to include in his definition of culture "human achievement" which, according to Niebuhr, is designed to lead one to the conclusion that the world of culture is a world of values. Culture is the social heritage of one generation of people transmitted to them by their predecessors and

[1] Amos N. Wilson, *Black-On-Black Violence* (New York: Afrikan World Infosystems, 1990), p. 9.
[2] H. Richard Niebuhr, *Christ and Culture* (New York: Harper & Row, 1951) p. 32.

transmitted through them to their successors.

In this venue of acculturation the young Black male begins the process of discovering his sense of significance as an African American male and begins the process of coming to grips with his life's purpose. Yet for the African American male the family must do something more than simply convey and bestow a sense of unity, management of the mind, muscles and heart, and a sense of belonging to a particular culture and family unit.

The Black family must give the Black male a strong personal Black male identity, one that is rooted in the reality that there is in America a Black culture that is rich and strong, so much so that it has impacted and influenced the world through technological advances, medical discoveries, excellence in music, art, nutrition, entertainment, rhythm and rituals. Families should help black men become proud of this rich culture and heritage.

Let me illustrate. When a young man was asked why he identified himself as a Black Christian instead of simply saying that he was a Christian, Jim replied, "I am a Christian by choice but I am Black by birth." Jim had been socialized to believe that his African American race and cultural heritage were so intertwined in his identity from birth that it needed to be emphasized in every dimension of his life and experiences.

In my travels in Israel I find it interesting that men will readily identify themselves by saying "I am Jewish." It occurred to me one day that people with a history of oppression are often socialized to emphasize their race and their culture. So it is with African Americans. Our history of oppression combined with the legacy of that oppression creates in the Black male a need to be proud of his race and culture.

Second in the context of the family Black males *must be equipped to initiate, develop and manage loving relationships.* Truth be told, most black men are quite effective at initiating relationships, especially with the opposite sex. The trouble they seem to have is developing and managing those relationships to make them last.

Relational skills are best developed within a family where the male child has the opportunity both to observe and participate in a loving environment with his parents and fellow siblings. It is in this context that the male child learns such valuable lessons in relationships, as how to communicate, how to forgive, how to listen and have respect for the opinions of others.

Barbara and Willis were well on their way to the marriage altar when their premarital counseling uncovered Willis's inability to trust people. This lack of trust was evident in Willis' temper tantrums whenever Barbara failed to report to him about every detail of her day. It turned out that Willis grew up in a family context where trust was never evident in the relationship between his mother and father.

Many black men evidence a serious deficiency in the area of positive interpersonal relational skills. This deficiency seems unusual in view of the fact that black men tend to be very charismatic and effective in initiating personal relationships, especially with women. This charismatic proficiency in initiating relationships usually conceals the lack of skill in developing and maintaining those relationships.

This inability to develop and maintain lasting positive interpersonal relationships is related to how the attitudes of all men in general and black men in particular are socialized to relate and communicate with women. Male attitudes toward women are expressed in terms of what it is they need them for. The attitude is shaped during their preteen years so that by the time Black boys become adult men they are settled in their minds as to the primary focus of their relationship with women.

In general boys are socialized in the home by the example of the father or some other significant male to discover girls at the physical level by way of being attracted to the external qualities of the young girl. The initial physical attraction often is followed through by physical contact in the form of petting and sex if possible.

By the time boys become men they have developed an attitude toward females that defines their need for them almost exclusively in terms of the physical. As a result of this physical focus men tend to communicate with women in friendship, courtship and marriage at the physical level with little concern for the holistic needs and virtues of the woman.

This attitude in men needs to be refashioned. In growing boys into men the family would do well to rethink how black boys are socialized in the home in terms of how they relate to other folk in general and women in particular. To this end mothers and fathers should spend more time supervising the social life of their sons, with a view to developing in them positive interpersonal relational skills.

The third area of family focus in terms of the socialization of black men is *equipping black men with strong self-esteem*. Self-esteem has to do with how the young boy feels about himself holistically. This includes his views on his physical appearance, intellectual abilities, family blood line, perceived self-worth and significance, among other things. Self-esteem is a positive inner spirit and attitude that fuels the young man's courage and confidence.

In Amos N. Wilson's *Black-On-Black Violence* under the heading of "Self-Contempt, Self-Concept, Love and Violence" Wilson wrote: "The essence of the Black-on-Black criminal is self-hatred or self-alienation. These can only be learned. Self-hatred can only occur as the result of the self having been made to appear to be hateful, ugly, degrading, rejected, associated with pain, nonexistent or devoid of meaning, and inherently inferior. Such appearances and associations are the fruits of White American narcissistic racist projections against the African American community."[3] The truth of Mr. Wilson's comments are well-documented and illustrated daily in the media's spotlight on the violent Black male and violence in the Black community. The Black family must contend with this negative media exposure as they build positive self-esteem in their sons.

Regarding self-esteem James H. Harris writes:

> While others may deserve the blame for the maladies that exist in the black community, we have to take control of the situation. Moreover, there is a need for a new method of ministering that will take into account the negative things that blacks do to themselves, such as black-on-black crime, teenage pregnancy, and community destruction. Though there are structural problems associated with these facts, the black community bears some of the burden for the problems and primary responsibility for the alleviation of these problems.
> There is a correlation between self-image and many other aspects of one's life. Persons who think a lot of themselves seem to be markedly different from those who do not.[4]

Equipping black men with strong self-esteem must begin in early childhood in the home environment. Parents must understand that self-esteem is not about who the boy is as such; it is not about looks, race or the color of his skin though all of these things are involved to some extent. Self-esteem is about how the young man feels about himself as a person. How a man feels about himself as a person dictates how he feels about his

3   Wilson, *Black-On-Black*, p. 77.
4   James H. Harris, *Pastoral Theology: A Black Church Perspective* (Fortress Press, 1985), p. 119.

intellect, looks, race, skin color and intellect.

The parents who socialize their son to feel good about himself have learned the secret of making the son feel significant and valuable as an individual in the context of the family and community. This is done most effectively by parents who pay special attention to their child in a way that makes him feel special.

Matthew was a brilliant man in the truest sense of the word. As a student he had a grade point average that evidenced his strong intellect. In addition Matthew was a very handsome young man; his company was sought by most of the young women who knew him. Matthew participated in sports and had the body of a weight lifter, yet he felt that he was not smart, unintelligent and ugly to look at.

Matthew's perception of himself was not rooted in the reality of his strong intellect nor the reality of his good looks, Matthew could not feel good about his good qualities because he did not feel good about himself. Somewhere in the environment in which Matthew grew up somebody damaged his self-esteem, and as an adult male his strong virtues could not override the dominating power of his low self-esteem.

It is my contention that the family, not the community nor the church, is responsible for equipping black boys with strong positive self-esteem. This equipping is best done by parents in general and fathers in particular who know how to make their sons feel like a special son. Fathers must make every effort to give their sons a sense of significance and self worth.

Fourth, it is in the context of the family that sons of Blackness are socialized to a concept of their Black male *gender identity*. The gender identity of black men is not about the age-old argument of male versus female superiority. It should be clear that women are equal to men in every way. The scope of male and female equality includes the intellect, functional abilities, emotional strength, and spiritual standing before God. However, the fact of male and female equality must not be perceived as meaning that there are no distinctions in the roles and functions of the male and female that are gender-based.

In teaching Black males concerning gender identity the focus must be placed on the differences that exist between men and women, those which make a difference in what it means to be a man and what it means to be a woman. Let it be understood that from a bibliocentric perspective both the man and the woman reflect the image and the glory of God. Scripture clearly reads, "Male and female He created them" (Gen. 1:27). That it takes a man and a woman together to produce or create a child is reflective of the image of God in both. It is also worthy of note that in the body of Christ gender differences do not make a difference in terms of one's standing before God (cf. Gal. 3:28). At the cross men and women stand as equals before God in Christ Jesus.

Gender differences do exist that make a difference in how the man and the woman are designed to function in their relationship with each other in marriage, in the church and in the community. The biological structure and design of men is different from that of women, a distinction that results from testosterone in men and estrogen in women.

This biological difference between men and women is most evident in the observable drive of teenage boys to assert their testosterone-driven desires to initiate, dominate and ultimately assume the leadership role in a relationship with the female. Women, on the other hand, tend to function best as responders to the initiative of the male.

In addition to biological differences that cause men to think and feel different from women, there are sociological differences in the home environment that contain different standards and expectations for the boy than those for his sister. These standards and expectations include the idea that the boy is to grow into a man capable of providing for a wife and children. Boys are socialized to believe that it is their responsibility to provide, protect and nurture their family. Women are socialized to function in a dependent role in their relationship with men regardless of their professional status in the market place.

It is also important to point out that there are spiritual differences that make distinctions in the spiritual functions of men and women. While in the body of Christ there are no male and female differences in terms of spiritual standing before God in Christ Jesus, there are gender difference in terms of Christian function. This gender-driven functional difference covers two primary areas, namely the family and the church. "For the husband is the head of the wife as Christ is the head of the church, his body, of which he is the Savior. Now as the church submits to Christ, so also wives should submit to their husbands in everything" (Eph. 5:23-24). "I do not permit a woman to teach or to have authority over a man; she must be silent" (1 Tim.

2:12).

Maintaining gender differences is not a popular view in today's politically-correct society. The feminist movement, led primarily by middle and upper middle class White women, has done a number on black women and in effect created a rather dismal and frustrating relational environment in many African American male-female relationships especially ones where the woman is a professional or there is not a husband or father in residence.

This less than positive unisexual attitude on the part of many black women has led to the feminization of a growing number of black boys. This feminization is not about homosexuality but about how the Black males are being socialized to function in their relationship with women. In other words, young black men have little sense of a distinctive male identity.

The feminization of black boys and the growing manliness of black girls is a residual effect caused by an attitude held by some Black women. In order to cope and camouflage disappointment in love, some women boast that they only need the African American male for what he has in his pants. They are not referring to the money in his pocket.

Fifth, it is from the home that black boys are equipped with *life values that reflect the history and traditions of African Americans* that are to blossom in manhood and give them good success. In the Village, historically speaking, individualism and separatism were not the prevailing attitudes. Instead, the prevailing attitude in the Black community has historically been one in which the needs of the community as a whole took priority over individual interests.

The historical value system that placed priority on the good of the community as a whole was reflected by the generous sharing of goods and services throughout the community among all who lived in it. There was the sharing of the gardens, the meat from the hog killings, and the joint caring, protecting, and disciplining of the children. Fellowship in the church took place around shared food and drink. Education was a high priority for all the children in the community and success was celebrated no matter who attained it.

In that historical venue, life was celebrated, marriage was honored, and children for the most part were born to married people. The old folk were respected, the sick was attended to and the dead was buried with dignity. The basis of this historic value system was the family Bible and the family church.

Today things are different in terms of life values held by black men. There is evidence of a loss of that historical sense of community with its inherent focus on that which was good for the community as a whole.

In terms of life values today there are four areas that must be established as top priority in the lives of African American males. First, boys must be taught to value their own life and respect the lives of others. Second, boys need to understand the value of a good reputation and thus develop the habit of speaking the truth in regard to themselves and others. Third, boys must have regard for the property of others and respect the right of the other person to maintain possession of that which is theirs. Fourth, sons must learn from the example of others a high regard for the institution of marriage and respect the sanctity of another man's wife.

The unfortunate reality today is one in which many sons are growing up in a family where the most valuable commodities they are exposed to are money, sex, drugs, and other forms of immediate self gratification. Thus in the minds of a number of black boys life evolves around the pursuit of things and pleasure.

Positive life values in the African American tradition teach boys to love people and use money and things. It does not teach boys to love money and things and use people. The young man who is developing positive life values demonstrates that positive process by his willingness to serve others sacrificially.

Finally the family is to pass on to the son *a functional religious belief system that is Christian based and focused.* As I watched the baptism of several professional athletes in a traditional Black church gathering, it occurred to me that these strong black men were in all likelihood responding to the religious seed that was planted in them by their parents, their mother in particular.

There is a tremendous emphasis today on reaching black men and I am personally excited about that reality. However, I am convinced in my own mind that the most effective way to reach black men is to train African American fathers in biblical truth so that they can spiritually nurture their sons.

As Christians we must understand that God sets forth specific responsibilities inherent in the role of a father. The father is charged with the responsibility of leading his family as a loving shepherd reflecting the compassionate leadership of God our heavenly father (Gen. 18:18-19). The father is to rule well his family not as a dictator but as one who loves his family unconditionally just as our heavenly father loves us (1 Tim. 3:4; 3:12). As a loving father he corrects his children not as a means of punishment but in order to correct their ways (Prov. 22:13,15). Fathers, in passing on their spiritual convictions to their sons, teach them the history and traditions of their faith. In his teaching he exposes the son to the history of the living God's involvement in his life experiences (Deut. 4:9; 6:7; 31:13).

The father is responsible to nurture his son's spiritual life and in the process of nurturing he points the son to the living God (Eph. 6:4). Finally the father who effectively passes on the spiritual heritage of the family to the next generation is one who knows how to encourage his children (1 Thess. 2:11).

In speaking to the issue of reclaiming the Village, I suggest that the first area of focus must of necessity be on the African American family structure and its spiritual status. I contend that the African American family today exists in a context of spiritual deficit. This spiritual deficit is most evident in the number of unchurched African American men in our community and the serious deficiency in basic biblical knowledge evident in the black men who attend church on a regular basis.

The family acts as the primary agency for socializing black boys so that they become Christians at an early age and thus are not spiritually fragmented as boys. Unfragmented boys will ultimately develop into whole adult black men.

When families fail in the positive socialization of their sons it seldom proves possible for the church and the community, the second and third agents of primary socialization respectively, to salvage the man. Thus the primary focus in reclaiming the Village must be placed on the African American family structure, especially concentrating on the role and significance of the African American male in that structure.

THE ROLE OF THE BLACK CHURCH

The second agency that functions in the socialization of black men is the Black church. The role of the Black church must be defined and viewed through the lens of Black culture.

Contextually speaking, the role of the Black church is to function as a primary agent of spiritual and social reconciliation, reconciling black men to God being the primary focus.

The instrument for reconciliation is the gospel of Jesus Christ and the vehicle through whom the gospel message flows in the Village is the Black preacher. The prerequisite to reconciliation between God and man is faith in Jesus Christ. Regeneration is then brought about through saving faith. The ordinances of the church are baptism and the Lord's supper. In the context of organized Black religion the preacher is viewed as the primary vehicle through whom God works to move His church and the community.

It is interesting to note that the church grew most rapidly when it was deeply involved during periods of serious social and economic struggle for the Black community in general and black men in particular. One such instance was the period from 1936 to 1962, a period of rapid social, economic and political change for the Black community. The same period saw a great deal of struggle, crisis and intense opposition against the upward mobility of black men. The church in this period became known as a place of refuge for the Black community and black men.

At the forefront of the Black church's ministry has been the objective to teach human worth. The church taught blacks that they were children of God long before the term *self-esteem* became a part of our vocabulary. In the midst of slavery, Jim Crow laws, and overt racism, the Black church accurately interpreted Scripture in a way that enhanced the self-esteem of the children and adults who were being dehumanized by human laws and customs. The liberation motif inherent in the life and message of the Black church continues to sustain so many of us who are products of its teaching. While educational institutions, law-making bodies and businesses failed to accord full humanity to blacks, the Black church was espousing a message of freedom and hope, challenging us to stand tall and be somebody in spite of the hostile and indifferent environment in which we lived.[5]

The Black church has five responsibilities in its role in the socialization of black men. These responsibilities include but are not limited to: *training and affirming traditional life values, developing a sense of purpose in terms of life mission, developing a Christ-focused spiritual belief system, and assisting in the*

---

[5]   Harris, *Pastoral Theology*, p. 115.

establishment of biblical absolutes by which life is lived on a daily basis.

In the history of African Americans no institution has contributed more to their positive socialization than the Black church. Yet many black men today seem uninterested in and even hostile towards the Black church. Perhaps it is time to remind black men of the debt they owe to the Black church for the contributions it has made and continues to make on their behalf in terms of their social, economic, family, educational and political survival.

The contributions of the Black church include but are not limited to psychological liberation from the curse of negative and destructive social habits, assistance in overcoming functional personal limitations and deficiencies resulting from years of social and economic oppression, such as drug and alcohol use and addiction, leadership development opportunities which included the opportunity to assume in the church leadership roles that were not available in the larger community, intellectual freedom to develop educationally and become theologians, professors, philosophers college presidents and such, developing a sense of family structure which encouraged the man's authority in the home, economic opportunity such as insurance agencies and business opportunities, and opportunities for social networking with others within the community to grow successful businesses.

Keeping in mind the fact that the Black church is a strong social institution combined with its long history of contributing to the positive socialization of the African American male, I suggest that the family in general and the father in particular is responsible for teaching positive life values to the children. It is not the church as such who should plant the seeds of positive life values in children but the church through its ministry to the family in general and the father in particular.

The church has the responsibility of reinforcing in children the life values that are put there by the parents. It must be understood that every family in general and every father in particular teaches family values to his sons by his own example. A major factor contributing to a dearth of black men in the church is the low value and often hostile attitude African American fathers attach to local church involvement.

The assertion that mediating values, perspectives, and the feelings they help to produce motivate criminal behavior, should not be construed to imply that conditions such as "poverty" do not contribute to criminality to a substantial degree. Furthermore, it should not be construed to imply that attitude, values, etc., need only be changed in order to change the criminal behavior of those who live in poverty without improving poverty conditions themselves. A condition and the experiential reactions it appears to evoke are derivative of the synthesization of the individual's perception of his "real" physical, behavioral, and social environment and the organized experiences and the motivations he brings into that environment. Consequently, significant changes in one stimulates related changes in the other and vice-versa.

Indeed the conditions under which the individual lives may significantly affect those with whom he associates. The perspectives, attitudes and values he internalizes provide or fail to provide the resources, opportunities and other amenities, the patterns of which determines whether or not he engages in criminal behavior. . .[6]

I suggested earlier that there are at least four things African American males must be socialized to value. I said (1) boys must be taught to value their life and respect the lives of others; (2) boys need to understand the value of a good reputation and thus develop the habit of speaking the truth in regard to themselves and others; (3) boys must have regard for the property of others and respect the right of the other person to maintain possession of that which is theirs; and (4) sons must learn from the example of others a high regard for the institution of marriage and respect the sanctity of another man's wife.

Only when these values become a part of the socialization process of black boys in the home will it be possible for the church to fulfill its responsibility of *reinforcing* these values by word and example in the context of its overall ministry to the family of liberation and reconciliation. If these values are not found in the home environment and thus not modeled before the male child it becomes very difficult to establish them as absolutes in the adult male even if they are saved.

As an Evangelical preacher for over three decades with a ministry focused primarily on black men and women, I am not at all convinced that our approach to evangelism and discipleship of African American men and women is entirely biblical. To be sure our focus on individualism in the church is derived from our western Eurocentric culture which places an

---

[6]   Wilson, *Black-On-Black*, p. 88-89.

almost exclusive emphasis on the individual. But I am increasingly leaning toward the position that this focus on individualism as opposed to the household and the church body may not be entirely biblical and is in conflict with Afrocentric culture.

Accordingly James H. Harris writes: "What is needed is a new type of linkage and interdependence between the church and the black community. This will help advance the quality of life of all blacks and hasten the process of achieving equality, fairness, and peace in our communities. More importantly there is a need for a new prescriptive theology-one that will help usher in a new day of freedom, justice and equality."[7]

I believe the New Testament model of evangelism is bent more in the direction of the family and the group. Thus, when an individual comes to faith, they often come to faith in the context of a family or a community so that the socialization process of the entire household is changed and the (*Village*) community is impacted for good.

The more powerful influence on a son's belief in God and the Bible most often comes from the example of the father rather than what he hears at church. For instance, I find it very difficult to teach young men respect for the institution of marriage when their fathers are immoral. It is hardly possible to develop in a young man respect for the life of another when his family context evidences a disregard for life. I am not suggesting that salvation does not change an individual entirely. It does. I am suggesting that in terms of life values, what the family establishes as valuable and or not so valuable in its socialization process is most often always present and influences to some extent the attitude and behavior of the young man who grows up in that environment.

Tony grew up in a family where the father was at times very cruel to him and his fellow siblings. He would often beat them for things which he thought they might have done. It was not unusual for Tony's dad to get him out of bed at midnight to rake leaves and grass from the yard. In this context of abuse he learned the value of lying to his father with a straight face as a means of avoiding cruel punishment. Later as a Christian young man Tony would seldom tell the truth when he felt threatened by the consequences.

Ben, on the other hand, was the kind of person who felt that

---

[7]   Harris, *Pastoral Theology*, p. 185.

moral purity was a standard for good girls but morality for boys did not include abstaining form sexual immorality. He felt that women should be faithful to their husbands but men were free to commit adultery so long as it did not become public and embarrass the family. Though Ben was saved he never developed any sense of moral values in this area. For him morality was a woman thing. Like his father, Ben expected his wife to accept his discreet immoral life.

It is difficult for the church to change or reverse the socialization of men which they have received and internalized from their family as they grew up. The church is effective when it can reinforce positive values first taught in the home. Black males are socialized in terms of their values first in the home. Those values are subsequently *reinforced* in the church.

When it comes to developing a life purpose, though the church is designed to take the lead in the socialization of black men. In thinking through the idea of socializing black men in the development of life's purpose I have observed that the Nation of Islam while making great strides in reaching black men and effectively resocializing them in terms of their ability to get off drugs, stay out of prison, and clean up their acts seems to be unsuccessful in resocializing these men in terms of their life purpose. Evidence tends to suggest that while the Nation of Islam is most effective in the inner cities in their membership recruitment efforts they tend to seek men from the college campuses to manage their international network of successful business enterprises. The inner city recruits are most likely to be found on the corner selling papers and bags of fruit.

This evident inability of the Nation of Islam to resocialize men as it pertains to life's purpose is rooted in the fact that the Nation of Islam accomplishes its religious and social goals in the lives of black men apart from a relationship with Jesus Christ and knowing Him as the living God. It is my contention that without a primary focus on the risen Lord Jesus Christ at the center of their person and the foundation of their hope no man can come to grips with his life purpose.

The Million Man March of October 16, 1995 more than anything in the recent history of black men in this country demonstrated the fact that black men are in search of purpose and significance as men in America. Minister Farrakhan spoke very proudly of this mega-gathering of black men in response to his invitation to them to come. However, there is little evidence that suggests that anything of substance has resulted from that gathering that has moved to fill the vacuum in the lives of black men in this country.

When it comes to *life purpose* the church holds the key in terms of effectively communicating that purpose from a divine perspective to men. As I suggested earlier one of the primary purposes a man must have in his life is to reflect the image and the glory of God. This is done by way of a man's creative skills, conquering ingenuity and his capacity for ruling over creation. In the book of Micah the prophet Micah sets forth a three fold purpose of man in the context of his relationship with God. "He has showed you, O man, what is good. And what does the LORD require of you? To act justly and to love mercy and to walk humbly with your God" (Micah 6:8).

Commenting on this passage, Dr. John A. Martin in the *Bible Knowledge Commentary* wrote:

> "Micah then told the nation (**O man** means any person in Israel) exactly what God did desire from them. God did not want them to be related to Him in only a ritualistic way. God wanted them to be related inwardly—to obey Him because they desired to, not because it was a burden on them. That relationship, which is **good** (beneficial) involves three things: that individuals (a) **act justly** (be fair in their dealings with others). (b) love mercy (*hesed*, "loyal love"; i.e. carry through on their commitments to meet others needs), and (c) walk humbly with . . . God (fellowship with Him in modesty, without arrogance)."[8]

Reflecting again on the Million Man March, it is interesting to note that the men who came to that march included most if not all of the social and economic groups from the lowest to the highest in this country. There were men who made their way to the march who had next to nothing; others went who had it all.

What these men shared in common was not a common social and economic status but a lack of established purpose in terms of their life purpose and mission. To put it another way, these men were seeking an answer to the questions "Who am I?" and "Why am I here?" The answer to these questions is the primary business of the church as it proclaims the gospel of Jesus Christ.

In terms of *life purpose*, the evidence suggests that more than a few African American men have bought into the idea that the whole purpose of life is to be found in the pursuit of material

_____
⁸   John A. Martin, "Micah" in *The Bible Knowledge Commentary* (Victor Books, 1985), 1:1489.

gain. Thus men socialize their sons to believe that money is the most important commodity they can obtain in life. In their pursuit of money men often sacrifice everything including their own life as well as the lives of their children. But when all is said and done, men at the top of the economic ladder find themselves still empty and insecure because contrary to what was promised, money does not deliver contentment and it cannot deliver or establish purpose in life.

Regarding wealth and crime in the Village, Amos N. Wilson writes:

> Wealth, the feelings and the associated ideas it evokes in some individuals, may motivate criminal behavior. Crime is not the monopoly of poor folk, nor is greed, alienation, and so on. We should note that a person or group is seldom if ever exposed to one environment exclusively, particularly in the United States. Poverty-stricken people know of and have been exposed to wealth. They are often keenly aware of the material and social benefits derived from being wealthy. This knowledge and experience, along with the internalization of cultural myths concerning rights and opportunities to acquire wealth, in conjunction with other ideas and feeling, interact with the current situation to determine behavior, some of which may be labeled criminal. Discrepancies such as between what is and what could be, what is and ho w it got to be the way it is, are "symptomatic compromises." It may be more the exposure to wealth. To the wealthy via direct and indirect experiences (e.g., reading, advertisement, etc.), which is the source of criminal behavior, more so than the exposure to poverty.[9]

It is common knowledge among students of Black history that the Black church has been for the Black male a primary contributor to their socialization in terms of life purpose. However, the church today seems impotent in its ability to impact black men as it pertains to their life purpose. Much of the spiritual impotence of today's church is related to the change of focus in the Black church which has moved to an agenda that places prosperity as the cornerstone of its message and ministry focus in terms of life purpose.

The late Dr. Martin Luther King Jr. in his letter from a jail in Birmingham, Alabama during the height of the civil rights struggles said ". . . the judgment of God is upon the church as never before. If today's church does not recapture the sacrificial spirit of the early church, it will lose its authenticity, forfeit the loyalty of millions and be dismissed as an irrelevant social club with no meaning for the twentieth century. Everyday I meet

---

[9] Wilson, *Black On-Black*, p. .90.

young people whose disappointment with the church has turned to outright disgust."[10] It seems to me that Dr. King's words are prophetic and describe the spiritual reality of the Black church today as we stand on the eve of the twenty-first century.

The third function of the local church in the socialization of black men is to equip them with a *Christocentric belief system* that is distinctively biblical. In this context, it is well to reflect briefly on the historical shaping of the belief system of African American men. The social and economic experience of black men in America contributed to the shaping of the belief system of black men. Black men, both slave and free, first heard the gospel message and were converted to Christianity through the preaching of White preachers most often in a tightly controlled and theologically manipulated White religious setting. In this setting both Whites and Blacks believed what they both heard and understood about the God of the Bible. Out of this understanding all men developed a belief system centered around the God of the Bible. Out of their respective belief systems emerged expectations of God in terms of His dealing with each in the context of their life situation.

For White Christians these expectations of God in terms of His involvement in the affairs of their lives were in accord with the existing Colonial-based Christian focused belief system. Out of their belief system emerged their distinctive world view which contended for prosperity and sustained racial superiority as evidence of divine approval and favor with God. Thus the belief system of White Christians had at its core expectations of prosperity from the hand of God in the context in which they lived.

The Black slave heard and believed the Bible stories and developed a belief system that was Christian based. Out of the Black slaves' belief system emerged their own expectations of God. For Blacks these expectations were in accord with the pain inherent in their oppressive life circumstances. The belief system of the slaves was rooted in the theological concept that the God of the Bible was the God of the oppressed and He was their deliverer as He was for the children of Israel when they were slaves in Egypt.

Thus while both the White oppressors and the Black oppressed of that day heard and believed many of the same

---

[10] Martin Luther King Jr., *Why We Can't Wait* (Penguin Group, 1964), p. 92.

things about the God of the Bible, their expectations of God which were rooted in their respective social and economic contexts were radically different. The difference in the expectations of God between the Black Christian slaves and the White Christian slave owners marked the difference between the social and economic context of prosperity that the White lived in and the social and economic context of pain that the Blacks lived in.

The slave held to a belief system that caused him to expect God to deliver him from slavery just as He delivered the children of Israel from slavery in Egypt and rain down judgment upon their White oppressors as He did Pharaoh at the Red Sea. From the same God White Christians expect prosperity which meant that their slaves would produce more of everything including children, grain and animals. The differences between the expectations of Black Christians and White Christians grew out of the differences that existed in the social and economic context in which each lived.

The church historically has been biblical in its perspective. Black people understood the Bible differently from whites. They have, without question, read and studied the same words of Scripture as whites; however, blacks have discerned a different message from the same words. That is why Nat Turner, a religious man, preacher, and visionary, led the insurrection in Southampton County, Virginia. He felt he was doing God's will—by ushering in an age of justice and freedom.[11]

The church must function today as an agency that is equipped to contextualize the gospel message in terms of its holistic, social and economic implications and applications so that black men develop a belief system that is not in conflict with either the Bible or their social and economic situation. I suggest that those who teach the Bible to African American men must be equipped to comfortably bring to that study the culture and the social and economic context of black men.

The fourth function of the church in the socialization of black men is to equip them with *a sense of self-worth.*Speaking to the issue of "Self-esteem in Context" James H. Harris writes: "The African American has been subjected to the most persistent and blatant forms of racism and oppression to be inflicted upon a people during modern times. This has been done in the midst of a society that speaks of freedom and equality in lofty

---

[11]   Harris, *Pastoral Theology*, p. 12.

philosophical terms without any recognizable intent to comply
with the moral obligation of its written or spoken words. Black
people have done well to maintain their sanity in the midst of
this constant and pervasive assault on their self-esteem."[12]

A sense of self worth is to some degree different from the
self-esteem about which I spoke earlier though it is built upon
the foundation of the self-esteem that is learned in the home
environment. This sense of self worth is perhaps best illustrated
in a brief historical reflection on the history of the Black church
in America. The first Black church was founded in the 1770s,
some time after the signing of the Declaration of Independence
in 1776. This was close to one hundred and sixty years after the
first slaves were brought to this country. Few if any first
generation slaves were converted to Christianity.

Driving the black people's desire to organize their own
separate churches and denominations following the
Emancipation Proclamation in 1860 was their perception that
part of the American conception of humanness included the
exercise of control over one's property. To Black people in that
historical context being human was to be free to do what they
wanted with their own property and resources. Thus the
founding of their own separate Black congregations and
denominations was for these pioneer church planters an
assertion of their humanity in a context that denied them such
recognition.

In that context Black people bestowed upon themselves a
sense of self worth through the church which gave them control
over some aspects of their own lives. This bestowal of self worth
by the church of that day caused these pioneer church planters
to seek ways of ensuring their freedom from the control of the
White person.

To this end many congregations and organizations
stipulated in their articles of incorporation the exclusion of
Whites from official membership and control of church property.
These stipulations must be viewed through the lens of the social
and economic context of those times in which these Black
churches existed. These Black churches were very poor and most
all of them were dependent to some degree upon benevolence
from a few Whites.

Through the years the Black church has been about the
business of bestowing self-worth upon black people in general

---

[12]   Ibid., p. 117.

and black men in particular. To this day in the Black community the church stands out even in the slums as the best kept facility in the community. It is where Black people socialize, entertain, network, wear their best clothes and drive their finest cars. It is also the only institution in the Black community that is dominated by the Black male.

Amos Wilson writes regarding the Black-on-Black violent criminal:

> The Black-on-Black violent criminal is what he is because he has been treated criminally at some point in his life, and/or treated to a history or a model of criminality. He is within a context that evokes criminal behavior not inhibited or redirected by effective opposing or alternative moral, intellectual, socioeconomic, cultural and valuational structures. The Black-on-Black criminal is violent because he has been violated, or perceives himself as such. He is vindictive. He wants to "pay the world back" for some insult he most often cannot name or define, an insult which occurred to him in the womb; an insult for which he wishes to vindicate himself, for that which occurred centuries before he or his parents were born—a history of unrequited grievances.[13]

To the extent that Amos Wilson is correct in his analysis of the mind and attitude of the African American criminal mindset the Black church must develop a ministry focus that not only focuses on the Village with a primary emphasis on reaching the African American male it must also develop a ministry focus that targets the White community with a view to changing the negative stereotypical views it holds of black men and creating positive work opportunities in the marketplace for black men.

In my view it is not possible to reclaim the Village without the positive involvement of the White community. For it is the White community that has primary control of power in this country. It is the White power structure that developed and maintains policies that exclude black men as equals with White men in the marketplace, politics, religion and the judicial system in America.

In his book *The Social Teaching of the Black Churches*, Peter J. Paris writes:

> The profound nature of the exclusion about which we are speaking cannot be grasped apart from an understanding of the integral relationship between person and society. Whenever persons are rejected by society, the result is a loss of place; the result is exile. Whenever a pattern of rejection persists from one generation to another and is firmly rooted in an ideology, the rejected ones become destined to a veritable permanent state of exile wherein

---

[13] Wilson, *Black-on-Black*, p. 77.

they have no sense of belonging, neither to the community nor to the territory. Since it is necessary for persons to be nourished by a communal Eros in order to become fully human, an imposed exile necessitates the formation of a substitute community, and, as we have seen that has been one of the major functions of the black churches. Born and reared in an alien sociopolitical context, blacks have had little hope for any sense of genuine national belonging. All attempts at self-actualization on the part of both individuals and the race as a whole have plagued with many and varied forms of social proscription, each of which has been based on a particular understanding of the nature of black humanity along with a corresponding institutionalized policy. For example, (1) slavery was based on the view that blacks were subhuman and hence needed to be owned and directed by others; (2) the American Colonization Society sought to repatriate this inferior race in Africa, because it contended that whites would never accept them as equals; (3) universal racial segregation and discrimination in the South (similar to that which was long practiced in the North towards freedmen) became the dominant social policy in the twentieth century for expressing the doctrine of racial inequality; (4) the legal demise of the Jim Crow system at mid-century has left in place large-scale urban ghettoization which, in turn, ensures for the foreseeable future the perpetuation of a racial underclass. All of these policies were designed to thwart the progress of blacks in all dimensions of their common life, and, perhaps worst of all, they have contributed to a sense of low esteem that blacks frequently have of themselves—a problem that the churches have sought tirelessly to correct.[14]

James H. Harris writes: "Self-esteem is the crucial movement towards true evangelicalism, and the church's role is to raise the level of consciousness in our people so the message of the gospel may truly be liberative. The Black church is called to actualize self-esteem in its ministry by developing programs that will specifically address this crucial need."[15]

THE ROLE OF THE BLACK COMMUNITY

There is a sense in which the term Black community refers not to a particular geographical community of African American people living in a certain city in America but to all African American people in this country. Yet the perception held by most folks who use or hear this descriptive phrase "Black community" is that all Black people live in and share not only a common geographic community but also a common socioeconomic lifestyle. It is important to note that this

---

[14] Peter J. Paris, *The Social Teaching of the Black Churches* (Fortress Press, 1985), p. 59-60.
[15] Harris, *Pastoral Theology*, p. 116.

perception of the phrase "Black community" is held by both Whites and Blacks.

African American people while sharing a common social, economic, political, cultural and religious legacy and heritage are quite diverse in terms of values, lifestyle and religious preferences today. Yes, there are those things that all African American people can only get in the demographic and geographic Black community such as hair cuts, certain food stuff, shoe shines and the Black church experience. However, this in no way suggests that all black men are the same. There are vast differences among black men in terms of their lifestyles and values.

Having said that, I must also point out that there is the reality of the existence of communities across this country that are entirely inhabited by African Americans. In these communities the common ground among the people is much broader than among those who live in integrated communities and are classified as white collar professionals.

There is a need for the church and the urban community to understand their interdependence. Neither the church nor the community lives for itself. A new sense of interdependence will enable blacks from all segments of society to understand anew the words of Paul to the church at Rome: "We do not live to ourselves, and we do not die to ourselves. If we live, we live to the Lord, and if we die we die to the Lord; so then, whether we live or die we are the Lord's" (Rom. 14:7-8).[16]

The Black community that is demographically Black has five basic structures around which it is built and upon which it stands and operates. These structures are production, distribution and consumption, socialization, social control, social participation and a mutual support system.

These five structural community pillars, are the avenues through which the community participates in the socialization of its residents in general and black men in particular. There are five areas in which the community interfaces with the family and the church in the socialization of black men: (a) developing values; (b) affirming self-worth; (c) providing opportunities to develop and practice social and economic skills; (d) demonstrating by way of models the principles taught in the home and by the church; and (e) provide a social network through which mutual communal support can be realized.

---

[16]   Ibid., pp. 31, 32.

I suggested earlier that there are at least four things African American boys must be socialized to value: (1) boys must be taught to value their life and respect the lives of others; (2) boys need to understand the value of a good reputation and thus develop the habit of speaking the truth in regard to themselves and others; (3) boys must have regard for the property of others and respect the right of the other person to maintain possession of that which is theirs; and (4) sons must learn from the example of others a high regard for the institution of marriage and respect the sanctity of another man's wife.

The primary socialization agency in the lives of young men must always be the home. What the home establishes in terms of life values is then reinforced by the church by way of its ministry of modeling the biblical ideal. The community is the context in which black boys develop proficiency in the application of the life values taught in the home and affirmed in the church. Inherent in the process of value socialization in the community is the observance and celebration of certain days such as June 19th (June Teenth) in Texas, Kwanzaa and the passing of Black cultural traditions from one generation to the next.

In discussing the socialization of black men in the community much has been said about the Black 'hood in America. Often a lot of what is said is mere rhetoric containing little if any real truth. Rather the Black community today bears little if any resemblance to the Black community of the past. To this end it is necessary to put the Black community in today's context.

The major population shift of African Americans from the rural agrarian south to the urban cities of the north and Midwest ended around 1970. This population shift is known as the Southern Migration. When the Southern Migration ended, the southern Black population had shifted from a high of 90% in the early twentieth century to around 52% in the 1970. This meant that for the first time there were more Blacks in the northern cities than there were in the agrarian South.

The migration of Blacks from the rural agrarian south to the large urban metropolitan cities in the north, significantly changed the religious, family, social and economic context in which African Americans lived.

Upon arrival in the Northern cites, these black men and women with their families moved into communities that were already crowded. These were communities abandoned by the

European immigrants who fled from the growing number of Blacks that moved into the community from the southern plantations.

One of the major problems seen in this new urban context was the inadequacy of existing housing and other resources to accommodate the increasing number of people in these urban communities.

In the rural south Blacks lived in a rather intimate social environment in which relationships within the community were strong and the extended family was a significant part of the social and economic infrastructure of the community. By contrast, in this new urban arena there was no such intimate social and economic context.

In an attempt to recreate the neighborhood with a communal flavor of intimate relationships, the southern immigrants transplanted their country churches to their new cities. However, time and circumstances proved unkind to the imported country church and its poorly equipped pastor as they struggled to fill the vacuum created by the new northern urban community in the lives of these Southern immigrants.

What was the urban ghettos of the southern immigrants in the 1970s have become the dangerous urban slums of the 1990s. The effect of these urban slum ghettos on the socialization of black men is generally negative. I note that "ghetto" is a reference to the race, or religion of the majority of the people who live in the neighborhood, i.e., Blacks, Jews, Catholic, Protestant etc. The word "slum" refers to the condition of the community in terms of the quality of the housing, streets, city services, etc.. There are no slum people, only slum living conditions.

The African American urban community today has a multitude of deficiencies limiting its ability to contribute positively to the socialization of Black males. These deficiencies are evident in the lack of visible positive life values in the community. In the urban Black community today two primary values are dominant, namely, money and survival. There is little evidence of life values that reflect a concern for life and respect for the lives of others. Few things in the community today reflect concern for the value of a good reputation and the habit of speaking the truth in regard to themselves and others.

Inner city young men seem to have little regard for the property of other people and even less regard for the other person's right to maintain possession of their property. In the inner city communities there are few examples of a high regard for the institution of marriage which include an unwavering respect for the sanctity of another man's wife.

Although urban communities are beset with many deficiencies in terms of their ability to contribute to the positive socialization of black men these communities have a number of long-term married couples and they are literally filled with churches. This suggests to me that any strategy aimed at reclaiming the Village must of necessity begin with a focus on the family and court the involvement of the church.

One of the primary functions of parents, teachers and various cultural institutions is moral education-guiding, training, and nurturing the young children in knowing, obeying, and affirming the culture's basic values. Hence, moral education can never take place in a vacuum; rather, it takes place in relation to a set of normative values. Harmony occurs in the context of mutuality (1) between persons and the society when the values of the latter are experienced by the former as self-affirming, that is, as a source of nurture for the self-actualization of persons; (2) between the society and persons when the values of the latter are supportive of those of the former, that is when persons have a spirit of patriotism aimed at enhancing the power of the larger whole. Similarly, disharmony occurs whenever the values of the society are experienced by persons as alien to their well-being and vice-versa. Thus, whenever particular social groups—religious, ethnic, economic, and the like—stand in opposition to the basic societal values, they necessarily threaten the entire social order.[17]

It was in the context of the communal vacuum born of the urban environment that the positive traditional life values of the Village began to fade and were eventually lost. For the Southern immigrant, the urban ghetto was a place of isolation in which the training and education of succeeding generations with traditional life values was at best difficult and at worse impossible.

In terms of the ability of the African American community in general to confer on black men a sense of self worth, it is interesting to note that when the great superstar O. J. Simpson lost his credibility and significance in the White community the Black community received him back into the fold with open

---

[17]   Paris, *The Social Teaching*, pp. 57-58.

arms and affirmed him as a significant somebody. This affirming attitude on the part of Black people is rooted in their history as a people with a compassionate spirit towards the underdog.

In the Black community there still is excitement when Black boys succeed in school, sports or any other endeavor. High School graduation is always well-attended by parents and friends of the graduates. In the Black community doing good is still exciting. This may sound like a contradiction to see the Black community as a place filled with social and economic deficiencies and disharmony in terms of positive life values and at the same time be a community that is intent on affirming that which is good. This reality is more of a paradox than a contradiction.

In terms of Black male socialization there is the ever-present need for positive role models. In the Urban community there are few African American heroes. I am not suggesting that there are none, for indeed there are many in the fields of athletics, entertainment, education, politics and academics. The problem is that in most instances the White community has stolen and appropriated the Black heroes from the Black community. When the White community no longer has any use for successful black men they are returned to the community with little if anything to offer in the form of models in the 'hood.

The African American community to some degree is not unlike a separate colony in that much of what occurs in it is controlled and manipulated by a power structure that is extrinsic to the community. A power structure does exist within the Black community. However this power structure is neither fully autonomous nor fully a creation of the citizens of that community.

As a result of this fragile community structure in the Black community today, it is seriously impotent in its ability to participate in the socialization of Black males in term of helping them develop holistically and become successful in the labor market. These deficiencies in the Black male most often result in few role models and poor networking in the community in terms of education, business, etc.

It is my contention that the Black church is the most viable option in the Village for reclaiming the Village. Speaking of the Black church in the context of the historical struggle of Black people in this country Peter J. Paris writes:

As we have seen, the black church has a notable history of founding educational institutions and promoting learning both within and outside the church. Closely associated with the educational programs of the respective churches, black denominational publishing houses were founded to enable black writers to participate in the production of study materials and to protect the children and laity from being exposed, either implicitly or explicitly, to racist propaganda. The publishing houses also provided an avenue for publication of monographs by blacks about blacks and especially historical studies of the churches and their leaders. As the progenitors of the black secular press, they constituted for many decades one of the race's chief means of gaining information along with editorialized comments on issues pertaining to the welfare of the race.[18]

It can be argued today that the Black church remains the possession of the Black community and embodies the cultural heritage of black people. Because of the financial clout of the black church and its ability to raise millions of dollars in cash and real estate, the Black church can hardly be dismissed or disregarded as the most likely candidate in reclaiming the Village.

Speaking to the issue of the moral realm in the Black community Peter J. Paris writes:

In the nineteenth century virtually all black leaders, ecclesiastical and otherwise, looked upon the slave experience as one of moral and social degradation. Consequently they assumed major responsibilities for "uplifting" the race by means of moral education. It was hoped that such training would result in the development of black men and women of good moral character, solidly grounded in the virtues of industry, thrift, patience, and goodwill—virtues that they considered necessary for legitimating their claim for full and equal citizenship rights. It did not take long, however, before black leaders perceived that their struggle entailed the task not only of rehabilitating the race from the effects of an oppressive past but also of confronting a rapidly rising tide of racial segregation that was destined to shape race relations for the foreseeable future. Nevertheless they continued to give high priority to the moral improvement of the race.[19]

This historical model of the involvement of the black church in the moral struggle of its people is in my view a relevant and functional model for the church today. In addition to its strong emphasis on worship and praise, the black church must give consistent and persistent attention to recovering the moral conscience of the Village.

---

[18]   Ibid., pp. 77-78.
[19]   Ibid., p. 62.

CHAPTER 4

GOD'S PATTERN
FOR DEVELOPING
UNFRAGMENTED MEN

I AM LOOKING FOR MYSELF.
HAVE YOU SEEN ME?

I met Fred at a singles seminar I was conducting. Fred caught my attention during the seminar because his questions were clear and to the point. Occasionally Fred would proudly respond to one of my questions to the group with answers that were well thought-out and biblically-based.

After the seminar Fred volunteered to take me back to the hotel. He said that he had a few questions he wanted to asked me in private and a few issues he wanted to discuss with me. On our way to the hotel Fred began by telling me an abbreviated version of his life. He was in his early fifties, was single again after having been married for nearly twenty years. He had a young son conceived out of wedlock since his divorce. Fred was retired from his job but busy doing a variety of different things.

Fred was a man who wanted to do the right thing for his son, which in his mind meant marrying his son's mom but marriage for Fred was a bit too much, especially since he had been there and done that before. As I listened to Fred confide about the mother of his son, his first marriage, and his skepticism about people and situations in general, it occurred to me that there must be something deeper inside Fred's mind that was causing him to be so unsettled at his age.

I finally turned the conversation away from Fred's son and toward Fred and asked him about his family background to which Fred responded, "I have no idea who my father or mother is. I was raised by a woman who took me in as a child." With this said Fred grew quiet. After a few moments of silence I said to Fred, "Have you considered the possibility that you may be the primary cause behind your problems of uncertainty and insecurity?" Fred answered, "Not really!" Another silent pause came and went and I continued, "It may well be, Fred, that you have spent most of your adult life trying to find yourself given the lack of identity you received as a child." I shall not soon forget the stunned look in Fred's eyes after hearing those words.

As a minister for nearly four decades I have seen countless numbers of men who like Fred are caught in the never-ending maze of uncertainty about themselves and their future that resulted from not having in place a strong self-esteem and a settled self-identity. In my view, positive self-esteem and positive self-identity go hand in hand. Deficiencies in the areas of self-esteem and personal identity contribute to the rise of a multitude of interpersonal relational problems between black men and their wives and children.

Regarding self-esteem, Matthew McKay and Patrick Fanning wrote:

> Self-esteem is essential for psychological survival. It is an emotional sine qua non—without some measure of self-worth, life can be enormously painful, with many basic needs going unmet.
> One of the main factors differentiating humans from other animals is the awareness of self: the ability to form an identity and then attach a value to it. In other words, you have the capacity to define who you are and then decide if you like that identity or not. The problem of self-esteem is this human capacity for judgment. It's one thing to dislike certain colors, noise, shapes or sensations. But when you reject parts of yourself, you greatly damage the psychological structure that literally keep you alive.[1]

Fragmented men are men who do not have strong self-esteem and thus do not like themselves as a whole. It is the fragmentation in the area of their self- esteem that contributes to the overall poor performance of black men in their relationships with their wives and children.

> Judging and rejecting yourself causes enormous pain. In the same way that you would favor and protect a physical wound, you find yourself avoiding anything that might aggravate the pain of self-

---

[1] Matthew McKay and Patrick Fanning, *Self-Esteem* (Oakland, CA: New Harbinger Publications), p. 1.

rejection in any way. You take fewer social, academic, or career risks. You make it more difficult for yourself to meet people, interview for a job, or push hard for something where you might not succeed. You limit your ability to open yourself with others, express your sexuality, be the center of attention, hear criticism, ask for help, or solve problems.[2]

Suicide mortality rates reach its peak in African American males between twenty-five to thirty-four and in White males at age sixty-five and over. Homicide and suicide are two of the leading causes of death among young Black males between ages 15 and 24. They are probably the leading cause of accidental deaths, and the many "suicides on the installment plan"—addictions, poor health habits, etc.—are included. Thus, black men kill themselves with their futures yet ahead of them, and White men when their futures are well behind them. One dies at the blossoming in the spring, the other after the first frost of autumn.

Apparently, the young African American who commits suicide is one who has grown old while very young. He has packed all the guilt, failures, shame, fatalism, pain, hopelessness, and cynicism of a lifetime within a lifespan of three decades. Somehow the cavalier optimism of youth and the willful self-confidence of young manhood have dissipated at or before the point of actualization and assumption of their powers to transform the world. Somehow Black youth and adults are born into and come early to exist in a different and ominous reality.[3]

It is out of this context of ministering to men who evidenced serious fragmentation in how they perceived themselves that caused me to think through the issue of the fragmentation of black men. For me the issue does not revolve around the argument of whether or not a significant number of black men show evidence of fragmentation in the area of their personal identity; I am convinced that most do. I am more concerned about how this fragmentation occurs, and what if anything can be done to correct it. There is an even more pressing concern, namely, is there a divine design for growing unfragmented men? I am convinced that there is such a design in the Bible.

It is to be noted at the very outset that like male babies of other races, African American males are not born with low or

---

[2]   Ibid., p. 2.
[3]   Amos N. Wilson, *Black-on-Black Violence* (New York: Afrikan World Infosystems, 1994), p. 157.

diminished self-esteem. The African American parent receives their newborn fresh from the womb with all the accompanying excitement as do other parents. Thus to the extent that the African American male grows into an adult with diminished self-esteem the conclusion indicates that the damage occurs in the environment into which the male child is born and grows up.

Speaking to the issue of what it means to be an African American male in America Amos N. Wilson writes:

> To be an African American male is to be confronted with bedeviling contradictions. It is to live with chronic feelings of self-consciousness. It is to experience the emptiness of deprivation; to be more often than not unfulfilled, unactualized; to be the object of the irrational and unpredictable hostility of others; to be perceived as a breathing, red-blooded stereotype; to be looked through; to be often regressed because the avenues of healthy self-expression and personal potentiation are closed against positive forward movement.[4]

While Wilson's profile of what it means to be black and male in America tends to be extremely negative and grossly generalized, there is a lot of truth in admitting that the environment is flawed with negativity.

As African American Christian men and women, we must concern ourselves with the reality that a number of black men, both Christian and non-Christian, reveal a diminished view of who they are in terms of how they feel about themselves. This diminished sense of self-worth shows up in the lives of African American men in the early stages of their development into adulthood, in their relational skills and social interaction. To this end I turn my attention to the issue of God's design for developing unfragmented men.

In Genesis 2:18-25 God gives us His pattern and design for developing unfragmented men. Let us note what God did not do after His observation about the man Adam: He was alone and it was not good for him. God was going to create from the man Adam one that corresponded to how God had designed and created the man (Adam). But there was a process to all of this.

The first thing that God did not do in responding to Adam's temporary condition of relational alienation was God did not provide for Adam that which he did not recognize his need for. Instead God led Adam through a sensitivity session, with a view to bringing Adam to the emotional and psychological point where he would recognize his need for a

---

[4] Ibid., p. 117.

corresponding helper (a wife).

In responding to Adam's real but yet unrecognized need for a creature corresponding to how he was created, God created a plethora of animals, which included all the different species, and Adam named each of the different species evidencing his fully developed intellect.

Having completed the assignment of naming all the different animals that God created, the Bible records, "So the man gave names to all the livestock, the birds of the air and all the beasts of the field. *But for Adam no suitable helper was found*" (Gen. 2:20, *italics mine*).

I understand the text to mean at least by implication that the man Adam, while in the process of responding to the assignment God gave to him to name all of the animals, examined his compatibility with the different species of animals. Adam found that God designed all of the animals to relate to others of the same kind but none were designed to fit holistically with him. Adam differed in characteristic traits from the other animals. Thus while it can be argued that the man was a part of the the same general circle of animal life, yet he stood unique and alone, above and apart from the animals of the world in terms of his inability to relate to them.

Another thing God did not do in responding to Adam's need for a corresponding helper is that He did not create another male to fill this relational vacuum in Adam's life. According to how Adam was designed by God he needed someone who could fit with him holistically in terms of his physical, social and emotional needs as well as his need to procreate. To this end God did not create a Steve for Adam, for in God's mind Adam needed an Eve, not a Steve, to correspond to how he was designed.

Having considered two things that God did not do in order to fill the vacuum in Adam's life in light of how he was designed, now consider what God did do. Having sensitized Adam to the fact that he was but one part of a two-part relational unit of one, God put Adam to sleep and took a rib from his side and created for Adam the woman Eve.

First Corinthians 11:9 tells us, "For also man was not created on account of the woman, on the contrary, woman on account of the man." In his commentary on Paul's epistles to the Corinthians Lenski writes regarding this text,

> "Man," without the article, any man whoever he may be; "on account of the woman," with the article, hence Eve; "woman," without the article some woman; "on account of the man," with the article, hence Adam. God made "a woman" for Adam but not "a man" for Eve. God could, indeed, have created both man and woman, Adam and Eve, in one undivided act. Today many think and act as though God had really done so. But the fact is otherwise. Nor should we think and say that at this late date God's creative act, which lies far back in time, makes no difference. The facts of creation abide forever. They can be ignored without resultant loss or harm as little as can other facts of nature.[5]

God's design for unfragmented men began with the understanding that God did not design men to exist in a relational vacuum. In other words, men are not designed to be alone. This truth must be taken into account in the context of how men are socialized to understand themselves in the area of their relational skills.

Gordon D. Fee on 1 Corinthians 9:11 writes

> . . . Man by himself is not complete; he is alone, without a companion or helper suitable to him. The animals will not do; he needs one who is bone of his bone, one who is like him but different from him, one who is uniquely his own "glory". In fact, when the man in the OT narrative sees the woman he "glories" in her by bursting into song. She is thus man's glory because she "came from him: and was created "for him". She is not thereby subordinate to him, but necessary for him. She exist to his honor as the one who having come from man in the one companion suitable to him ,so that he might be complete and that together they might form humanity.[6]

Simply put, a man by himself is merely one of a two-part relational unit consisting of male and female, which when joined together form a single unit of one whole person and personal relationship. Thus men must be socialized in a manner that equips them to understand their need for a physical companion, spiritual companion, reproductive companion, economic companion and emotional companion. This companion must be one who corresponds with how men are designed by God to function in society.

The female companion that God designed for the man is one with whom he is physically and emotionally designed and equipped to relate to holistically. When a man and a woman are joined together the results should be their ability to

C. H. Lenski, *The Interpretation of St. Paul's First and Second Epistles to the Corinthians* (Columbus, OH: Wartburg Press, 1946).

Gordon D. Fee, 1 & 2 Corinthians in *New International Commentary on the New Testament*, p. 517.

communicate positively and bond together holistically as one, forming a new single world between the two of them consisting of both of their life goals, objectives and values.

It is necessary to emphasize again that it is genuinely impossible for any man to function as the "help meet" of another man. The male body is not designed to fit together with another man's body, nor is a man emotionally designed to fit as the companion of another man. This physical impossibility has a corresponding impossibility in the internal design and structure of the male emotional make up. Men are not designed by God to correspond to one another as a mate. God designed the female to fit together with the male as his mate.

It is also necessary at this point to note that Adam, unlike all the other animals God created and Adam named, was created to reflect the image and glory of God. Thus, the man Adam was created with a moral code by which he was to live. This inherent code of morality distinguished Adam from all the other animals in the world. There is therefore an inherent connection between manhood and morality.

It is in the context of the relationship between a man and the woman who is his wife that the concept of family is born. Inherent in God's ideal, idea of marriage and family is the concept of a distinctive morality that ultimately distinguishes man from all of the other animals in the world.

Regarding the moral realm of humanity in general Peter J. Paris writes:

> The moral dimension of life comprises of the most distinctive differences between human beings and other animals. Morality is expressive of the capacity to determine the quality of human activity by making choices in accordance with understandings of good and bad, right and wrong. As moral agents, human beings are able to perceive others as subjects, and in their encounter with them they may choose to treat them either as subject or as objects. Similarly, all human beings claim rights that obligate others to respect their dignity as subjects. Paul Tillich described this claim as the locus of the moral act per se. In fact he argued that morality is born only in the act of treating the other as a person, since to do otherwise would be an objectification of the other: hence destruction of the other's personhood, and not only that but also a corresponding loss of the agent's own personhood.[7]

It is my contention that the development of unfragmented men according to God's design demands a Bible-based code of

7   Peter J, Paris, *The Social Teaching Of The Black Churches* (Fortress Press, 1985), p. 60.

morality at the heart of which is the family that consists of a man, his wife and their children. It is not possible to build an unfragmented man without first structuring a solid moral foundation. Thus in reclaiming the Village the moral foundation must first be restored.

The current state of the moral foundation in the African American Community and the crying need for the restoration of that foundation is most vividly evidenced by the current epidemic status of teenage pregnancy. Joyce A. Landers, speaking to the issue of teenage pregnancy in an article "The State Of Black America" said: "There is no other problem in the black community today that is more threatening to future generations of families than teen pregnancy, a problem of monumental proportions that is producing the womanchild and manchild on unprecedented levels. It is a problem that will affect three generations—the teen parents, their children and the grandparents."[8]

Commenting on the same issue James H. Harris writes:

This problem jeopardizes the stability of the black family and sets the black community back in its efforts to progress socially, economically and educationally. It becomes increasingly difficult to finish school, get a job, and become self-supporting when there are children to raise. Consequently, many of these young people will have to seek government support and they will be trapped in the vicious cycle of poverty throughout their lives. "At any given time, sixty percent of children born to teenagers outside marriage who lived and were not adopted, received welfare."

Clearly, there is a negative intergenerational effect of teenage pregnancy that lingers on and on in such a way that many years afterward, few have been able to overcome the socioeconomic impact of raising a child while being a child . . .

The church must intervene in the personal lives of our young people by encouraging them to postpone sexual activity until marriage and adulthood. How many of us have heard these teenagers explain that a baby gives them hope and something of their own, another human being to love and provide for. This is a sad phenomenon because the "reality principle" suggest that teenage pregnancy harbors difficulties that are long lasting. The love for the baby can soon turn to hate and resentment and apathy when one has to abandon the promises of the future in order to fulfill the responsibility of raising a child . . .

Inasmuch as teenage pregnancy is an epidemic problem in the black community, every black church needs a comprehensive Family Life program to assist in training, nurturing, encouraging and teaching teenagers (male and female) about responsible relationships that begin with thinking well of themselves and respecting others. Before there can be any substantive social

⁸   Joyce A. Landers, "The State Of Black America" (New York: National Urban League, 1986) p. 65.

change in society, black youths must develop a positive self-esteem that will manifest itself in reversal of some of the current trends and practices in the church and in the community.'

* James H. Harris, *Pastoral Theology: A Black Church Perspective* (Fortress Press, 1985) pp. 124-25.

CHAPTER 5

THE PATH TO WHOLENESS

BLACK MALE SENSITIVITY

Derick and Rose had been married for more than twenty five years during which time they had done quite well materially. They had accumulated a good deal of money, owned a number of cars and quite a bit of real estate here and there in the city. However, their marriage had not been a happy one for a number of reasons; but for Rose one thing stood out above all the others. Derick, according to Rose, had no sensitivity at all to either her many qualities as a professional woman nor was he sensitive to her many needs as a woman.

Derick, on the other hand, felt that he was a perfect husband and frequently complained that his wife was unaware of how well off she was to have a husband like himself who took care of all of the affairs of the family. Derick's problem is not unlike a number of men I have ministered to over the years. He is out of touch with his needs as a man. I did not say that Derick is out of touch with the needs of his wife Rose; I said he is out of touch with his own needs.

Derick assumes that he understands his wife Rose very well. However his understanding of his wife is not his problem. Derick's problem is that he is a fragmented man who does not understand himself. This lack of self-understanding has made him out of touch with his holistic needs as a man. A man out of touch with his needs as a man is hardly capable of being in touch with the needs of his wife and children.

Sensitizing men to their needs holistically begins in my view with helping them redefine themselves in terms of how

God designed men. Men tend to define themselves as a complete unit in and of themselves. This means that a man will tend to focus only on his business of doing things and gathering stuff which in his mind makes him who and what he is.

To the extent that a man defines himself as a complete unit in and of himself, to that extent he will be limited in his ability to recognize his needs holistically. Thus he will tend to focus on fulfilling those needs that he feels and recognizes. For a number of men their most felt needs are in the arena of the physical and the social often at the exclusion of the interpersonal.

In pursuit of the fulfillment of his felt physical and social needs a man will often acquire for himself those things that contribute to his self aggrandizement in these areas. Among the things that men collect are cars, clothes, and women, all to be used to serve him in a way that maintains his concept of being complete in and of himself.

At a recent premarital counseling session I asked a young man to list the things that he recognized he needed his young bride-to-be for. While his response did not surprise me, his dishonesty did. He said he needed her for everything.

"Like what?" I asked.

"Well, you know," the young man replied.

I suggested to him that there were probably two things and only two things at that point that he recognized he needed this young woman for as his wife. Namely, "as a Christian man," I said, "you need her as a means of sanctifying your sex life, and you someday plan to have children. Oh yes, and you think she will be faithful to you as a wife and support you in your ministry, right?"

To say the least, such straight talk startled the young man but he could not deny the accuracy of my suggestions.

The number one complaint I hear from wives of Christian men is that they are insensitive to their needs. My number one response is that the man is out of touch with his own needs as a man designed by God as one part of a two part unit. The greatest need most men have in the area of sensitivity is knowing their own needs holistically.

To this end consider with me Ephesians 4:23-24, "to be made new in the attitude of your minds; and to put on the new self, created to be like God in true righteousness and holiness." It should be noted at the very outset that in order to change how you think and see the world you must first be born again.

Having been born again one must then decide to take off and lay aside the old way of thinking and acting. This includes giving up certain habits, addictions, entertainment, and relationships, not as a means of conforming to some code of religious legalism or newfound humanism but as a means of enriching one's walk with the risen Christ. Then one must make themselves ready to put on the new self.

Having put off and laid aside the old self, it is now possible to move to the renewing of the mind. The Christian man must come to the conclusion that there is no future in their old life of worldliness. The only hope that any man can have of developing into an unfragmented man who is in touch with his needs as God designed him to be is by laying aside the old life, so that he can go about the business of renewing his mind in order to put on the new self that is in the image of Christ.

The putting off of the old secular mind and laying aside the old secular agenda must precede the putting on of the new self. It is impossible to put on the new self, with its new attitudes and agenda, and use it to cover over the old self; the only thing that can be done with the old self is to pull it off and lay it aside, so that you can put on the new self.

The old self is tracking with the lust of deceit; it is characterized by sin and sin is always deceitful. Sin has the power to look at life and misinterpret reality, deceiving a man into thinking that what is a lie is really the truth and what is the truth will appear to be the lie. It is the deceitfulness of sin that causes men to see themselves as a single unit of one, rather than seeing themselves as one part of a two part unit. It is the deceitfulness of sin that interprets male homosexuality as unperverted reality or an alternative life-style.

The prerequisite to being able to dress yourself in the new self is being renewed in the spirit of your mind. The word *renewal* in this text (Eph. 4:23) is a present passive infinitive. This means that it is the responsibility of the believer to allow their minds to be in the process of renewal. The focus of this renewal is the spirit of the mind, which is a reference to the new person that the believer has become in Christ. The word *renewal* means to "be in the process of spiritual transformation." The text is saying that a prerequisite to putting on the new self is a spiritually-transformed mind.

In my view far too many men in the church are not in the process of having their minds renewed, i.e., *created to be like God in true righteousness and holiness.* A primary contributor to this stagnate spiritual state is the fact that a number of men in the church have a secular agenda as opposed to a spiritual agenda in life, thus they tend to hold on to their faith in the same way that they hold their credit card or life insurance policy; it is theirs to be used when needed in a crisis situation.

The Christian man whose mind is in the process of spiritual renewal is one who is being impacted emotionally, intellectually, vocationally and even physically by the spiritual transformation through which he is moving in the power of God the Holy Spirit.

There are seven benefits that result from the spiritual transformation of black men in which they put off the old self, put on the new self and are renewed in the spirit of their minds. *They develop a new world view, new life values, become predictable, develop strong and lasting relationships, understand intimacy in the context of marriage, develop new life motivation and a clear life mission.*

A new world view. I have suggested that African American men are victims of cultural brain washing. I have also said that one of the results of cultural brain washing is what I refer to as a loss of world view. By loss of world view I am referring to the tendency of African American men to have a narrow view of the world in terms of their place in the world and their potential for contributing to the good of society in general. This narrow world view is most evident in the limited investments of time, money and wealth black men in general tend to make in their families, church, community and in historical Black cultural and educational institutions. Far too few African American men reveal any interest in becoming a world leader in the political, economic or religious arena.

It is essential that I point out at this point that the spiritual transformation to which I am referring (cf. Eph.4:23) is not the fruit of Black religion as such, nor is it the product of genuine Black Nationalism; the spiritual transformation to which I refer does not automatically result from being born again. The renewed mind, *created to be like God in true righteousness and holiness,* that evidences spiritual transformation is the product of Black male spiritual mentoring. At the heart of this mentoring is an emphasis on developing a spiritual agenda that reflects a commitment to personal holiness in private and in public. It has a strong focus on the Great Commission and it places a high priority on the value of family life.

One of the first indications that I look for in a Christian man who is in the process of being transformed and renewed in the spirit of his mind, is a loss of self-focus and a move towards an agenda that has service to the Lord Jesus at its core. A man with such a focus is moving in his understanding of himself in the context of his relationship with God.

In the gospel according to Luke, chapter 5:1ff we have an example of men who received a new world view. In this text Jesus takes Peter and his boat out into the deep water to catch fish. You will remember that Peter and the other disciples of Jesus were for the most part common men who made a living catching and selling fish in the marketplace. After having gone out with Jesus where the water was deep and having caught a multitude of fish, Jesus said to these men "From now on you shall be fishers of men." I take it that Jesus gave these common men a new world view that changed their focus from catching fish for the local market to catching men for the kingdom of heaven. It is essential that we note that this new world view Jesus gave to Peter and his fellow fishermen followed the experience of their spiritual transformation.

New life values. In the context of Black culture the desire for riches is perhaps one of the most prevailing attitudes to be found in the market place and in the church. Greed can be found in the most conservative circles of Evangelical Christianity. It is to be noted here that this evil vice called greed has especially flourished in America over the past ten or so years, beginning about 1980 with the rise of right wing religious political Conservatism. Riding on the shoulders of the marriage of Evangelical Fundamental religion and Conservative Republican politics greed has negatively affected every major significant institution in our country. This includes the financial institutions, the various branches of government, the religious institutions, the social and educational institutions, and the family.

With this in mind we must note here that Evangelical Fundamental Christian doctrines in and of themselves are not a defense against greed. In fact in some instances Evangelical Fundamentalism seems to promote greed, i.e., prosperity Christianity.

In his book on *Black-on-Black Violence* Amos Wilson had the following comments regarding adornment and Black-on-Black criminality:

> It is through his dressed ostentatiousness, his conspicuous consumption that the African American, offended by White racism, fight back. Consumption and display are his weapons of choice, which, as paltry substitutes for substantial revolutionary preparation and action, have been selected to defy the incursions by and restraints of his enemies. If he cannot defeat them, unbalance them. Neutralize them, perhaps seduce or convert them, he can at the very least, gain their begrudging and envious attention. He achieves reality and higher social standing through getting the attention of the other particularly the others who would ignore, dismiss or demote him only when he is seen by those Europeans who have insulted him when he impress them with his buying power. . .
>
> Through the monetary worth of his possessions, his jewels, his clothes, cars, houses, rents, he, in a relatively safe way, compensates for the worthlessness of being Black in America.[1]

The desire for riches is one of the three most serious and persistent threats to the testimony and family life of African American men, the other two being pride and immorality. Those who desire riches must understand that such a desire leads to temptation, a trap, many foolish and harmful desires that plunge men into ruin and destruction (cf. 1 Tim. 6:9-10).

Few things in the African American male experience have proven to be sources of greater struggle than money. Several different reasons explain why this is the case. The struggle results from the fact that black men are currently ranked fourth in annual income in America behind White men, black women, and White women. Increasingly they are falling below Hispanic Americans.

This low ranking of African American males in annual income translates into insufficient funds with which to provide for themselves and their families. At the other end of the spectrum are those black men who for any number of reasons find themselves in the peculiar position of having more money at their disposal than they are prepared to manage. For these men this too is a struggle.

In terms of new life values the issue of money and the value that is attached to it must be settled. Inherent in coming to grips with the value a man places on money is the source from which he gets the money and the price he is willing to pay to obtain and retain money.

In developing a balanced attitude toward money a good

---

[1] Amos N. Wilson, *Black-on-Black Violence* (New York: Afrikan World Infosystems, 1990), p. 141.

passage to consider is Philippians 4:11-13. "I am not saying this because I am in need, for I have learned to be content whatever the circumstances. I know what it is to be in need, and I know what it is to have plenty. I have learned the secret of being content in any and every situation, whether well fed or hungry, whether living in plenty or in want. I can do everything through him who gives me strength." I take the text as saying that in the life of a believer there will be times when one has more than enough to live on and other times when there is hardly enough to get by on.

To manage this kind of change in circumstances and at the same time guard the integrity of your testimony before the church and the world, one needs to learn the lesson of contentment. This means having a sense of a divinely bestowed sufficiency no matter what your financial or social situation may be. Learning to cope with shifting circumstances through the experience of living through and trusting God in and through the struggles of abundance and deficiencies, is a must in developing a balanced attitude towards prosperity and poverty in general and money in particular.

The new values system that results from this renewed mind equips the Christian man with an attitude that empowers him to believe that he is able to do everything, including handle prosperity and poverty through Christ who is his strength. In this context it is important to note that Philippians 4:11-13 sums up the essence of human needs as food, clothing and a place to stay. Thus it can be said that so long as a man is able to meet these basic needs for himself and his family, he does well to be content.

To speak to the issue of developing new life values one must of necessity include a word about lifestyle. The lifestyle of a man is most often a clear reflection of his attitude towards money and things. The issue here is not simply a matter of modesty versus extravagance; it is a matter of faith and contentment versus greed and frugality.

Billy is a good example of what I have in mind. He was a man who had a lifestyle that reflected modesty and humility. Billy would seldom spend money on himself or his family. He would drink water rather than spend money on fastfood when he was on a trip. In the minds of the many people who saw Billy he was a modest, humble man. However, in reality Billy was a man who loved money above all else. He seldom gave anything to anybody; in fact at the age of fifty Billy still held on to most of the possessions that he had ever purchased in his life. Billy had all of the outward markings of a man who lived a modest lifestyle but in reality he had a deep and abiding love for money.

It may be difficult to understand and even more difficult to accept as practical truth but the Bible teaches that Christian virtues are more important in life than money because Christian virtues can empower a man to maintain a wholesome and balanced attitude towards money and things. This is due to the fact that virtues are of the heart and not of the flesh and the head as money tends to be.

I call attention to use of the action word "flee" (1 Tim. 6:11) by the biblical text in this context of dealing with money, or more specifically with the desire to get rich. "But you, man of God, flee from all this," refering to the "love of money" mentioned in v. 10. This implies that when it comes to money a casual cursory attitude will not do. The man who distinguishes himself as one who has a new value system evidences that by fleeing from what other men are pursuing, namely the acquisition of money and things.

Note also that God uses the same word "flee" in reference to immorality in 1 Corinthians 6:18. This again implies that the solution for escaping the pull of moral seduction, as well as escaping the pull of economic seduction, is one and the same, "to flee."

Finally as it pertains to new life values, the Bible teaches that there is no virtue in being poor; neither is there any condemnation in having money. The church has the responsibility to lead men who have money in developing a biblical perspective on how to manage their wealth. This means challenging men to emotionally, psychologically and spiritually divest themselves of any and all love of money. The bottom line is to help them understand that God gave them what they have to enjoy but not to trust as a source of security. Instead those who have money must use it to do good, to be rich in good works and be generous and ready to share.

Predictability. The man who has a renewed mind will develop a pattern of behavior and a relational attitude that will cause him to become predictable among those who know him, i.e., his family and associates in terms of his values, attitude and behavior. The issue of predictability is in effect a focus on the issue of Black male integrity.

There are few subjects that have been more carefully investigated over the past few years than has the integrity of black men in general and those in leadership in particular. The media fills itself with images, reports and stereotypes that suggest to the world that most black men are seriously deficient in the arena of integrity.

To question or suspect a man's integrity is to assault the very fabric of the man's manhood. For in the final analysis a man's effectiveness in life over the long haul stands or falls not so much on his wealth, credentials, intellectual abilities or social network but on his own personal integrity. In addition the integrity of a man's family is inseparable from the integrity of the man. It has been my observation over the years that young black men tend to be rather careless with their integrity, evidencing little apparent regard for how essential their integrity will ultimately prove to be in the context of their family, community, and vocation.

At the heart of the black male's management of his integrity are the crucial choices he makes of his running buddies who share his convictions of holiness in private and in public. The man who keeps his integrity free from dishonorable purposes develops an attitude that embraces the truth that as a Christian man he is God's vessel for noble purposes. He has been set apart unto God, and he is to be useful to the Master and prepared to do any good work.

In the context of predictability it must be mentioned that young men face certain risk factors that are inherent in the very nature of being young. These risk factors are referred to under the umbrella of youthful lust. They include such things as *impatience, intolerance, love of argument, self-assertion and partiality.* These youthful tendencies are seriously intertwined in the very fabric of the young man's attitude and each tendency has the potential of damaging the young man's integrity and negating the effectiveness of the young man's pursuit of success.

There are other attitudes in addition to the five I have listed above that could be included under the heading of youthful lust, I have listed the ones most common. The question comes then, how does the youthful Black male deal with these and other lusts? The answer is still "Flee." In Paul's letters to Timothy, he used this word "flee" at least twice; once in 1 Timothy 6:11 in his instructions on the wrong attitude towards money, and then in 2

Timothy 2:22 in his instructions about youthful lust. It seems to me that the conclusion can be drawn that a young man's attitude toward money and his youthful lusts are serious issues that must be settled if he is to have any kind of integrity in his home, church and community.

The young man who desires to be predictable in his attitude and behavior must learn not to struggle with the power and influence of money but to flee from it. The key word is "flee." The same is true with youthful lust. You do not struggle with it, nor do you deny the presence of such tendencies. You just "flee." Escaping the terrible trap of youthful lust not only means running from them, it also means pursuing *righteousness, faith, love, peace* and *the company of spiritual people.*

It is my contention that predictability is the mark of spiritual integrity. It is also an essential key to success. Black men must rethink the idea that predictability is evidence of a weak man and that strong men are unpredictable and difficult to figure out.

Strong relationships. A common belief exists that black men are most often serious servants to their wife and children. However, there may be room to question the soundness of such assumptions. The facts actually suggest that more than a few men are determined to be served by their wives rather than serving them. This attitude is most prevalent in the expectations that the young husband brings to the table in preparation for marriage. In that setting the young husband-to-be makes it very clear that he is committed to providing up to half the family income but he is not as willing to commit to performing half the household and family chores.

It is my opinion that the absence of a servant's heart is a primary contributing factor to much of the exploitation that occurs in the family life of a number of our young black men. To this end I suggest to young men that they trust more of their relationship to their heart and tilt their heart towards being a servant to their family.

As It pertains to being a man with an attitude that contributes to building strong and lasting relationships, I suggest four things: *refuse to be quarrelsome, learn to be kind to everybody, be patient when you are wronged,* and *be willing to correct those who oppose you with a spirit of gentleness.*

Intimacy. In the context of a renewed mind the African American male must seriously consider his attitudes towards sex and sexuality. However, this consideration is often viewed through the lens of the longstanding and prevailing negative stereotypse of black men as it pertains to male sexuality in general and black male sexuality in particular. I find two things most troubling about the stereotypes of Black male sexuality, which are the idea that black men are more generously endowed than White men in their genitals and the notion that all black men are sexual studs. I am not troubled about the fact that such stereotypes persist in the minds of others about black men. But what is troubling to me is that black men not only believe such stereotypes, but genuinely believe that genitalia size makes a difference in their ability to achieve maximum satisfaction in their sexual performance and experiences.

While reveling in the false notion that black men are superior to other men in their sexual equipment and performance, many black men have neglected to develop a sense of intimacy. Thus I have found over the years that many of the wives of black men express the idea that they are having frequent sex but enjoying it less. The missing ingredient is not in the sexual equipment, nor the use of that equipment but in the attitude that is driving the equipment, namely intimacy.

I recall an incident that occurred when my wife and I were doing a singles seminar in Arkansas. One of the single women said to me, "Are you suggesting that a person marry a man without ever having sex with him?"

"Yes I am," I replied.

"Well, what if after you get married you discover that you do not enjoy sex with him?"

"Why would you not enjoy sex with him?" I responded.

"Suppose his penis is too small?"

"My studies suggest that there is very little if any difference in the size of adult male genitals," I responded.

"That's not true and I know it," the sister replied. At that point I deferred to my wife to continue the discussion.

Intimacy is about attitude, atmosphere, time, etc. It has little to do with actual sexual intercourse, genital size, or sexual performance. The problem men have is the source from which they acquire their sex education. For the most part no small number of men testify to the fact that the source of their sex education is the streets. Few men receive any sex education from either their home or their church. Thus, I find in most instances even the Christian husband has a street-level attitude toward sex, devoid of any sense of sacredness.

In his renewed mind, the African American Christian man comes to understand that it takes time to be intimate. This means learning to manage his impromptu libido so that he and his wife have time to create an aura conducive to intimacy. This atmosphere is influenced by auditory (music), visual (environment), and other sensory stimuli. This awareness results from a man having come to the conclusion that it is possible to engage in intercourse on a regular basis and not be intimate. An open and honest conversation with his wife will reveal that she most often prefers intimacy before, after and even when intercourse is not forthcoming. She does not define intercourse as intimacy.

Intimacy is an attitude of sexuality in which the couple takes the time to create a romantic setting in which they both are relaxed and comfortable. It must be a place that is private and nonthreatening. In this setting each responds to the internal and external senses of the other. The environment is enhanced with that which smells good and feels good. This requires mutual physical appeal, mutual romantic appeal and mutual environmental appeal.

It is important to note here that spiritual renewal impacts and enriches not only the public external dimension of a man's life, it reaches into the deep inner personal dimensions of life so that even his private sexual attitude and performance is changed for the better.

New life motivation. From the window of my office at the Institute for Black Family Renewal I am looking at a young African American man who might be twenty-two years old standing where he has stood for the past six months selling crack cocaine. This young man, along with several others, works four- to six-hour shifts, seven days a week supplying the drug habits of men and women who come from all over the city of Dallas and from every strata of society in terms of social class.

As I watch these young men I cannot help but wonder what it is that motivates them to do what they do every day. The one thing that seems to surface as the primary motivating factor in the minds of these young men is survival. These young black men seem to have no sense of tomorrow. They tend to live from one day to the next, just surviving.

It is my contention that men without positive life motivation are men without a vision for their lives. Having a life vision means having a clear mental image of what it is that you were born into this world to do. Without such an image it is impossible to be motivated to think and do that which contributes to the good of others.

Dennis is in his mid forties and has been married for almost twenty five years. He and his wife have one daughter who is now in college. He serves and has served as a leader in my church for a number of years. When Dennis was in his early twenties, he too was caught up in the survival mentality which led him to alcohol of every kind on a daily basis. As a soldier in the military Dennis sent me pictures of himself from all over the world in a drunken stupor surrounded by a variety of alcoholic beverages. I still have those pictures.

One Sunday morning after listening to a sermon where the gospel was preached, Dennis gave his life to the Lord Jesus and began the long road of spiritual transformation. His mind was renewed and he developed a new motivation for living. I subsequently married him to his lovely wife and he became a man who lives to serve. The catalyst that effected change in Dennis was not just his salvation; that was the starting point. The change was the result of Dennis coming to grips with his life vision through a number of years of personal discipling.

Clear life mission. Concurrent with the birth of a life vision in the renewed mind of the African American Christian male is clarity on his life mission. I suggest to you that a man without a life vision is a man without a life mission. The absence of vision and mission in a man's life is a primary contributing factor to the increasing number of young black men who spend their days and nights doing nothing but growing old or worse, trafficking in the underworld economy.

Consider Jephthah, one of the judges of Israel . He was the son of a prostitute, hated by his brothers, disinherited and thrown out of the house by his fellow siblings because his mother unlike theirs was a prostitute. And in the land of Tob where he settled he became a leader of the bad guys in the hood. But later when circumstances so dictated, his own people sought him out to become their leader in a time of crisis.

Jephthah is an example of a man who was a born leader but

was stripped of the opportunity to lead in a constructive context for reasons beyond his control. Therefore, he found people to lead in the destructive context in which he found himself. Such is the case with many young Black men today. They have no opportunity for constructive leadership in the venue in which they live so they lead where they can. Leadership is about ability and courage, not so much about the setting.

In my view there are merits for young black men who are highly motivated to lead and who do lead. However, due to the fact that the opportunities for leadership are in a negative environment, they end up leading their peers in doing bad things. These young men need to be reached with the gospel and be discipled so they can develop a new mind with a God-focused life vision and mission.

The path to wholeness for all men in general and the African American male in particular is a path that leads to the church where he is evangelized and discipled. Since it can be argued from the Bible that God Himself created man for the purpose of reflecting His image and His glory, it seems only natural to conclude that any effort designed to develop unfragmented men with spiritually renewed minds, created in the image of Christ and who are therefore sensitive to God's purpose for their lives, must be rooted in the gospel of Jesus Christ. Thus the preaching of the gospel must be liberating and transforming as it is preached to African American males.

CHAPTER 6

THE BASIC NEEDS OF AFRICAN AMERICAN MEN

There was a time in the not so distant past when the needs of African American men were defined stereotypically as consisting of the desire for a big luxury car, loud, colorful and flashy clothes, a White woman or a very light skinned African American woman and a fasttrack night life. This stereotypical definition of the essence of the needs and ambitions of the Black male contributed to the wealth of many White men, not because they necessarily believed that such a definition of the needs of black men were accurate or true but because so many black men themselves had been socialized to believed that such was the essence of their needs.

It is common knowledge that a black man can in most instances easily get a loan from almost any bank or credit union in order to buy an expensive automobile to be financed over any number of months. However, in most instances, that same bank will not lend the same man an amount of half the price of the car if it were for any other purpose, such as an investment in a small business. The stereotypical view of black men is that they value and cherish big luxurious fast cars. Thus they will make the car payments above all else, because in the mind of most financial institutions it is the black man's car that defines for him the essence of his status in life.

There are untold thousands of African American men who due to a lack of understanding of their own needs as a man over the years trusted themselves and their career to others who stripped away the economic fruit of their talents in entertainment, sports, academia, and politics. In all too many cases gifted and talented men received in return for their labor only the fragrance of the wealth they generated.

In that context there were seldom any critical comments from the media about the contractual salaries these men received for their services. Today there is growing evidence that things are changing. High-profile successful African American men are increasingly coming to grips with their needs in a holistic way and taking charge of their own lives and careers. Thus the media is increasingly critical of the dollar figure that Black professional athletes and other men are demanding for their services.

In our country today, African American men rank lower than African American women in annual income in a country where men in general are perceived to be the primary breadwinners. This is evidence that in America the needs of black men are perceived to be something less than that of White men. It is really unfair when you actually think about it that no matter what credentials or talents a black man has, to be Black and male in America is to be defined as one who is on the prowl for women, sex and fast living. Even worse is to be perceived as something less than a primary provider for his family. But the truth is that African American men have a hierarchy of needs that are not unlike the needs of other men in America.

Recently my oldest daughter and her husband were flying to Hawaii for a vacation. They were seated in the first class section of the plane. It so happened that on this particular flight there were no other African American males seated in first class. My son-in-law's presence in first class provoked the flight attendant on this flight to repeatedly asked him what it was that he did for a living. They insisted that he must be a professional athlete. It is difficult for a black man to step beyond the stereotype of "muscles, not brains" as that which defines his profession. My son-in-law is on his way to becoming a university professor, but his gender and his color could not convey this to the stewardess.

I think it can be said without fear of contradiction that how a man defines his needs will dictate how he prioritizes his life in terms of his time, talent and money. For a number of African American men a successful career is the essence of their needs. For these men, usually young professionals, anything and anybody that is not a part of their career goals is a distraction. Thus it is not unusual to find men who have successful careers but fragmented family relationships. The problem in most instances is how these men define their needs which often does not include positive family relationships. These men are like one dimensional high-tech machines on their way to the village of success.

To the extent that a man narrowly defines his needs or allows his needs to be defined so that the definition does not include the full scope of his person and function as God designed him to be, to that extent a man is himself susceptible to serious exploitation and most often will feel compelled to exploit the people and situations that he encounters in an attempt to fill the vacuum created by the narrow definition of his needs.

Keith is an example of a man who was so determined to succeed in his career as a banker that he defined the essence of his needs as a man by his career goals. The narrow scope of Keith's definition of his needs did not include a positive relationship with his family. Though Keith could never bring himself to admit that he needed a wife he could not deny or dismiss the compelling presence of his sex drive.

In his pursuit of sexual pleasure, scraps of intimacy and strains of companionship, Keith was in and out of a number of relationships with women. Keith, like a number of men I have met over the years, has the kind of definition of his needs as a man that is so narrow that it pushes him into exploitative relationships with women. These fragmented and exploitative relationships was for Keith a serious source of guilt as a Christian.

In my view a man has several basic needs that must be met if he is to function as an unfragmented man in the African American Village. First, a man needs *a family which is designed to meet his many interpersonal needs for companionship, intimacy, headship, a reproductive context and security.* Second, a man needs *a life mission,* i.e., a job which provides security, stability and fulfillment. Third, a man needs *a social context which provides for his relational needs and affirms him as a man who is a significant somebody.* Fourth, a man needs *a relationship with God through Jesus Christ which will give him a sense of unity within himself and with others.*

First, *a man needs a family which is designed to meet his many interpersonal needs for companionship, intimacy, headship, a reproductive context and security*. There are few men of whom it can be said that they do not need a family, meaning a wife and children. Those men for whom a wife and children are not essential are men who have the gift of celibacy and are called to a ministry context in which being single is a necessity. It is my opinion that the gift of celibacy mentioned in 1 Corinthians 7:9 is tied to ministry and calling. Celibacy is not a matter of birth in which a man has a diminished sex drive. It is not a matter of selfishness or lack of opportunity to marry. Celibacy is a matter of ministry and divine calling.

Men who do not have the gift of celibacy do well to include in their hierarchy of needs "Family." This need for a family must be defined in such a way that it is distinct and distinguishable but isolated from a man's career and his basic sex drive. Since God designed men so that they need a wife, i.e., one that fits with how a man is designed, each man must seek to understand the needs he has within himself that a wife is designed to meet.

To say that a wife is designed to fit together with how a man is designed by God is to say that just as the male and the female sexual organs are designed to fit together in a process by which the two become one, so it is with the man and the woman who reside within each other's body. They too are designed to bond together at the emotional and social level so that the two become one in a similar manner to the fitting together of the physical bodies.

In Genesis 2:18 God makes the observation about Adam that he is alone and that the situation is not good for him. From that observation that God makes regarding Adam being alone, I suggest that as a young man moves towards adulthood his body begins to communicate to his mind that he is alone and that it has a growing need for someone to share itself with. This sense of need signaled by the body of the young man to his mind is what I call loneliness. Adult men have a need for someone to fill that vacuum called loneliness in their lives. That somebody is a wife which together with the man constitutes a family.

The vacuum of loneliness is a felt need that can best be satisfied in the context of marriage in which companionship takes place. Companionship means sharing yourself with another at the level of the emotions and the spirit. In this context it can be said that a man and his wife are kindred spirits, i.e., they are bonded together at the level of their physical bodies and their human spirits.

The first time the idea of companionship in marriage caught my attention, I was performing the funeral of Mr. Arnwine who had been married to his wife for well over fifty years. I watched his wife as she stood over the casket viewing his body for the last time. As she stood there brushing her hand over his head and quietly weeping, it occurred to me that as Mrs. Arnwine stared into that casket she saw a large portion of herself in that casket in the person of her husband with whom she was bonded for life. Within a few short months after we buried Mr. Arnwine, his wife sat down one day on the front porch of her home and died. She lost her passion for life in this world once her companion in this life was gone. She had expressed to her children that her greatest desire was to be in heaven with her husband.

Companionship is the fruit of emotional and spiritual bonding that takes place in the relationship between a man and his wife over time as they share themselves with each other in the context of changing times and changing circumstances.

In the context of the family where companionship is taking place, a man experiences the fulfillment of his need for intimacy. Intimacy is an attitude that reflects a man's sense of sexuality in an atmosphere of romance. Intimacy is not so much about sexual intercourse as it is about sexual stimulation. Sexual stimulation is no doubt a primary need of most men. This need for sexual stimulation is best met between a man with his own wife.

In premarital counseling, I most often find that the bride-to-be is woefully unaware of her soon-to-be husband's need for sexual stimulation of the kind that arouses his libido. This means that he is stimulated by what he sees, smells, hears and touches in the context of sexuality. Thus the wife in order to meet the need of her husband for intimacy must be secure enough in herself to dress and function as her husband's lover, woman, and friend.

The man's need for a family is also reflected in his compelling compulsion to provide and protect the one who is dependent on him, i.e., the need to be the head of a woman. I have seldom found a man regardless of his social or economic status who in his relationship with a woman did not want to be in charge. In my view this drive to be in charge of his relationship with a woman is in accord with how God designed men in the beginning.

Men who are married to the kind of woman who feels

compelled to be in charge of the relationship tend to want to have a secondary relationship with another woman in which he is in charge and the woman adores him for who and what he is. I call these kinds of relationships paradoxical male and female relationships. A better title may well be fragmented husband and wife relationships.

I have said that most men need a family in which his need for companionship, intimacy and headship can be met. There are two additional needs that a man has that are met by his family: the affirmation of his manhood and the need to reproduce himself in his children.

The Bible has much to say about the need of a man for a family. "Drink from your own well, my son-be faithful and true to your wife. Why should you beget children with women of the street? Why share your children with those outside your home? Be happy, yes, rejoice in the wife of your youth. Let her breasts and tender embrace[e] satisfy you. Let her love alone fill you with delight. Why delight yourself with prostitutes, embracing what isn't yours? For God is closely watching you, and he weighs carefully everything you do" (Prov. 5:15-21, *The Living Bible*).

Clearly this text instructs the young man to explore and experience the essence of his sexual fantasies that emanate from his maleness in the context of his own family with "the wife of his youth." Sexual activity outside of the family is not only said to be unwise but it also brings the behavior of the young man under the judgment of the living God.

After God fashioned Eve from a rib He extracted from Adam's side, He woke Adam from the sleep He had brought on him and presented the woman Eve to him, Adam took a look at Eve and immediately broke out in a song. " 'This is it!' Adam exclaimed. 'She is part of my own bone and flesh! Her name is 'woman' because she was taken out of a man.' This explains why a man leaves his father and mother and is joined to his wife in such a way that the two become one person" (Gen. 2:23, *The Living Bible*).

This excitement on Adam's part over God's gift to him of the woman is evidence of Adam's recognized need that he as a man had for one who was like him yet different from him in so many ways. It is my contention that what Adam saw in the woman Eve was a reflection of his glory, just as he saw himself as a reflection of God's glory. "For a man ought not to have his head covered, since he is the image and glory of God; but the woman is the glory of man" (1 Cor. 11:7).

Regarding a man and his children the Bible speaks in the affirmative but only in the context of his own family "Behold, children are a gift of the Lord; the fruit of the womb is a reward. Like arrows in the hand of a warrior, so are the children of one's youth. How blessed is the man whose quiver is full of them; They shall not be ashamed, When they speak with their enemies in the gate. (Ps. 127:3-5, NASB).

"Your wife shall be contented in your home. And look at all those children! There they sit around the dinner table as vigorous and healthy as young olive trees" (Ps. 128:3, *The Living Bible*).

In the midst of all the talk and hype about reclaiming the Village, I feel it necessary to suggest that unless and until African American men are socialized in such a way that they refuse to buy into the stereotypical definition of their needs held by others, they will continue to define their needs in the narrowest of terms and inconsistent with how they are designed.

Black men must choose to define their own needs, to include their need for a family as a distinct and distinguishable need they share with other men regardless of race and social class. Unless and until this self-definition of needs occurs and spreads among black men on a consistent basis, it will not be possible to move towards reclaiming the Village.

A word about what happens when stereotypical definitions are imposed by others on the African American male or when by his own narrow definition "family" is not included among his primary needs. One of the symptoms of a fragmented man is that he tends to narrowly define his needs in a way that reflect in its narrowness his fragmentation. Thus he will have a definition of his needs that is totally career focused or totally pleasure focused. Men who have a fragmented concept of their needs as a man will most often not place much value on having his own family. This does not mean, however, that he does not seek to get what he feels he needs in the area of companionship, intimacy, and children along the road to success. It simply means that his definition of his needs as a man does not include "family," which is a reflection of his social and spiritual fragmentation.

I watched the 1997 basketball draft in which a number of young African American men became the one out of ten thousand to be chosen to play professional sports. One young man in particular caught my attention by his insistence that he was going to buy his parents a house and a car. As I listened to this young man I thought to myself, "That's great," and it is. Then I began to wonder what will he do to meet his own needs as a man as it pertains to his own "family." The probability is that this young man has defined his needs as a man only in terms of his career as a professional athlete. To the extent that this is the case he will evidence serious fragmentation in his relationships with women.

Curtis worked for a company that occasionally sent him and others in the company out of town on business. Once he and his co-workers arrived in the city of their destination, the attention of the men quickly turned from business to pleasure. The pursuit of pleasure took the men into various hot spots in the city where there were topless this and bottomless that, kind of bars.

As a Christian these kinds of places and their activity grieved Curtis' spirit so he decided to inform his boss that he was not going to continue to go with them to the bars. His boss responded, "It's OK, Curtis. No one will tell your wife where you went and what you did."

Curtis responded, "I am a Christian and I am not interested in this kind of activity."

"That's OK, too, Curtis. Nobody is a saint. God won't mind you having a little fun," said Curtis' boss.

"Well," said Curtis, "I will meet you all back at the hotel. You see, I am not concerned about you all telling my wife nor am I trying to be a saint. The fact is I do not need this kind of action. I have all I need in this area in my family." With that said, Curtis took a cab back to the hotel.

Now this attitude and action by Curtis did not set well with his boss or his co-workers but it fit quite well with Curtis' spiritual convictions. It takes the courage of a man's convictions to empower him to define his own needs and order his behavior accordingly on a consistent basis.

Second, *a man needs a life mission*, i.e., a job which provides security for himself and his family. A man's need for a job is endemic to his very existence as a man. This idea is evident in the first instructions God gave to Adam namely to subdue the earth and rule over it. In addition God placed the first man

Adam and his wife Eve in the Garden with the instructions to manage it.

In speaking to the issue of a man's need for a job it is important to point out that in the sequence of the creation narrative in the first chapters of the book of Genesis God gave Adam a family with specific instruction as to how to function as a family man, and then He (God) gave the man (Adam) a job. This is an important sequence to note because it suggests that a man is to get his sense of identity, self-esteem and sense of significance from the context of his family, not his job.

Work does not define a man but rather it allows a man to express his manhood in a constructive manner that enables him to meet his needs and contribute to the good of others. It is the man who understands his mission in life who is able to view his work as a means to an end, and not an end in itself.

Few of us have missed seeing the group of clean-cut young African American men in the streets selling papers, fruit and other items. These young men in my city of Dallas in Texas are of the non-Christian Muslim religion. A good number of these young men have been recently released from prison. I find it most interesting that the Muslim religion include among the requirements of their faith-work. As a matter of fact Muslims boast of having close to full employment among their members. Their choice of jobs ranges from the menial to the highly professional. Perhaps the Muslims are in tune with the fact that work is endemic to manhood in terms of expression of manhood.

The unfortunate reality today is that the church is not given to insisting that men be given productive work. Black preachers tend to be willing to leave black men sitting and standing idle on the corner in the village, while we beat upon them in our sermons in the pulpit for not finding a job. Men who do not work for whatever reason are either idle because of their fragmentation or fragmented as men by their idleness. Fragmented men tend to reflect their fragmentation is a variety of destructive ways.

When all is said and done, a man has some basic needs which cannot be met by a job. These needs include companionship, intimacy and identity. The man who seeks to fulfill such needs through his job will ultimately be disappointed. By the same token there are some needs that a man has that can only be met by his involvement in constructive work. These needs include such things as security, stability, a sense of significance and productivity. In our country today the largest rate of unemployed youths are Black, and more than 40% of unemployed adults are black men.

Unemployment among men is an unhealthy thing in that it contributes to the fragmentation of the man so that he loses his sense of self worth. Let me be clear here and say that while a man receives his sense of self worth from his family as a boy in the environment of his home, it is his ability and his opportunity to do constructive work that nurtures and maintains that sense of self-worth as an adult male. A job is endemic to any expression of manhood.

Robert is an example of a man who defined his need for a job in such a way that it callused over his sensitivity to his need for a family. In the mind of Robert's family it was his job not they whom he needed. In the mind of Robert's wife he was married to his job.

When Robert received notice that his firm was closing it was evident to me that with the loss of his job Robert had lost the very thing that gave his life significance and made him feel useful. Without his job Robert was unable to recognize himself. Unfortunately he had not developed the kind of relationship with his family that allowed him to relate to them in a constructive manner. Thus in short order Robert had neither job nor family.

In the context of the relationship between manhood and employment it is necessary to speak to the issue of affirmative action. In this venue James Harris writes:

> Affirmative action should be the essence of equal employment opportunity. However, aside from what is should be, it is an effort to eliminate the vestiges and causes of endemic discrimination in every phase of society. From the outset, equal opportunity in employment was in effect passive acceptance of past inequities while agreeing not to perpetuate or aggravate the said inequities. Therefore, equal employment opportunity is in effect acceptance of the status quo. Conversely, affirmative action is an active systematic program instituted to redress grievances and to hire and promote a proportionate number of minorities.[1]

It is my contention that a job is endemic to the whole idea of manhood and thus unless and until it is possible to provide meaningful employment for black men, a great portion of their

---

[1] James H. Harris, *Pastoral Theology: A Black Church Perspective* (Minneapolis MN: Fortress Press, 1991).

basic needs will go unfulfilled and the idea of reclaiming the Village will remain merely an idea.

Third, *a man needs a social context which provides for his relational needs and affirms him as a man who is a significant somebody in the context of the community.* One of the most evident virtues that black men have is the ability to initiate conversations and relationships with anybody, anywhere and at anytime. To be an African American man is to be gifted with a strong positive social attitude.

In a recent ABC television special entitled "Black & White: Why Can't We Live Together" Tom Brokaw interviewed one White woman who said that she did not shop at a certain mall because she was frightened by the young black men who congregated in them. Mr. Brokaw asked the woman if she had ever experience any harm from any Black person. "No," she replied, "but their gathering in groups tends to frighten me."

This tendency to gather in groups and hang out, is characteristic of most Black males. They gather and hang around talking loudly, teasing, high-fiving each other, listening to music and bragging about nothing. This social tendency on the part of black men is perceived to be less than cultured behavior and even intimidating to White people in general. It is rooted in the culture of African American men as a part of what it means to be a black man. The fact is black men tend to be very sociable in any given context. This tendency is not evident among White males. Thus it is often perceived to be less than civilized behavior on the part of black men.

Most black men can meet a woman at a checkout counter in any store and walk out with her name, address and phone number without ever holding up the checkout line. It is also true that there is a thing that exists between black men that allows them to almost instantly meet and relate to each other on the corner, in the church and on the job.

It is in this context of understanding and defining their social need that many black men become very vulnerable and susceptible to hurt and exploitation. There are two extremes that characterize the behavior of black men in the context of relationships and their social networking. At one extreme is their tendency to give too much credit to White men in terms of their abilities, success and integrity. At the other extreme is the tendency of black men to give black women too little credit in terms of their availability, integrity, attitude and sensitivity.

These two extremes in the mindset of African American men contributes significantly to their constant struggle to develop and maintain lasting positive relationships. In pursuit of social acceptance by White men on their terms, black men keep trying to acculturate so they can possibly assimilate. To this end they strive to perfect their functional abilities in the area of their professions. Frustration comes when most black men ultimately find their efforts to achieve acceptance as an equal with White men is unattainable. At the same time the suspicious attitude black men harbor toward black women contributes to his perception that she thinks he is beneath her in terms of social class.

In my view African American men must be socialized in such a way that they are not so vulnerable in their social life to exploitation and rejection by White men and are not suspicious of the attitudes of black women. This means learning to manage that part of his make up that consists of both the spirit of the lion which makes him strong and courageous and the spirit of the lamb which makes him gentle and vulnerable.

Fourth, a man needs a relationship with God through Jesus Christ which will give him a sense of unity within himself and with others. In the African American church, black women outnumber black men on an average of eight to one. Conversely in the non-Christian religion of the Nation of Islam black men outnumber black women by a similar count. This suggests two things: The black church in the minds of African American men is not today user-friendly; and black men have a recognized need for a relationship with God.

It is a man's relationship with God through Jesus Christ that brings unity of purpose and direction into his life. Salvation begins the process of moving a fragmented man from the pit of fragmentation to the path of wholeness.

In this section I have suggested that the African American man must be socialized in such a way that he understands that to the extent that he is out of touch with his holistic needs as a man living in the context of North American, he is in fact out of touch with reality.

Understanding his needs means recognizing that as a man he is a physical being and thus has all the physical needs that other men have. He must not define these physical needs in a way that renders him insensitive to the other needs he has as a man. By the same token, as he seeks to meet his felt physical needs, he must exercise discipline so that he is in charge of the drive to meet his physical needs rather than those needs being in charge of him.

A few years ago comedian Richard Pryor said that the reason black men are always holding themselves in the seat of their pants is because what was in their pants is the only thing they have that the White man has not taken from them. The feeling is they had better hold on to themselves lest the White man take that too.

As comical as these words were at the time Mr. Pryor spoke them, there is a sense in which African American men do define their manhood by what is in the seat of their pants. In a singles conference not long ago a single professional sister said to me, "The only thing we (African American, single, professional, black women) need the African American male for is what is in his pants." I suggest that such a declaration is an attempt to deny a need for what is not available. Black men are more than physical beings; they have so much more to offer than what is in their pants. And I think that deep down this sister knows this.

As I have reflected on the Million Man March held in October 1995, it has occurred to me that one of the many messages that echoed from that significant gathering was the fact that African American men have a serious vacuum in the area of their spirit and emotions. Black men are sick and tired of being viewed and defined stereotypically as not quite ready for primetime in terms of who and what they are. The strong signals that are flowing from African American men today is that they are men of compassion. They care about people and situations and want to be cared for.

One African American man in his frustration said, "If you cut my flesh I will bleed real blood just like other men; the same is true when you hit me in my spirit. My emotions will bleed and I will cry like any other hurt man does."

Recently I saw an African American woman with a little black boy who was about four or five years old. As she was entering the store apparently the little boy did or said something that set her off. She turned and began to curse this little boy who I learned later was her son with the most foul words I have ever heard. When she finally quieted down the little boy was crying, and she said to him, "Stop that crying. You are a man. What I said did not hurt you!" I thought to myself what a shame this woman has such a warped view on the feelings of black men. This woman would never have taken a knife and cut her son to the bone, so that he would bleed and possibly die from the wound, yet with her words she cut her son to the bone and could not recognize the wound, nor see the blood streaming from his emotions in the form of tears..

Black men are more than strong, well-built bodies. They are equally endowed with spirit and feelings. In addition it must be recognized that black men are men of strong intellect. I call attention at this point to the fact that most of the men and women who are perceived as heroes by African American men are either entertainers or sports figures. We give too little credit to black men who are gifted in the area of academics.

The young golfer Tiger Woods is a good example of the making of another athletic hero for the African American community in spite of the fact that young Tiger Woods steadfastly resisted the efforts of the White-dominated media to make of him an African American golfer. He clings tenaciously to the idea that he is not really an African American.

In the context of Black male intellectualism there is a tendency on the part of African American men to do two things that are hindrances to their coming to grips with their own intellectualism. First they give White male intellectuals far too much credit in terms of the prevalence of intellectualism among White male and the substance of what Whites define among themselves as intellectualism. The second thing black men do is disregard much of the work of their own Black intellectual brothers, choosing instead to adapt the White intellectual as the only model of genuine intellectualism.

Over the past two decades on the staff and faculty of Dallas Theological Seminary, we have graduated a number of men who have proven themselves to be strong intellectuals and yet few in our student body view them as such. They choose instead to exalt the White male intellectual as the sole representative of true intellectualism in the field of biblical studies. This tendency on the part of Blacks to disregard their own intellectuals may indeed be one of the negative side-effects of integration.

Integration with Whites in the field of education both sacred and secular was perceived by the generations born prior to the sixties and seventies as the path to acceptance and equality. Such was the goal of the Civil Rights Movement.

However integration in many ways has proven instead to be an obstacle in the path of those of ebony hue who are still cast aside and viewed as not quite ready for primetime.

Finally black men are productive men and must be socialized to perceive themselves as such. This means rejecting the stereotypical notion that they are in fact best fitted for that which requires little more than muscles and studding. Black men are capable of producing the highest good in the most technical context of our time. To this end black men must refuse to permit themselves and their sons to be socialized to believe that they are equipped to do little more than survive via their muscles.

The African American male today stands in need of a word from God. This word from God must address the issues of fragmentation and unity. It must speak to the pressing needs that black men have to feel and be accepted as equals with other men. The agent through which that word from God is most likely to come is the church.

Speaking to the issue of the church as an agent of change James Harris writes:

> As a pastor I have asserted that the church is a change agent; however, it is more than that. Because the church is equipped with the gospel of Jesus Christ, it has the power to transform lives. Individual and community transformation is the end result of worship. Those who worship god week after week should not display the same actions and behavior as those who do not. Their perspective and attitude should change, and they should also be able to help change others.[2]

---

[2] Harris, *Pastoral Theology*, p. 92.

CHAPTER 7

BLACK MEN AND
FAMILY RESPONSIBILITIES

I n Memphis, Tennessee in the month of May 1997 at the time when the city was celebrating what is called Memphis in May. It happened that on this particular weekend near downtown Memphis a fifteen year old African American male shot and killed an eighteen year old African American male. In the aftermath of the killing the fifteen year old said that he killed the older boy because he wanted to become a member of a local gang and that was his assignment in order to join the gang. In other words, the fifteen year old paid his admission fee into the gang with the life of an eighteen year old.

The boy who did the killing demonstrated with the murder of that eighteen year old on that day that his most pressing ambition was to become a member of a local gang. The eighteen year old who was killed had a very different life ambition. He was a college student with a scholarship and was actively involved in community service. On this night he had simply joined in the celebration of Memphis in May in downtown Memphis.

As I listened to the reporters comment on the tragedy of this incident and watched the mothers of the two young men grieve over the death of what amounted to both their sons, it caught my attention that in neither case was there a father present. It seems that both boys were products of a family that functioned as best it could without a resident father. The absence of a father-in-residence most often means the absence of an ideal biblically-based family structure and foundation. This fact must not be lost in the modern day feminist rhetoric about the need for a resident father being unnecessary. Every Christian who in obedience to the word of God holds marriage in honor and must acknowledge the fact that when it comes to a healthy family structure and function, a father-in-residence is essential.

A few days after this tragic incident in Memphis, a thirteen year old African American young man who lived in a small town in Arkansas got into an argument with his older sister about washing the dishes from the evening supper. The young boy got so angry that he went into a rage and took a .357 magnum pistol and shot his sister to death. He then grabbed his sister's five month old baby and crushed its skull and snapped the baby's neck. While still enraged, he turned on his mother and shot her, just missing the young child she was holding in her arms.

The whole neighborhood was shocked by the evident rage of this young Black thirteen year old. The community expressed their surprise in view of the fact that this young man did well in school and was never in trouble.

Finally the camera turned to the father of this young man whose response was "I have nothing to say." The evidence suggested that this young man was the product of a family in which the father-in-residence was uninvolved in the life of his children. A father who chooses to be uninvolved in the lives of his children or who is negatively involved will likely find himself trying to manage a family that is dysfunctional.

There is a long history in this country in both the White and Black communities of failing to acknowledge or of disregarding the role and function of African American fathers in the management and development of their children. During slavery the Black male was not given any respect, role or authority in the lives of the children he fathered. In the context of slavery the children of black men for all practical purposes belonged to the slave master and the mother of the children.

In more recent times the African American father is perceived to be under the power and the authority of his wife who, in the minds of the larger community, is the real leader and authority in the home. The idea of the female-dominated family enjoyed a major emphasis in the Moynihan Report that came out during the Nixon Administration in the 1960s. In the contemporary 1990s, reports by such men as Bill Moyer and other news correspondents have emphasized again and again the same stereotypical view. They still report the Black family functions essentially without the influence and or constructive involvement of the Black father.

I am reminded here of the shock on the faces of the many public school and college administrators' faces when I show up to attend to the affairs of my children with or without their mother. I encountered many aggravating experiences with school administrators in predominantly White public school systems, colleges and universities. They preferred not to deal with me as a respected, in-resident, positively involved African American father. I finally concluded that these administrators and educators needed to understand that I was one of a multitude of Black dads who are not mentioned on the evening news. We cannot be counted among those frequently mentioned but invisible Black dads who contribute nothing more than spermatoza to the parenting process. For thirty years I have pastored a multitude of African American men who are in-resident positively involved fathers. We are members of that African American community of black men who do not make good copy on the evening news.

One of the women's liberation's staunchly-held notions is in my opinion more than a little bit destructive to the families of black men. That view states that women can do just fine with or without an in-resident father. This feminist driven view in essence contends that the only thing that is really required of the male in the parenting process is his sperm. Reality proves otherwise, and the disproportionate number of single mothers we have in our community trying to grow sons into whole adults with too little success is here to prove it. When it comes to a family's normal functions, an in-resident father must be factored into the process.

It is necessary for every African American woman to recognize and acknowledge the need for a man to head the family and lead it in its many diverse responsibilities and functions. Men on the other hand need to know what their responsibilities in a family are and how the family is to function in order to meet those many responsibilities. In addition, the man who decides to have his own family must be equipped to manage himself and his family so that it functions in a healthy and constructive manner.

In Genesis 3:1 when Eve decided to have a conversation with the Devil as he appeared in the Garden of Eden in the form of a snake, interestingly the text says that Eve, having been persuaded by the Devil to eat of the forbidden fruit, gave it also to her husband (Adam) "with her." I take it that while Eve was having this extended persuasive conversation with the Devil about what God had said, Adam was present the whole time and neither said nor did anything to prevent his wife Eve from disobeying the word of God. In a word, Adam abdicated his role as head of the family, leaving it to his wife Eve to function in his role as head of the family. The results of Adam's tragic decision remains with us to this day.

Eli, a priest in the nation of the Jews, had several sons who were ungodly and demonstrated their wicked attitude by disregarding the sanctity of the tabernacle. Those boys had sex with women inside the place of worship, the tabernacle, and stole meat that was being offered to God as a sacrifice on the altar. The immoral and irreverent attitude and behavior of these boys was sin in the eyes of God. Their father knew what they were doing but did nothing to correct their behavior. Eli the man of God chose to abdicate his responsibility as a father and failed to confront his sons about their evil doings. His failure caught the attention of God and brought his whole house under judgment.

> And the LORD said to Samuel: "See, I am about to do something in Israel that will make the ears of everyone who hears of it tingle. At that time I will carry out against Eli everything I spoke against his family—from beginning to end. For I told him that I would judge his family forever because of the sin he knew about; his sons made themselves contemptible, and he failed to restrain them. Therefore, I swore to the house of Eli, 'The guilt of Eli's house will never be atoned for by sacrifice or offering' (1 Sam. 3:11-14).

King David is a third example of a man who chose to abdicate his responsibilities in the management of the function of his family. In the tragic incident of Amnon's incestuous rape of his half-sister Tamar, his brother Absalom killed him. Having killed his brother, Absalom fled the country and remained a fugitive in another country until his father's friend interceded for him and David consented to let his son Absalom return home to the city of Jerusalem. However, Absalom's Dad, King David, stipulated that his son Absalom could come back to the city but he was restricted from the palace house and the presence of his father.

Then Joab went to Geshur and brought Absalom back to Jerusalem. But the king said, "He must go to his own house; he must not see my face." So Absalom went to his own house and did not see the face of the king. In all Israel there was not a man so highly praised for his handsome appearance as Absalom. From the top of his head to the sole of his foot there was no blemish in him. Whenever he cut the hair of his head —he used to cut his hair from time to time when it became too heavy for him —he would weigh it, and its weight was two hundred shekels by the royal standard. Three sons and a daughter were born to Absalom. The daughter's name was Tamar, and she became a beautiful woman. Absalom lived two years in Jerusalem without seeing the king's face (2 Sam. 14:23 -28).

I call attention to the fact that Absalom was in the city with his father King David for two years and yet David never said a word to him about anything. This means that King David refused to confront him about the murder of his brother Amnon. Absalom, perhaps in reaction to his father's rejection of him, pulled off later a revolution in Jerusalem that dethroned King David.

It is my contention that much of the Black on Black crime in the African American community today perpetuated by young African American teens and young adults, is a reflection of the absence of in-resident father in many families. In families where a father is in resident, those few do not confront their sons about their attitude and behavior.

My observations over the years as a pastor suggest that a number of the bad actors and violent young men who wound and kill people have in-resident fathers who provide their boys with the best of everything but will not confront them about their attitude and behavior. This must change if there is to be any hope of reclaiming the Village.

While it is true that the African American community has a disproportionate number of single parents, we must be careful to guard against the frequently published idea that married couples are the norm only in the White community. The Black church bears witness to the fact that married couples are not the exception in the Black community no more than the White Community. Yes, there are more women in most Black churches than there are men but for the most part the women in the Black church are married.

The challenge we face today in the context of the African American family is first rejecting the stereotypical idea that African American men are generally irresponsible fathers unwilling to head their own families. We must also disregard the idea that the men on the corners doing nothing are representative of the majority of African American men. They are not. Finally we must determine to look beyond the images of black men in the media that on a daily basis connect crime and violence to African American men. Rather we must see instead the multitude of men who in fact are good men doing a good job as head of their families.

The church must increase its efforts to reach black men with the gospel of Jesus Christ. Then, by way of discipleship, teach men the word of God which will in time move them out of the arena of biblical illiteracy. It is in the context of discipleship and mentoring that African American men must be taught the responsibilities and function of a family. It ought not be assumed that men know what a family's responsibilities are and how it should function.

This focus on the function of a family is built upon the premise of the biblical idea that God designed the family structure to be monogamous in terms of the relationship between the man and his wife. A monogamous relationship means that a man is to have only one living wife in his life. The biblical idea of monogamy is established in Genesis 2:24 and reiterated in Matthew 19:1ff.

God commanded Adam to cleave to his wife. The husband-wife relationship has a higher priority than the relationship a man has with his parents. In Genesis 2:24 God establishes the marriage relationship as the most valuable relationship that a man has. In fact a man's marriage is the only lifelong exclusive covenant relationship he has. This means that men are to value their relationship with their wife above parents, children, friends and job.

The man who is most prepared to head a family and lead it in its many diverse functions and responsibilities, is one who understands that he must place a high priority on understanding his need for a wife. Out of this understanding of himself will come the value the man will place on his wife as a person and as his corresponding helper. It is this understanding of himself combined with the value he places on his wife that a man develops a level of commitment to his family that will sustain the marriage for a lifetime.

The primary responsibilities of the husband/father are to provide for the basic needs of his family, make provision for the education of all of the children born into that union, teach family life values, build self-esteem in the children, lead in the development and management of the spiritual environment in the home.

In answer to the question of what is the primary function of a family, most men respond by saying that from their point of view the the family is there to meet their needs. When asked to list their number one need as a husband, most men say sexual satisfaction. Few men are very specific about their needs beyond the need for sex. To be sure sexual satisfaction is important, in that it affirms their manhood.

This section focuses on answering the question of what an African American man must know about family responsibilities and function and how to be equipped to lead and manage a family in contemporary America. The man who decides to marry needs to know the what and the how of family responsibilities and function in order to structure and lead a family that is not dysfunctional. A poorly structured family will most often function in a manner that will fragment the children born into that context. These children will most often grow into fragmented adults, thus continuing the cycle of fragmentation in the Village.

In terms of family function the first responsibility a man has is as the primary provider, keeping in mind that a majority of men go wife-shopping with their eyes, not their mind and heart. These men are looking for a wife who will meet their number one felt need which they often define as sexual satisfaction. The flip side of that felt need, which is not perused through the passion of his eyes but is nonetheless his responsibility, is his duty to "provide" for his family the basic stuffs, such as food, clothing, shelter, etc. This side of the relationship demands the involvement of the mind, heart, muscles and spirit of the man as an effective primary provider.

It is important to note that on average the young men who comes to the marriage altar brings with them all the necessary equipment to peruse and in time achieve his most felt need of sexual satisfaction. However, in all too many instances those same young men are woefully ill equipped to attend to the flip side of that need which is to "provide" even the most basic needs of woman who is the object of his passion. In this context, I suggest that the issue of functioning as the head of a family must begin with equipping the young man with the ability to think beyond the press of his libido and focus on his responsibility to function as the primary provider for his family.

It has been my opportunity to observe over the years as a pastor who has counseled and married numerous couples, that the ability of the husband to provide the basic necessities of life for his family, is as essential as sunshine is to growing a healthy garden. A man who is limited in his ability to "provide" the basic necessities for his family regardless of the income of his wife most often finds himself in a fragmented family situation especially when children enter the picture. In the mind of more than a few African American men, having a wife who earns more money than he does compares to having weeds in your garden. It simply does not look or feel good.

The process of preparing the African American male to manage his family in such a way that it functions in a healthy manner begins when the young man is yet a boy. The wise parent instills in their son the idea that he must be equipped to manage his libido when it kicks in during his early teen years. He should be equipped to provide for his family when he elects to take a wife, most often in his mid-twenties. He must not prematurely negate his opportunities to adequately prepare himself to be a provider. This preparation includes getting an education, work experience, and a marketable skill. How well parents prepare their son in these two areas will determine for the most part how healthy the young man's family will be as a result of hie being able to meet the needs of his family.

In a family in which the husband is equipped to provide the basics for his family, companionship, love, and positive life experiences most often follow. In other words a man equipped to provide the basic needs for himself and his family is likely to have an attitude and a home environment in which the nurturing and bonding virtues of companionship, love, and positive life experiences can take place.

A family that is headed by a mature man and structured to function in a healthy manner creates a healthy framework in which love and companionship can grow. It is difficult for a man to develop and maintain a family structure in which his love for his wife and children can be nurtured if he is stressed out by a lack of finances and the resulting deficiencies in basic necessities.

Jacob is an example of a young man who married young primarily to avoid fornication as a Christian young man. He and Melody married when he was nineteen and she was eighteen. At the time of their marriage Melody was already pregnant with their first child. They have had three additional children. They have been married now about five years.

Everybody who knows Jacob can testify to the fact that he is a very fine Christian young man and he could hardly have married a finer young woman. However, over the five years of their marriage Jacob has struggled to provide the basic necessities of food, clothing and shelter for his family. Melody is willing to get a job but the cost of quality childcare and the level of her labor skills makes that option unattractive.

Jacob is indeed a fine young man in the truest sense of the word. However, in terms of employment skills he is very limited. Though he works very hard, even sometimes working two and three jobs, just to provide the basics for his family, oftentimes there is simply not enough money to go around. This financial shortfall contributed significantly to Jacob's repeated bouts with depression and frustration.

It sometimes seems to Jacob that being and doing what is right in the eyes of God has its downside. Having your own wife and children, as opposed to living in immorality and not being an in-resident father, is priced beyond what Jacob can afford to pay.

The finest Christian man who takes a wife in obedience to the word of God but is ill equipped to provide the basic necessities for his family will find himself feeling trapped and frustrated by his family. When it comes to having a family it is not sufficient for the man to be saved and committed to morals and righteousness. The family requires of him the ability to provide the basic necessities for that family. It is true that God will provide, however God's provision for a man to take care of his family begins in the early years of that young man's life as he is equipped to make it in the marketplace of life.

I refuse to marry men who are unclear on how they will provide for their family. In my view, to marry a Christian man so that he can have sanctified sex but cannot provide for his wife is to put a man in a situation in which in the mind of God he is worse than an infidel. "If anyone does not provide for his relatives, and especially for his immediate family, he has denied the faith and is worse than an unbeliever" (1 Tim. 5:8).

In his struggle to provide for his family Jacob is developing an attitude towards his wife and children that tends to define them as a burden too heavy for him to carry. Jacob has few options as to the quality apartment and community in which he can live. His options run along the lines of poor to slum quality housing. Thus Jacob's management of his family is increasingly less structured along the lines of love and companionship and more along the lines of frustration and worry. As a result the atmosphere in Jacob's home environment is increasingly negative and stressful for the wife and children.

Jacob's problem is not unlike a number of African American men I have met over the years as a pastor. Men who are saved and committed to living for the Lord. However, they were not equipped as boys and young men to manage their libido in a way that did not lend itself to immediate self gratification. Neither were they equipped to provide for themselves and their family at a level above poverty.

This observation has nothing to do with the quality of the character of the young men, nor does it reflect any deficiency in their spiritual commitment. The point of my observation is that a man's ability to provide the basic necessities for his family is in many instances on the same level of significance in the healthy function of his family as is his character and religious commitment.

In my view, to reach a man with the gospel of Jesus Christ and disregard his ability or inability to provide for himself and his family the basic necessities of life is in effect to abandon him to a life of frustration in which his faith in God is little more than spiritual fire insurance good only at death. "Make it your ambition to lead a quiet life, to mind your own business and to work with your hands, just as we told you" (1 Thess. 4:11).

My son is nineteen years old and in his mind he is madly in love with a very fine young woman who is eighteen. I am fully aware that he is totally equipped to peruse and acquire in time sexual satisfaction with this young woman. Both my son and the young lady are saved. However, this does not at all suggest that their sex drive is not strongly active. I hope that in parenting my son, I have equipped him to manage his libido so that he has time to complete his preparation for providing for himself and his family.

As my son would say, I must tell you straight, most if not a majority of the men I know who have dysfunctional families are not men who are unbelievers, mean, lazy or immoral. These men are saved and committed to living for the Lord. Their problem tends to reside in their inability to adequately provide the basic necessities for their family. The average young man has little to no idea of what it will cost to provide the basic necessities for a wife and children. It is important that I point out here that many of these ill-equipped men are sons of middle class parents. These middle class moms and dads parented poorly in terms of equipping their sons with the necessary skills with which to provide for themselves and their family.

These young men are perhaps best defined as a cut flower generation in that they are only equipped to survive and flourish as members of their parent's household. On their own, they soon wither and fade into failure. In other words there are many fine Christian young men in terms of their appearance and attitude who are essentially ill-prepared to leave home and build a life for themselves as either a single young man or one who is married.

I am suggesting that it is increasingly common to find middle class African American parents who in their parenting ill-equipped their sons, fine Christian young men though they may well be, to leave their father and their mother and cleave only to their wife. James Harris writes:

> The black church has a responsibility to teach its constituents the value of economic independence so blacks can launch an all-out effort to become producers and not simply consumers. The process of education is important here because schools and other institutions are not concerned about teaching economics independence or interdependence. It is up to the black church to systematically redirect the energy and thought processes of its members beginning when they very young.[1]

The second primary function of a family is to provide for the education of the children. The emphasis lies in the education of children as it pertains to the father's involvement. In the education package of the African American male, I place academics, social skills, interpersonal relational skills and survival skills.

When a young man takes a wife I suggest delaying the birth of their firstborn for two years to allow adjustment time between the husband and his wife. During this two-year adjustment period, I suggest that a foundation be established and an environment created into which a child can be born and developed into a whole adult. To put it another way the first two years of marriage without children gives the young husband

---

[1] James H. Harris, *Pastoral Theology: A Black Church Perspective* (Minneapolis,. MN: Fortress Press, 1991), p. 48.

time to gain an understanding of what the functions of a family are and how to manage the family in such a way that it functions in a healthy manner.

The effective education of children in my view is rooted in the ability of the father to provide a residence for his family in a community with a quality public school system. Having a quality school system must not be understood to mean a suburban school system nor necessarily an integrated school system, it is to be understood to mean a system that is committed to quality in education in that it is about the genuine education of the children in the system regardless of their race, social class or culture. It is not possible for any father to provide a better education for his children than what the public school system in the community in which he lives provides. If he can afford it, parochial, private or chartered schools are other options. There are many vanguards, academies and magnet schools that one may attend without the restrictions of district boundaries.

Young Christian men who marry to satisfy and sanctify their sex drive must be equally concerned about the children who result from that satisfaction. It is quite possible for a single man to live and do well in an inner city, but it is less suitable for a wife and children. Thus endemic to the education of his children are the options the young father has as it pertain to choice of residence and the quality of the public schools in the community in which he chooses to lives. Children who get a functional education in a less than quality school system are the exceptions to the rule. Praise the Lord for the thousands of exceptions to the rule during our country's "separare, but equal" era. The support and concern of the Village balanced the scale.

The necessity of a functional education is such that no father can risk taking up residence in a community in which the school system is ranked low in academic accomplishment. Neither can he risk subjecting his young, impressionable children to the daily bombardment of racial slurs, overt discrimination and mainstreaming in the "better" schools. Choosing who will be the caretakes of your children for most of their waking hours is an important decision. More than education is at stake.

It is the responsibility of the family to function in a manner that contributes to the academic development of the children. The education of children includes developing positive social and interpersonal relational skills. In this context I must distinguish between the young man who marries and is equipped with few economic options in terms of choice and quality in housing, community and public education and those who are not. The difference includes more than the lack of opportunity for quality education in the public school system. It also means that the man who is able to choose his place of residence in terms of the quality of the housing, community and public school system most often can afford to have sufficient room to accommodate the addition of children into the home.

The lack of space means the absence of privacy for both parents and children. When there is inadequate space for privacy children often are exposed to the intimacy between their parents and thus are prematurely exposed to what is from the child's point of view pornographic at worse and promiscuity at best. As a rule parents do not invite their children into the bedroom to observe their sexual activity. Yet a number of children are frequently exposed to such bedroom activity because of the lack of space and privacy in the home.

Positive interpersonal and relational social skills means having a family context in which the environment is conducive to learning to respect the privacy of others as well as learning to share and participate in the world of others. Developing positive social skills means learning how to give and take, how to laugh and cry, how to seek forgiveness and how to forgive.

In the context of the overall development of positive social skills children develop interpersonal skills that contribute to their ability to get along with others who may be very different from themselves. They learn how and when to speak, above all they learn the value of listening and thinking.

For close to twenty years I have served as executive director of an Early-Childhood Development Center in an inner city church. I have often observed the interest and knowledge of sexual intercourse many of the young children bring to the center. I learned that the knowledge the children had of sex was not from what they saw on television as I had assumed but from what they saw in the parent's bedroom at home. I frequently stress to young parents the need for privacy in their homes. But I realize that for a number of parents privacy is not an option due to their income level and the resulting living conditions.

This lack of privacy contributes to sexual abuse in many homes between siblings. This sexual abuse is not limited to the girls in these homes as is commonly thought. A number of boys are abused as well. Few parents give any consideration to the impact of sexual abuse on their sons. Yet there are no small number of men who are sexually dysfunctional because of being sexually-abused boys.

I have seldom met a man who had poorer interpersonal and general relational social skills as did John. John was a man with many hang-ups especially as it pertained to his relationship with his wife. He could hardly hold a conversation about sex and yet he would frequent places where prostitutes hang out. Sometimes John felt like he was gay. Other times he felt as if he was at least bisexual. As I met with John over an extended period of time and gained his confidence, he shared with me one day how as a boy he was repeatedly sexually abused by an older girl with whom his mother often left him. According to John this abuse is among his earliest negative memories as a child.

As it pertains to the education of children the husband/father must be equipped with the abilities and the opportunities to have an income that empowers him with positive choices in terms of residence. The choice of residence must be in a community that has a strong public education system and sufficient space in the house to accommodate the family's need for privacy. The lack of economic choice in the context of education will most often contribute to the fragmentation of the children in the home.

It is the function of a family to teach by word and example what is commonly referred to as traditional family values. These values are transferred in the home environment to the children as they are modeled by the parents. The church and the community reinforce and affirm these values. Affluence does not equal better. The media bounds with horror stories of kids-of-means committing suicide, overdosing on drugs, cheating on tests, aborting or giving birth to and then killing the baby, practicing Satanism, executing their parents and mass-murdering their classmates. One may choose to reside in a community that does not hold the same traditional values or respect said customs of the family. Many upwardly-mobile blacks reside in virtual isolation in their ivory towers (homes) all week and seek socialization in the havens (churches) in communities they escaped for a "better" life. A part of the Village is still working.

I suggested earlier that there are at least four things African

American boy must be socialized to value: (1) Boys must be taught to value their life and respect the lives of others; (2) Boys need to understand the value of a good reputation and thus develop the habit of speaking the truth in regard to themselves and others; (3) Boys must have regard for the property of others and respect the right of the other person to maintain possession of that which is theirs; and (4) Sons must learn from the example of others a high regard for the institution of marriage and respect unwaveringly the sanctity of another man's wife.

At this point it is important to state again that the options the husband/father has in choice of a community in which to live is based on his economic status. This environment will enhance or diminish the potential for transferring traditional family values. The couple who lives in a low income housing community, with poor public education, deficient church and pulpit ministry, is likely to find that the community has a greater influence on their children than they hav.

It is important to point out here that good people in inner city low-income Black communities are at a serious disadvantage in comparison to Black communities, whether inner city or suburban, that are not in economic decline or abandoned by city services. The disadvantage is in the values that are prevalent in the community.

The inner city tends to have a value system that revolves around economic survival and immediate self gratification. It is not unusual to find life in the inner city held at considerable less value than in communities that have higher income and stable family models. In the inner city black men tend to place a higher value on money than they do on life. They also tend to risk more to get money than black men in other communities, simply because they have less to risk. In the inner city a less conservative moral code exists so that fidelity in marriage is less prevalent and families tend to be less stable and teen pregnancy more common.

When the place of residence is driven by financial limitations so that the choices are limited to low income communities, the husband/father will most often find it much more difficult to manage the function of his family so that positive traditional family values are transferred to the children.

I have said earlier that it is difficult even impossible except is a few rare instances for a father to get for his children an education that is superior to the education that is available in the public educational system in the community in which he lives. The same is true of a father's ability to transfer traditional family values. It is rare indeed to find children who do not reflect the values of the community in which they grew up.

I married my wife in the community center of the low income housing in which she lived. In reflecting on men who grew up in that community over thirty years ago, those who made it to adulthood with traditional family values are the exceptions, not the rule. Today nearly forty years later that low income community is in serious decline in every respect. The children who grew up in that community are almost always the least equipped with functional positive family values.

The tendency today on the part of a number of us who grew up in low income communities is to think that there is nothing really so bad about low-income communities because, we hasten to think and say, folk in the suburbs have as many poorly parented children as do folk in the inner city. The truth is the inner city poor communities today are among the worse places in this country to raise a family. Yes, there are children in stable Black communities that are poorly parented but these children in spite of their parent's failure are privileged to have options in terms of education, security, religion and values.

There is a significant difference between the child who has the opportunity to get a quality education, positive life values and such but chooses to reject them and the child who never had such opportunities. This is the difference that exists between the option to choose the best and not having an option at all. There are many African American males who are born into families and community contexts in which they simply have very few if any options in terms of choice in these important areas of their lives.

The husband/father who is equipped to provide the basic necessities of life for his family will find it less difficult to communicate positive family values to his children. Due to his less restricted choices in terms of community in which to live, he is most likely to choose a community that is characterized by stability, strong moral standards and a high premium on life. In other words, latitude in the choice of community in which to live provides the husband/father the option to choose a community with schools, churches and community values that are most consistent with his own.

In my view the family that functions in such a manner that

it communicates biblically based family values must have at its head a man equipped to provide the basics for his family, including a stable healthy community environment, a good public school system and a strong community church.

It is the function of a family to equip the members of the family with strong positive self-esteem. To lead his family in this function the husband/father must himself have his self-esteem in tact. This means that he is a mature man, literate, educated, and has a job which provides him with adequate income to live in a community that he feels good about. For the man of whom these things are not the case, self-esteem is likely to be a problem for both him and his family.

Self-esteem is about feeling good about yourself. It is about an attitude that embraces the idea that you belong and are a significant somebody. Self-esteem is developed in the home in the children as they are affirmed and loved by their parents in both words and deeds. It is confirmed in the church and community in the models each present.

To the extent that a man is himself deficient in his own self-esteem, to that extent he will struggle in leading his family in developing in his children positive self-esteem. In this context self esteem must be nurtured in the Black male child by both parents. Nurturing positive self-esteem requires positive family relationships and life experiences.

Regarding self-esteem in black youth, James Harris writes: "The most serious manifestation of a lack of positive self-esteem is seen, however, in the alarming number of sexually active and promiscuous teenagers. These young people do not seem to be concerned about the biblical concept of fornication."[2]

Finally in terms of family function it must operate in a way that develops and maintains a strong spiritual life. I chose to list the husband/father's responsibility to lead his family in the development of a strong spiritual life last on the list of family responsibilities and functions. It is not of less significance than the other family responsibilities but, because it is often perceived to be a panacea, it negates the need to emphasize additional important functions and responsibilities of the family when listed first.

In the context of the spiritual life James Harris says it well:

Individual salvation has as a necessary correlate the salvation of the community. Worship properly understood and practiced

[2] Harris, Pastoral Theology, p. 124.

facilitates the salvation of both. Inasmuch as the black community is victimized by so many internal and external injustices, it needs to be saved. However as long as we think of salvation as an individual, personal experience, instead of a community experience, we fail to understand the Exodus event as a paradigm, not only of liberation, but also of salvation. Contrary to what blacks were taught during slavery, salvation apart from liberation is inconsistent with the gospel message. To be "saved" is to be a new creation, and a new creation implies complete transformation.[3]

It is extremely difficult and almost impossible for a man to use his faith in God to override his lack of preparation in terms of his being equipped to provide for his family. It is not wise to live in a slum community and expect not to be impacted by the attitudes and values in that community. Nor is it Christian to think that the ability to provide for the family is the essence of what it means to be the spiritual leader in the home. Men who neglect their families in order to earn more money is likely to have a dysfunctional family due to benign neglect.

Developing the spiritual lives of children demands of the husband/father that he leads in the development of a Christian home. A Christian home is one in which both parents are saved and committed to living for the Lord on a daily basis. In a Christian home, Christ is the central focus and the family has a spiritual agenda that is focused on being salt and light in their home, on their job and in the community.

The husband/father who leads his family in this function is himself given to prayer, bible study and sharing his faith. He is a man of biblical conviction and lives out those convictions in a transparent way so that his family is exposed to his consistent commitment to holiness in public and in private

[3] Ibid, p. 193.

PART 3

THE PROCESS OF DEVELOPING UNFRAGMENTED AFRICAN AMERICAN MEN

CHAPTER 8

THE MEANING OF MANHOOD

MANHOOD MEANS THE WILL TO WORK

There are a multitude of ways to define manhood in the context of contemporary Black America. Topping the list are definitions that focus primarily on money, biceps and sexual conquest. In the language of the streets a real man has "Nuts." My nineteen year old son, who is well versed in street language, tells me that the difference between a Butterfinger and a Baby Ruth is that the Butterfinger has the potential but does not have the "Nuts" to pull it off. In the Village that same difference exists between Black males and genuine African American manhood. Being a male means having the potential but it takes a real man to pull off the function of genuine manhood.

It will be impossible in defining manhood to arrive at an adequate definition without including a definition of the will and the skill to work. This approach includes within its scope the skill and the will to work and makes the distinctions between what it means to be an African man wrapped in genuine African American manhood as opposed to what it means to be merely an African American male.

Including the will and the skill to work within a definition of genuine manhood also makes a distinction between genuine manhood and genuine womanhood. This is not to suggest that the will and the skill to work is exclusively a man-thing because it most certainly is not. It suggests, however, that women in general tend not to define themselves by their work regardless of the nature of their work. Women tend to define themselves more by their family and their work is an addendum to that identity.

> To the woman He said, "I will greatly multiply your pain in *childbirth*, in pain you shall bring forth children; yet your desire shall be for your husband, and he shall rule over you." Then to Adam He said, "Because you have listened to the voice of your wife, and have eaten from the tree about which I commanded you, saying, 'You shall not eat from it'; cursed is the ground because of you; *in toil* you shall eat of it all the days of your life. "Both thorns and thistles it shall grow for you; and you shall eat the plants of the field; *by the sweat of your face You shall eat bread*, till you return to the ground, because from it you were taken; for you are dust, and to dust you shall return" (Gen. 3:16-19, NASB).

An interesting thing about this passage is that the curse on the woman that resulted from the fall focused on her function as a mother while for the man the focus of the curse was on his function as a provider "by means of the sweat of his brow."

The Apostle Paul, in writing on the issue of the role of women in the church, discusses their function, not their spiritual gifts. He quotes the passage in Genesis 3 as the foundation upon which the role of women in the church is built. Paul writes, "Let a woman quietly receive instruction with entire submissiveness. But I do not allow a woman to teach or exercise authority over a man, but to remain quiet. For it was Adam who was first created, and then Eve. And it was not Adam who was deceived, but the woman being quite deceived, fell into transgression. But women shall be *preserved through the bearing of children* if they continue in faith and love and sanctity with self-restraint" (1 Tim. 2:11-15).

Even more interesting to note that in this text there is a strong inference to the fact that childbearing for believing women has a redemptive element in it. In nearly forty years of Christian ministry I have met few if any Christian women who did not desire to have children. No matter what they did professionally, having children meant more to them than did their jobs. Christian women tend not to define themselves by their work as men do.

I suggest that a bibliocentric definition of manhood includes within its scope the will and the skill to work. To make such an argument brings out from others the objection that the Apostle Paul's argument is culturally biased and thus not applicable to the contemporary African American cultural context. I respond that the link between womanhood and motherhood did not originate with the Apostle Paul but in the Garden of Eden before and after the fall. Nor does the link between manhood and work originate with the Apostle Paul but in the Garden of Eden before and after the fall.

As a biblicist I am compelled to reject the argument that the biblical emphasis on manhood and work and womanhood and mothering is purely cultural. I believe the biblical emphasis is consistent with how God Himself designed the man and the woman to function as a two-part single unit reflecting His image and His glory through the ages.

Any holistic attempt to reach black men today with the gospel of Jesus Christ must include such considerations as job opportunity with upward mobility and in many cases it must include the development of job skill. I have found it impossible to develop men in the faith without the man having a job in which he can express his manhood.

The contention that manhood means having a job is rooted in the belief that God designed men to obey and worship Him. This attitude of worship and obedience is deeply related to man's need and desire for work as an expression of his humanity. The man who does not work most often struggles with his identity and security in the context of his family and community.

"The LORD God took the man and put him in the Garden of Eden to work it and take care of it" (Gen. 2:15).

In his commentary on Genesis John H. Sailhamer writes regarding this verse,

> The author had already noted that God "put" man into the garden (v. 8b). In v. 15 he returned to this point and recounted the purpose for God's putting man there. Two important points from v. 15 are in danger of being obscured by the English translations. The first is the change from v. 8 in the Hebrew word for "put." Unlike v. 8 where a common term for "put" is used, in v. 15 the author uses a terms that he elsewhere has reserved for two special uses: God's "rest" or "safety," which he gives to man in the land (e.g., Gen. 19:16; Deut. 3:20; 12:10; 25:19), and the "dedication" of something in the presence of the Lord (Exod 16:33-34; Lev 16:23; Num 17:4; Deut 26:4, 10). Both sense of the terms appear to lie behind the author's use of the word in v. 15. Man was "put" into the garden "in God's presence" where he could be "safe," and man was "put" into the garden "in God's presence" where he could have fellowship with God (3:8).
>
> A second point from v. 15 that has often been overlooked in the EVs is the specific "to work it and take care of it." Although that translation was as early as the LXX (2nd cent. B.C.), there are serious objections to it. For one, the suffixed pronoun in the Hebrew text rendered "it" in English is feminine, whereas the noun "garden," which the pronoun refers to in English is a masculine noun in Hebrew. Only by changing the pronoun to a masculine singular, as the LXX had done, can it have the scene of

the EV's, namely "to work" and "to keep it." Moreover, later in this same narrative (3:23) "to work the ground" is said to be a result of the fall, and the narrative suggest that the author had intended such a punishment to be seen as an ironic reversal of man's original purpose. . . If such was the case, then "working" and "keeping" the garden would not provide a contrast to "working the ground."

In light of these objections, which cannot easily be overlooked, a more suitable translation of the Hebrew would be "to worship and to obey."[1]

I find Sailhamer's comments on this passage quite insightful yet not in contradiction to the traditional view that work was inherent in man's responsibility in the garden, i.e., God put Adam in the garden to work. I suggest that there is no dichotomy or conflict between a man's responsibility to work, i.e., the traditional view of the text, and a man's responsibility to worship and obey the living God, i.e., Sailhamer's view that God put man in the garden to worship and obey Him. To separate worship and work is to isolate the one from the other, so that it is not possible to speak to both from a biblical perspective. Any separation between work and worship builds a wall between the secular and the sacred, so that it is not possible for the man or woman of God to prophetically speak to the secular regarding ethical and social issues with a view to evaluating that context.

In speaking to the issue of evangelicalism and social politics James Harris writes: "The history of the evangelical movement suggest that there has never been no absolute dichotomy between religion and politics in the sense that some conservatives would have us believe."[2]

The fall of man adds the burden of toil and sweat into his work responsibility that God had given him in the garden before the fall. Under the curse, caused by the fall into sin by man, creation took on an attitude that caused it to be in a state of constant conflict with man and thus man's work became a situation that is most often neither pleasant nor effortless. It is my contention that in the mind of God work and worship are combined in the package of manhood in any cultural context.

Endemic to the idea of manhood is the will and the skill to work. There may well be a spiritual connection between a man's will to work and his will to obey and worship God (cf. Eph.

[1]   John H. Sailhamer, "Genesis" in *Expositor's Bible Commentary* Frank Gaebelein, ed. (Grand Rapids: Zondervan Publishing House, 1990), 2:44-45.
[2]   James H. Harris, *Pastoral Theology: A Black Church Perspective* (Minneapolis,. MN: Fortress Press), p. 6.

4:28).

The will and the skill to work must be distinguished from the desire for and the pursuit of money as an end in and of itself. The man who has the will and the skill to work is equipped to function in accord with how men were originally designed by God and in accord with the new man that is created in Christ Jesus through salvation. The man who only has a passion for the acquisition of money ultimately finds himself in conflict with both himself and the living God.

God created man in His image for the purpose of reflecting His glory. He put all of creation at man's disposal so that man could subdue and rule over it. It is my contention that one of the ways man expresses the image of God in himself and reflects the glory of God in this world is by means of his work and his worship.

Inherent in a man's will and skill to work is the ability to be productive and contribute not only to his own welfare but also to the good of others. In addition it is through a man's work that he affirms and nurtures much of his humanity in general and identity as a man in particular. An idle man is likened to a man in shallow waters in terms of his concept of who God is and his concept of his own manhood.

My dad died when he was fifty-seven years old. At the time of his death I thought he was an old man whom I loved dearly but whose time had come. Today I am over fifty-seven myself and it does not seem old at all. It now seems to me that my dad died prematurely, thus I have taken the time to reflect on what might have contributed to his early death.

When my dad was fifty-two years old, in my desire to move him to what I thought at the time was a better life off the farm on which he had lived and labored all of his life, I moved him and Mom to the big city of Dallas in Texas. In the city my dad had little to do, and for the first time in his life he was idle. My dad could neither read nor write, so finding a job that he could do in the city was difficult even in those days.

As I look back on that decision to move my father to the city so he could have what I believed to be a better life, I know now it was not at all a better life for him. When I moved my dad from the farm I moved him away from his job and thus away from all that defined his manhood and gave him his identity for over half a century. In five short years after I moved him from the farm to the city, he died. In retrospect it is clear to me that most of his five years spent in the city were spent in a state of depression and social isolation.

In my view, work is a necessary part of manhood and thus must be factored into the definition of what it means to be a man. The problem my dad had was living without a job through which he could continue to express his manhood. It was not a matter of not having money, we made sure he had money and most everything else that he needed. It is important to say again that a distinction must be made between the value that is placed on having money and the value that is placed on having a job. For the Christian man the issue is having a job not just money. "He who loves money will not be satisfied with money, nor he who loves abundance with its income. This too is vanity" (Ecc. 5:10).

At this point I need to put in a word of caution about men and work. I have observed over the years a tendency on the part of many families to push their sons into the labor market at a very early age. Sometimes the place of employment is not a healthy environment for adult men, much less young boys. The motivation for such parents pushing their sons into the marketplace is not so much the money but the idea that boys need to know how to work.

I agree that it is good for parents to teach their sons a strong work ethic. However, in all too many instances, parents push their sons into the labor market prematurely in terms of the young man's physical, emotional and psychological maturity. Often I have seen young men crippled for life by their exposure to an environment on the job that is so negative and hostile that it breaks their spirit.

In Ephesians 4:28, the Bible speaks to the issue of a man working in order to be empowered to give to those who have need. This verse speaks to the issue of working with one's own hands in order to be able to give to the poor set against the backdrop of stealing as the wrong alternative to work.

The sin of stealing is not limited to pickpockets and burglars. It can disguise itself in respectability which may go undetected in church pews. The moral sanctions of even a purely secular society can perhaps curb the more obvious crimes of avarice. Christian motivation, however, can penetrate to the root of this deep-seated sin. "We are members one of another." Christian love is derivative of the love of God, seeking not its own. Like the love of God, it is prepared to give to those in need.

It is significant that the verse recommends to the thief honest work with his hands. Modern psychology would applaud. The humble toilers of the earth know something of the coastlines of civilization's stores which then are enjoyed and all too often wantonly squandered by idle hands. The defection from the churches of the working man of modern times may call, by way of remedy, for a rediscovery of Christian vocation in the world of shared manual labor. "We labor working with our own hands" (1 Cor.4:12), says Paul of himself and his apostolic band. Christians may well look with fear upon a life of idle wealth. They might at the judgment stand under condemnation of the eighth commandment.[3]

"Make it your ambition to lead a quiet life, to mind your own business and to work with your hands, just as we told you" (1 Thess. 4:11).

This verse connects work with a quiet life and a lifestyle that is characterized by personal inner peace and a public testimony not given to meddling in the affairs of others. The will and the skill to work with their own hands was to distinguish these believers from the unbelievers. It is interesting to note that the will and the skill to work is given here as a mark of holiness. This is especially noteworthy in the context of a day when many churches are filled with men and women who have never worked and have no intention of ever getting a job. According to this text, the will and the skill to work is just as significant in a man's Christian testimony as is his will to avoid immorality and other sins.

I am impressed with the Nation of Islam's emphasis on work as a part of what it means to be a member of that particular Non-Christian religion. I find that the Muslim ministers live and minister even in the most depressed slum communities. In those slum communities they have their mosques and there the people gather to worship. What impresses me most is that to be a Muslim is to have a job. The skill and the will to work in the Muslim faith is a high priority.

In the Christian church, especially in many of the urban communities, most often the minister does not live in the community, but what is even worse in my view is that the folk who are members of the church all too often evidence neither the will or the skill to work. Christianity is often preached and modeled as the kind of religion that lends itself to

---

[3] *The Interpreters Bible*, Vol. 10, p. 700-701.

accommodating the lazy.

I frequently make the argument that in the Village there is a tendency to bestow upon money the value that the Bible ascribes to Wisdom. Wisdom is best defined as the ability to distinguish between that which seems to be important but is really not and that which seems to be important and really is. "For wisdom is protection just as money is protection. But the advantage of knowledge is that wisdom preserves the lives of its possessors" (Ecc. 7:12).

The overemphasis on money in our community is a primary contributing factor to the number of young men who pursue money, not a job, and are willing to do most anything to get the money. I suggest that it is time to change the focus of our values from money as an end in itself to jobs and money as a means of providing the necessities of life. For it is the job that ultimately satisfies the need of a man, not money in and of itself.

The rationale for the argument I have sought to make for prioritizing the will and the skill to work over the pursuit of dollars as an end in itself grows out of my experience as a pastor. Over the years I have observed men who believed that a man was suppose to have certain things like, a car, money in his pocket, clothes and such. These men, many of whom were without either the skill or the will to work, found a way to get the money and things that made them look and feel like men even though they had no job; they simply had money and things.

In time the money and things these men had acquired through a variety of means gave way to the vacuum in their manhood that such things were suppose to fill but could not. These men ultimately discovered most often in their mid-life that money and things acquired for the most part by way of scheming and manipulation lacked the substance necessary to fill the vacuum in their lives that was created by the absence of a relationship with God through Jesus Christ, combined with the absence of the will and the skill to work.

In addition these men found that money and things in and of themselves do not fit them for the responsibilities inherent in manhood. As a result of this recognition many of these men found themselves trying to find for themselves an identity and a place where they fit in society at middle age. In most instances at this stage of their lives they simply could not find themselves or their place in society.

When I say that manhood includes the will to work I am saying that the will and the skill with which to get and maintain a job is in fact a God-ordained role and responsibility of men. I am suggesting that there is much that is missing and unhealthy in terms of Black male and female relationships in contemporary Black America which tends to define the roles of the man and woman in unisexual terms. While it is not possible to defend the conservative Christian idea that is prevalent in some church circles that wives are to be homemakers only, it is possible to defend the idea that in the male and female relationship a primary role of the man is to work and provide for himself and his family.

"But if anyone *does not provide* for his own, and especially for those of his household, he has denied the faith, and is worse than an unbeliever" (1 Tim. 5:8). Unless we are willing to view this passage as merely a cultural statement fit only for the social and economic context of a bygone era, we must as a matter of intellectual honesty accept this text as saying that there is a biblical and spiritual link between a man's faith in God through Jesus Christ and his will and skill to work.

This role and function of the Christian man is clearly different from that of women as set forth in Titus 2:3-5, "Older women likewise are to be reverent in their behavior, not malicious gossips, nor enslaved to much wine, teaching what is good, that they may encourage the young women to love their husbands, to love their children, to be sensible, pure, *workers at home*, kind, being subject to their own husbands, that the word of God may not be dishonored." Again the issue of culture and context is raised. A consistent single, as opposed to a dual, hermeneutics (the science of interpreting scripture) demands that one conclude that the Bible places a higher priority on motherhood for the Christian woman than it does on work in the marketplace. For men the biblical focus places a higher priority on work as opposed to housekeeping.

The man should understand and define his manhood with a primary emphasis on the will and the skill to work as a part of that which sets him apart as as a male wrapped in genuine manhood and marks him as distinct and distinguishable from the role and function of a woman. He does not include in that understanding the idea that such a definition of himself and his role means that he is superior to women; it simply specifies a difference in function and responsibilities in the context of the family and community.

MANHOOD MEANS
FUNCTIONING AS THE HEAD OF THE FAMILY

The story is told of two young children, a boy and a girl ages four and three, playing house in the backyard of their family home. The young boy went off to work in the imaginary morning and came home in the imaginary evening. The young girl met the young boy who was her pretend husband at the door with greetings of adoration. In a little while the little girl prepared the imaginary table for dinner at which they both sat down with their imaginary children and ate their imaginary meal.

After the meal the young boy arose from the imaginary table and went out into the garden and picked up a stick and returned to the imaginary house and drew it back to hit the young girl who was his pretend wife. The little girl screamed, "Don't hit me with that stick." The little girl's scream drew the immediate attention of her parents. When the parents asked the little boy why he was going to hit the young girl with the stick, the young boy replied, "Because we are playing house and I am the husband and I was going to beat her so she would know that I am in charge."

It was three o'clock in the early morning when the phone rang, awakening my wife and me with the sound of borderline hysteria. When I answered the phone, the person on the other end screamed into the phone, "Pastor Lane!" and then the phone was hung up. A few minutes later the phone rang again. I answered and the person on the other end screamed, "This is!" and again hung up. By the time the phone rang a third time, my wife and I had figured out to whom the female voice on the other end belonged. I answered the phone the third time and immediately called out the young woman's name and she answered me.

"Jackie," I asked, "What in God's name is going on over there?"

"It's Mel!" she said, "I think he has lost his mind!"

"What is Mel doing to you?" I asked.

"He is trying to beat me, because I will not agree with him about some crazy business idea that he has."

"Put Mel on the phone," I told her. "Mel, what is the problem?"

Mel's reply stunned me. He said, "I understand from your teaching that I am the head of my family. This means to me that I am in charge and my wife must do what I say. The only thing I know to do when she refuses to do what I say is to whip her into submission." I could not understand how it was that Mel had gleaned from my teaching on family structure such an understanding of what it means to be the head of the family.

Henry was eighteen years old when he came to talk with me about getting married. In his conversation with me, Henry pointed out that he was eighteen, soon to be nineteen years old. He went on to point out that he had finished school and was a committed Christian. "Look at me, Pastor Lane. Do I not have the body of a full grown man?"

"Yes, you do," I replied.

"Well," said Henry, "Since you agree that I am a man and I am saved, in obedience to I Corinthians 7:1-9, I am ready to get married. For the Bible clearly says that in order to avoid fornication let every man have his own wife."

"Henry," I said, "You have the right idea but I must call attention to the fact that your focus is on your maleness, not your manhood. You are considering marriage as a male and as a means of obtaining for yourself a sanctified active sex life. You are not focusing on marriage as a means of expressing your manhood."

Henry illustrates a problem that I have seen in a great number of young Christian men over the years. Young men who are committed Christians, having grown up in the church, decide to marry in response to the demands of their libido with little regard for their preparation to function as the head of the family.

Headship has to do with how a man and his wife perceive their respective roles in the home. Failure to do this will most often cause serious conflict and emotional damage in the relationship over time. At the very outset of the relationship it is necessary for the couple to address the issue of roles and responsibilities in marriage. When all is said and done, the man will feel compelled to define his role as the one in charge.

Having spent close to four decades in Christian ministry during which time I have counseled and married literally hundred of couples, I have seldom seen a couple who entered into marriage where the husband did not rise to the surface as the one in charge of the family. Regardless of who in the relationship had the most education or earned the most money, the man ultimately surfaces as the head of the family.

I am fully aware of the stereotypical notion that black women dominate their men. I have met more than a few black women over the years who were determined not to have any man in charge of them in a relationship. I am here to say that in most if not all such cases the African American man still emerges as the one in charge. In view of the fact that in the Black male and female relationship the man will ultimately surface as the head of the family it is necessary to define from a biblical point of view what "Headship" means in the context of the Christian family.

To define "Headship" as male royalty and the home as the man's castle is to suggest a home environment in which the man thinks and functions as the superior one and thus he will evidence a dictatorial style of leadership as the head of the family. In such families, the wife regardless of her education or profession will of necessity have to become something less than a total human being compared to her husband in order to escape abuse in the marriage at the hands of her husband.

Thomas was the kind of man who viewed himself as king of his house. He loved money and things. Lois, his wife, was highly educated and quite an intellectual. In terms of knowing how to manage things Lois was definitely superior. Yet in order to avoid being abused physically and emotionally by Thomas, Lois often demonstrated a spirit that was something less than who she really was. She felt compelled to submit to the dictatorial leadership style of her husband. What is amazing to me is the fact that Thomas views himself as a Christian man who leads his family in accord with the Scriptures.

The husbands who misdefine "Headship" generally develop a style of leadership that ultimately forces the wife to live like a tenant in her own house. She is treated like a share cropper on a southern plantation. She is made to feel like nothing more than the property of her husband to be used for his pleasure at his discretion. This kind of husband controls all that the wife is and all she earns without the slightest concern for her interests, needs or desires. Thank God that "Headship" is not about control or domination but freedom and security.

The Greek word "κεφαλη" translated head in Ephesians 5:23

does not mean ruler as in royalty, monarchy or autocracy. It is a word used for the top of a pillar, the mouth of a river, the bow of a ship or the head of a body. The word "κεφαλη" also does not mean "above and separate from" but rather it means "in unity with that which it serves as head."

In the Scriptures "κεφαλη" implies the kind of unity which a body and head share. Unlike a mere ruler this concept of headship demands an integral unity with the body over which it has authority. The head identifies with the body so that if any part of the body suffers the head suffers with it (1 Cor. 12:6).

The Christian concept of "Headship" in the family means having the authority to decide and lead in the context of equality between the husband with his wife. Scripture speaks of three such headship concepts: God the Father is the head of the divine union the Trinity (1 Cor. 11:3); Christ is the head of the one body, the church (Col. 1:18, 24); and the husband is the head of the one-flesh union of husband and wife (Eph. 5:23).

In each of these concepts of "Headship," the significance is that of a preeminence over in the context of equality with. Thus in the Trinity, Christ rightly claims equality with the Father, (John. 5:18; Phil. 2:6) and yet the Father is the head of the Trinity (1 Cor. 11:3). In the church Christ is the firstborn of many brethren and is not ashamed to call us brethren (Rom. 8:29; Heb. 2:11), yet Christ is the head of the church (Col. 1:18, 24). In marriage the husband and wife stand as equals in the body of Christ (Gal. 4:28) yet the husband is the head of the wife (Eph. 5:23).

Clearly the Christian concept of "Headship" does not mean superiority. It does mean that the husband is to preside over the family as its head. Thus to define manhood as depicting one as the head of the family is to suggest that manhood connotes being mature enough to function as a self-giving head of one's own family. It means being motivated by a sacrificial love for his family that parallels the love he has for himself. This image of "Headship" implies that the husband and his wife identify so closely with one another that they are essentially a single unit likened to the unity of a man's physical head and physical body.

No one can decide their own gender. One is either born a male or a female. It is equally impossible for any individual to choose their race or ethnicity. However, it is well within the boundaries of any male to decide for himself whether or not he will live his life as a mere male or develop his maleness into genuine manhood.

I have suggested earlier that manhood means having the will and skill to work. In this section I am suggesting that manhood means functioning as the head of the family.

According to 1 Corinthians 7:8-9, the choice to remain single is a valid choice for those who have the gift of celibacy and are called to minister in a context in which being single is required. In such situations genuine manhood is expressed in and through the ministry to which the single man gives himself completely.

The man who chooses to marry of necessity must be able to function as the head of his family. This ability to function as the head of his family means understanding that as the head the husband must be equipped to manage himself, his wife, his children and the affairs that are involved in their lives. Genuine manhood in terms of preparation to function as the head of one's own family begins with a man's learned ability to manage himself. This self management means learning about himself so that he understands himself to the point at which he is in touch with his own holistic needs, emotionally, physically, spiritually, economically and domestically.

This process of self knowledge and management for African American boys should begin no later than age twelve, at which time they should be given increasing responsibility in controlling their heart, their head, their sex drive and their muscles. This training in self management means that parents understand the parenting process and that at this stage of the child's development they manage rather than dominate their son's development. The process of learning to manage himself, when done well, equips the young man with the ability to keep himself from becoming involved in relationships and social situations that hinder or even stifle his progress towards completing high school, college or vocational training. In addition, it will keep him from sexual promiscuity and the likelihood of siring a child prematurely.

In the context of self management there are two areas in the lives of African American boys that tend to be undermanaged. These two are the intellect and the libido. Far too many black boys get ushered into adulthood with negative psychological baggage and undesirable sexual baggage. This baggage will most often show up in marriage as a hindrance to effective management as the head of the family.

As a pastor who has done countless hours of premarital counseling I have often wondered how it was possible for a young man to take on a wife and manage her, when it was evident that he had not yet learned to manage himself. The young man who is ill-equipped to manage himself will most often seek to manage his wife through control and total domination. Neither he nor she will experience any freedom in the relationship.

The man who has learned to manage himself comes to the marriage altar equipped to manage his wife as the head of his family. In 1 Timothy 3:4 one of the qualifications for becoming an elder in the church is that as a husband, the man is able to manage his household well. In Ephesians 5:25 the idea of headship can be defined as management. Thus the husband has the responsibility of managing his family as the primary authority over the subordinates in the home, namely his wife and his children.

As the manager of the family the husband must have family plans, goals and objectives that fit well with the family's overall spiritual agenda. As a manager, the husband/father must be able to communicate in a positive way with each family member. He must be able to inspire positive attitudes in each family member. He must be able to protect the family and provide it with security. All of the affairs of the household must be cared for under the watchful eye of the husband who manages of the family.

The husband who manages his family well must manage the following with distinction:

1. The nurture and development of the spiritual commitment of every member of the family in terms of convictions, attitudes and behavior.
2. A positive atmosphere in the home.
3. His family's prayer life, Bible study and church attendance.
4. The financial provisions and stability of his household.
5. The modeling of godliness in such a way that positive family values are transferred to the children.
6. The demonstration that hearts surface in the relationship as more important than heads at the interpersonal level where feelings are in the fray of things.
7. The growth and development of his children's social

skill, academic education, relational skills, survival skills.

8. His family's passages through the seasons of life.

A husband must be equipped to nurture his wife in such a way that he earn her respect and confidence. This is accomplished as she and he over time merge their iidual ambitions and goals into a new world view in which the talents and aspirations of both can be pursued and attained in an atmosphere of freedom.

I had pastored Jackie for more than ten years when she brought Willie in to meet me and to talk about the possibility of marrying him. Jackie was a very beautiful young woman and was highly successful in her career. Willie, on the other hand, was a man with few accomplishments and clearly showed evidence of having poorly managed his own life.

After a few visits I said to Jackie, "I suggest that you think about breaking off your engagement to Willie. I do not think he will be a good husband to you."

"Why not?" Jackie quickly responded.

"Well, Jackie," I said, quite frankly, "I think you are more woman than Willie is equipped to manage as a husband."

"But why, Pastor," Jackie replied, "what on earth could you possibly mean?"

"I do not mean anything sexual," I replied. "I mean that you are so successful at managing yourself and have acquired much at an early age; Willie, on the other hand, evidences poor self-management and seems to have had very little vocational success. I cannot imagine how it will be possible for him to do a better job at managing both you and himself given how he has poorly managed just himself. In other words, Jackie, Willie is indeed a handsome man and may even be a good man but his lack of success at managing himself suggests to me that he is deficient in that area of his manhood that would empower him to function as the head of his family."

Like so many Christian women, Jackie believed that Willie's faith in God automatically equipped him to function as the head of a family. Indeed salvation settles forever the issue of a man's relationship with God through Jesus Christ. It does not, however, fill in all the missing pieces of a man's life. At best salvation provides the basic potential for developing in time genuine manhood through consistent mentoring.

The husband who is equipped to manage himself has learned to manage himself over time under the tutelage of a persistent mentor. It does not happen overnight. He must therefore understand that it takes time to get to know his wife and learn how to manage her effectively. Over a period of two or more years the husband should know his wife well enough to effectively manage her. It is only after this process of effective management is in place that the couple should seek to have children who must also come under the management of the husband.

The management of their children by the husband/father begins at conception and continues through the development of the child/children into adulthood. This management includes tending the nest during pregnancy so that the mother is well-provided for in terms of atmosphere, medical care and general emotional security. The father manages the spiritual development of the child/children with a view to developing in each child biblically-based spiritual convictions that will guard their hearts and protect their lives. Secondly, the father must manage the education of the child/children by way of choice of residence and consistent involvement in the education process with both teacher and student. The father manages the transition of the child into adulthood; this includes dating, courtship and the general social life of the child/children.

In the context of "Headship," manhood means being equipped to manage the "family affairs." In some respects a family is not unlike a company or organization and lends itself to a similar process of organization and administration. The family must have specific family goals and standards by which to operate in order to ensure unity and a healthy home environment. The family must have values and priorities that motivate it to function constructively. To ensure mutual support and deal with issues and individual concerns, family meetings must be held on a regular basis. In this context the father functions as manager. He delegates responsibility, enforces the principles of individual responsibility and accountability, and rewards achievement.

Nathaniel was a good man in the truest sense of the word. He worked hard all the time and provided well for his family. Nathaniel and his wife Sarah had three children, two girls and a boy. As I ministered to Nathaniel and his family it became increasingly evident to me that Sarah was not happy. I called

Nathaniel into my office and asked him if he and his wife were having problems. Nathaniel said "Well, Pastor, I really don't know what it is that's bothering Sarah. God knows I work my butt off trying to provide the best for her and the children."

With Nathaniel's consent I later called his wife into my office and asked her if she and Nathaniel were having a problem. Sarah's response did not surprise me because I had heard it so many times before.

Sarah said to me "You know, Pastor, Nathaniel is a good man. He works hard all the time trying to provide the best for me and the children. Don't get me wrong. I do my part but Nathaniel tries so hard to give us things." And then Sarah added, "but you know, Pastor, I would trade all of the things Nathaniel gives me and the children for the simple gentle words 'Sarah, I love you.' You see, Pastor, Nathaniel only knows how to give things to me and the children. He really does not know how to love me as a wife and the children as his children."

Like so many men Nathaniel was strongly determined to provide for his wife and his children, believing that by so doing he was carrying out his responsibility as a husband and a father. The truth is that more than a few African American men struggle in the area of evidencing and expressing their love for their wife and children. However, a number of African American men believe that the wife who demands of her husband more than things of comfort is in effect a nagging wife to whom too much is not enough.

The husband who understands "Headship" to mean loving his wife and children is mature enough to trust his heart to his wife and children. This means being able to say such things as "I love you," "I need you," and "You are my priority." The husband who is equipped to love his wife and children knows the value of having a home environment in which hearts are more important than are heads and people are more important than things.

Each time I visit The Holy Land in the State of Israel I am struck by the age-old tradition of the way of the shepherd with his sheep. In Israel there are thousands of sheep each belonging to a particular shepherd. It caught my attention that experienced shepherds do not drive sheep; the sheep are led. Sheep have a tendency to follow the leader which in many cases is a goat. No matter what may lie in their path the sheep will follow the goat that is leading them. Sheep do not lead sheep because by nature they are followers, not leaders.

The shepherd's responsibility is to care for the sheep in accordance with the nature of the sheep. This means leading and not driving the sheep from one place to another. The shepherd understands that the sheep depend on him for daily provisions, protection from predators, and comfort from the scorching heat or bone-chilling cold. I conclude that the quality of life to which the sheep are exposed is in direct proportion to the quality of the shepherding provided by the shepherd.

It is my contention that "Headship" in the context of the Christian home can be compared to shepherding for like the shepherd and his sheep the husband/father is responsible for the provision, protection and comfort of his family. The man who is equipped to shepherd well his family also provides for them intangibles: love, companionship, life experiences, security and stability.

Like a good shepherd the husband/father leads his family with both heart and head and provides for them holistically. The husband/father who shepherds his family leads with wisdom as he seeks to mold his family with life values that are biblically based.

In summary I have sought to make the point that manhood means being equipped and empowered to function as the head of the family. I have defined "Headship" as the authority to lead in the context of equality. Functioning as the head of the family means being able to manage one's self, wife and children. To be the head of the family is to be a shepherd to the family.

A few consequences result when a man fails in his function as the head of his family. One of these is a wife who feels lonely and while in that state tends to crave a relationship in which she is shepherded well. This unsettled emotional state of the wife tends to expose her to lustful men who feel a need to conquer lonely women. This troubling scenario is not uncommon in the church and tends to further destabilize an already unstable husband and wife relationship.

Sue was married to a preacher and they had two small children. Sue asked to see me one day and when she came in it was soon evident that she had a problem. As I listen to Sue tell me her story it suddenly occurred to me that Sue's problem was infidelity.

I said to her, "You are having an affair."

After a few minutes of silence followed by an outburst of

anger, Sue asked me, "How did you know?"

I said, "Before I tell you how I gleaned from your words the fact that you are having an affair, let me first tell you how you got involved with the man with whom you are having an affair.

"There is a man in your life who perhaps on your job one day began to compliment you on how you looked. And then he began to make comments to you about how good you smell. One day he came by your desk and stopped to talk to you, and much to your surprise he spoke very few words choosing instead to listen to you. In time you began to look forward to spending time with this man for he made you feel special. He told you often how pretty you were and how good you smelled. He even commented often about how smart you were. Truth is you liked hearing these things. The problem is your husband, though he is a good man, never treats you this way and you wish he would.

"This thing between you and this co-worker went on for a while and one day he did not come by and you thought it was just a coincidence. Two or three days went by and when you did not see this man you began to miss him. Finally he came by and you asked him where he had been to which he replied, 'Around.' With this said, your co-worker disappeared again and this time you did not see him for a whole week. When he came by this time he suggested to you that he wanted to spend time with you alone. You knew right away what he meant but you rejected the notion of having an affair for after all you love your husband dearly.

"Two weeks passed and you did not see or hear from your co-worker. Though you hated to admit it to yourself the fact was you missed him dearly. In fact you missed him so much that you decided to give in to his request for time alone with him in exchange for time with him in which you heard the words you desperately needed to hear because they made you feel so much like a woman of worth."

Sue is an example of a wife who was poorly shepherd by her husband. Her infidelity resulted from the vacuum left in her life by a good man who was ill-prepared to shepherd his wife. Sue was not a bad wife; she was a vulnerable wife who got caught up in the wind of lust by a man who preys on such women. Sue's husband gave her everything but what she needed most . . . himself.

MANHOOD INCLUDES THE WILL TO PARENT

It is my contention that a man's desire to parent the children that he sires is as natural and as strong as his desire for sex and sexual satisfaction. Many African American men list sex and sexual satisfaction as their number one priority in their relationship with their wife. It is interesting to note then that in pursuit of sexual satisfaction the number one concern expressed in premarital counseling by a majority of young men is the ability to function sexually at a level that will maximize satisfaction for themselves and their mate. For many the path leading to maximized and satisfying sexual experience is perceived to be related to the size of their genitals. The consensus seems to be that genitalia size is an essential ingredient in maximum sexual performance and that it either affirms or diminishes genuine manhood. In addition African American males are socialized as young boys to view and relate to females at the physical level with a view to using them as instruments of sexual pleasure.

In the African American community boys are generally expected to demonstrate their maleness by way of sexual promiscuity, thus affirming the fact that they like girls. Even in the church boys are held to a more liberal moral code than are girls. I have found as a pastor in the African American community for more than thirty years that most African American fathers expect their sons to have "gotten them sum stuff" by the age of eighteen. If he does not demonstrate a strong interest in females and sex on or before his eighteenth birthday, most fathers are concerned that something is wrong with "that boy."

I am reminded of a conversation I had with a co-worker regarding my son when he began to evidence an interest in females at about age fifteen. My co-worker commented that my son's interest in females was a good thing and I should be glad that he was interested in girls for, said my co-worker, "He could be interested in boys." Truth is, my co-worker had a point.

I am fully committed to the moral principles set forth in the Bible.

It is *God's will* that you should be sanctified: that you should avoid sexual immorality; that each of you should learn to *control* his own body in a way that is holy and honorable, not in passionate *lust* like the heathen, who do not know God; and that in this matter no one should *wrong* his brother *or take advantage* of him. The Lord will punish men for all such sins, as we have already told you and warned you. For God did not call us to be *impure*, but to *live a holy* life. Therefore, he who *rejects this instruction* does not reject man but God, who gives you his Holy Spirit (1 Thess. 4:3-8).

However, I have found over the years that this principle of sexual abstinence and moral purity is seldom strongly emphasized to boys in the church. For the African American young man virginity is taught in many instances in the form of a suggestion rather than a command from the Lord.

Ed was thirteen when his father became ill and in time died of AIDS. For the first time in his life, Ed was confronted with the fact that his dad whom his mother had divorced some years earlier was a homosexual. This knowledge about his father seriously unsettled Ed, so much so that he began to question his own sexuality. His concern over his own sexuality grew in intensity as Ed moved up into his teens with little felt desire for involvement with females.

By age fifteen, Ed was more concern about not being homosexual than he was about his Christian moral convictions. With a view to convincing himself that he was not homosexual, he started to pursue sexual involvement with females. By age twenty one Ed could boast of his many sexual conquests and that he had sired five children whom he was ill-equipped to father. Ed's sexual promiscuity might have confirmed that he was not gay but it did not affirm his manhood because even though he was equipped to function sexually and beget children he lacked the manhood necessary to parent them.

In Genesis 1:28 we have the first command God gave the man whom He created in His own image ". . . be fruitful and multiply and fill the earth." In Psalms 27 and 28 the Bible discloses the view that children are evidences of God's blessings. And in the account of Abraham and Sarah we see the same, "So Sarah laughed to herself as she thought, 'After I am worn out and my master is old, will I now have this pleasure?' " (Gen. 18:12).

The Scriptures are replete with statements that having children is consistent with the will of God. Children, according to the Scriptures, are a blessing from the Lord, and according to Genesis 18:12, there is pleasure inherent in the process of begetting children. This is not to suggest that sexual intercourse is to be restricted to the pursuit of pregnancy. Sex is a gift from

God and is intended for pleasure from which according to God's plan children are conceived.

In this day of ours it seems as if boys and men are socialized to think of their relationship with females almost exclusively in physical terms. It is the pursuit of sexual pleasure which in many instances include extreme eroticism that drives more than a few men in their relationship with females. This kind of thinking on the part of no small number of African American boy and men contributes greatly to the fifty-one percent of African American children being born out of wedlock.

To suggest that genuine African American manhood means the will to parent is to suggest a distinguishable difference between African American men who sire children and are not married to their mothers and men who sire children only by the woman to whom they are married but for some reason get divorced from that mother. The difference between these two groups of men, neither of whom are in-resident fathers, is illustrated by a principle I learned growing up on a farm in Lake Providence, Louisiana.

Mr. Shed Nickoles was one of a number of men I knew growing up as a boy on the farm. The interesting thing about Mr. Shed Nickoles was that he loved milk but he did not own nor did he want to own a cow. When asked why he refused to get for himself his own cow since he loved milk so much, he would always answer, "I don't like cows that well and I simply detest the idea of having to care for the calf that is born to the mother cow so she will produce milk. I prefer to get my milk wherever I can and be done with it. No cow, no calf, just milk is all I want."

Mr. Shed Nickoles was a man who even though he loved milk detested the idea of having to care for a cow and a calf in order to have his own milk. He preferred to get what he wanted from the cow and leave the caretaking of the cow and the calf to others.

So it is with some men in their relationships with women. They love the physical pleasure derived from the relationship. The trouble is, these men only want what the woman can give them in terms of pleasure; they have no desire for a lasting loving relationship with any woman.

In general, it can be concluded that the man who decides to marry a woman indicates by that decision and action his desire to commit himself to a family. In most instances, a top priority for such a man is sex and sexual satisfaction.

In the language of Proverbs 5:17ff this man is one who determines to drink water from his own well as opposed to spewing his semen in the streets. This decision to commit to having a family implies at the very least that such a man is willing to parent the children that results from that relationship.

On the other hand, the man who begets children outside the marriage bond evidences a lack of commitment to the woman choosing to get from her the pleasure of sex without any binding obligation to her or the child/children that might result from that relationship. Like Mr. Shed Nickoles, this is a man who enjoys the pleasure the woman provides him with but cares little about the woman and cannot stand the idea of parenting any children that might result from his sexual encounters with the woman.

The male sperm is an essential ingredient in the conception of children. This is a matter of male biology and has little to do with the character or the general emotional, economic, psychological or spiritual status of the male. Though it has often gone unrecognized by the parents of teenage boys and girls, the fact is, the sperm from a young male barely in his teens is enough to impregnate a girl who is also in her early teens. This being the case, it is time that we change how we socialize African American males so that how we manage the social lives of our teenage boys and girls reflects the reality of their reproductive potential.

That conception is a matter of biological fertilization between male sperm and female egg at whatever age demands that we distinguish between that which reflects male biology in childbearing, namely sperm, and that which reflects genuine manhood, namely, the will to parent.

While a teenage boy can beget a baby because he is a male child, it cannot be said that his getting a female pregnant means that he is a man. Manhood in this context can only be reflected in the will and the ability to parent the child. Teenage boys are ill-equipped to parent because they are not mature men no matter what their economic status happens to be.

Genuine African American manhood in the context of the male and female relationship is reflected in the will of the African American male to parent the children that result from that relationship. The first priority for the man is to establish the kind of contractual relationship with the woman that binds him spiritually and legally to the woman and any and all children that might result from that relationship.

This means entering into marriage with a view to remaining in the relationship for a lifetime. The man who has the will to parent evidences that desire by way of marriage before there are any children. Marriage in this context demonstrates to the mother and the child that the father is committed to being an in-resident father.

When I asked Mary how long she and William had been married, she replied, "We have been together about twelve years."

I noticed the absence of the word *married* in Mary's reply and so I said to her, "My question was how long have you been married to William?"

Mary laughed and said, "So you caught that, did you?" Then she added, "We are not married."

I suggested to her that should she and William decide to marry I would be happy to assist them in the preparation. Mary implied that marriage would add nothing but a piece of paper to what she and William already had.

Increasingly I find young women who are of the opinion that marriage is nothing more than a piece of paper that adds nothing to the marriage. These young women think that so long as she and the man have feelings for each other that is all that matters. But marriage is much more than a piece of paper. The will to marry speaks volumes about the man's intent in terms of commitment to the woman and the children. Specifically it says that the man is willing to legally give his name to the child along with whatever he acquires in his lifetime in terms of material assets/estate.

Men who are willing to marry and have their children in the context of that marriage are saying that even if the marriage fails and ends in divorce he will not divorce his children. He is committed to being their father, providing for their overall welfare, protecting them, correcting them and modeling wisdom before them.

Chapter 9

"Baggage" and the African American Male

I t is my contention that every African American male carries baggage, regardless of who he is or what his social, political, economic or spiritual status may or may not be. And it really does not matter whether or not they recognize and acknowledge the fact that they carry baggage. To be African American is to have baggage.

Every African American male at the personal level carries baggage that includes the legacy of slavery and the residual effects of segregation and cultural brainwashing. I am well aware that a growing number of African American men believe it is time to put the whole slavery issue behind them and move on. I also know that many young White men today deny any connection or responsibility to the historic event of slavery. The Clarence Thomas's and Ward Connley's of our day often refer to their own boot straps as the means by which they attained their respective success. The fact remains that to be White in America is to have benefited from the fruits of free slave labor and to be Black in America is to have been impacted by the legacy of slavery, segregation and cultural brain washing.

On a recent trip to New York City my wife and I took a ferryboat out to see the Statue of Liberty on Ellis Island. As I viewed Ellis Island up close I was filled with the realization that of all the people visiting that monument recalling with gladness their ancestors' arrival as immigrants, only to African Americans did Ellis Island mean nothing.

Our ancestors did not choose to come to the New World as immigrants; they were brought here by force as slaves. I was so gripped by a sense of detachment at the personal level that, I stayed aboard the ferry deciding not to tour the beautiful complex. As I walked away from the window of the boat and sat down beside my wife with my head down, I was fully aware of the fact that my personal baggage as an African American male was tugging at the fabrics of my mind and emotions.

To be sure the slave system above all else had a crippling effect on the establishment, maintenance and growth of the African American family as it struggled to develop in accordance with the accepted pattern of family structure in North America. The impact of the crippling disruption of slavery, segregation and discrimination against the African American family life was exceedingly cruel and vicious.

There were several facets of this personal social emasculation of the African American family. First, the African American family was broken up at the inception of the slave trade with the capture and shipment of young west African men from a variety of tribes to the Americas. Second, the slave traders revealed a total disregard for the African family and kinship unit. Third, the captors' preference for young men in the prime of their life combined with their lack of interest in trading females resulted in the development of a North American slave system that was primarily young, Black, African and male. Fourth, these young African men worked and lived in the most inhumane conditions and were treated by their captors as mere animals with no sense of humanity, family or kinship bond.

I am addressing the issue of contemporary African American males and their personal baggage. It is necessary, therefore, to be specific about the slave conditions that have left us this legacy: the everpresent personal baggage that inhabits the lives of all African American males today.

In the North American slave system which was a closed Black skinned, race-based slave system, there was no legal foundation, sanction or protection for marriage as an institution among slaves. There was the exploitation of slave women by slave owners and overseers for both pleasure and profit, often in full view of the Black male who more often than not was father, husband or brother to the woman being physically and sexually abused.

There was systematic denial of any role for the Black male

as husband and father. There was willful separation of family members including children, who were sold off to different plantations. There was a complete absence of societal support and protection for the African American family as a physical, psychological, social and economic unit.

The legacy of slavery may be less evident today and less direct in its impact but the vestiges of it are no less insidious. There never has been a time in the history of African Americans in this country in which they have experienced systematically at the personal level and generally as a race of people the kind of social support from the larger society that would even approach the intensity of the negative impact of slavery on the Black family in America.

In slavery African American men were subjected to a social, political and economic situation in which conformity to either the norms of his native male dominated African culture from which he had been snatched and brought to America or the norms of the Anglo American male dominated culture in North America was even remotely possible. In slavery the African American male was cast in a public and private role of perpetual childhood. In order to obtain the good favor of his master he had to subscribe to a paternalistic relationship with his White owner and overseer. He was compelled to surrender all claims to respect as an adult male and any hint of independence.

The American slave system was one of infantilization. It was designed by the slave masters to prove to himself and the Black African slave that males whose skin was black were mentally and emotionally inferior to White males. This inherent inferiority of the Black slave was understood to mean that they could only survive in a dependent childlike relationship with his White master.

The African American male in slavery was consistently and systematically denied the role of husband and father. At most he was his wife's assistant, breeding partner and in some instances was perceived to be his wife's possession. The laws of most southern states did not recognize the paternal relation of children as belonging to their Black slave father. The paternal responsibilities for the children were assumed by the mother of the children and the slave master. Male slaves were not the head of their households; the slave owner was the head. The male slave did not have the authority to discipline or exercise any authority over the children he sired; this was a role reserved for the slave master.

In slavery the African American family was generally defined as consisting of the African American mother and her children apart from any reference to the father. It was the mother who stood in defense of the children evidencing the will to endure cruel and unusual punishment when it came to the possibility of being separated from her children.

During what is commonly referred to as the Southern migration African Americans moved in great numbers from the agrarian South to the industrial North. When the Black southern immigrants moved into the Northern and Midwestern metropolitan cities they found a social and economic situation that encouraged the same pattern of family structure prevalent in the segregated south, namely a matrifocal family structure. In other words the economic environment favored the Black female.

This matrifocal family structure was rooted in the fact that in the cities the African American female could obtain and retain a job much easier than the African American male. Black women became domestic servants and worked more frequently and received higher wages than black men.

This economic situation gave preference to the Black woman in the labor market at the exclusion of the Black male in a society where the man is normally regarded as the one responsible for the support of his family. Naturally it caused the black man to feel deeply inadequate and inferior to his wife and men of other races. This caused serious frustration in the home and often led to frequent separations and the emergence of a number of households in which the mother or grandmother became the dominant figure.

The high number of Black female-headed households often gives the impression that the Black family is highly disorganized and in general dominated by women. However, it could well be said that the matrifocal family structure arose in that historical context as a means of stabilizing the Black family in a difficult social and economic situation.

The Southern migration which brought many Black families from the agrarian South into the larger industrial cities led to the ghettoization of Black families. These rural and mostly under-educated Black families moved into communities that segregated them from other ethnicities. A "ghetto" is not a description of the living conditions but a reference to the enclosed culture and religion of people who live in a certain community. Thus the cities into which these southern Black immigrants moved already had ghettos filled with Jews, Italians, and Germans, etc. Each group was insulated in its own world.

In these "ghettos" the Black family did not find a social and economic support system that was significantly different from the South. Making things worse was that the fact the "ghettos" deprived them of the extended family and Village that existed in the rural South. Thus an already weak family structure became even more fragmented by the "ghetto" context.

In these cities as in slavery and the rural segregated South, the African American male was the one most seriously impacted by the "ghetto" experience. His role as provider, protector and model for his family was in effect completely eliminated by the city's "ghetto" social and economic system.

There was no system in place in the urban Black "ghetto" to assist the African American male in functioning as a husband and father in his family as was available for foreign immigrant men and their families. The pattern of family life for the African American developed in a markedly different way from that of the larger society and foreign immigrants. One of the results of this economic and educational disadvantage for the African American male was a proliferation of female headed households.

The urban "ghetto" in conjunction with the subsequent welfare system elevated the Black female to the position of being the most important and enduring figure in the Black family. This elevation of the Black woman over the Black man in the urban "ghetto" by the welfare system and the larger society is reminiscent of what happened under slavery.

The virtual demise of the African American male in his role as provider of the Black family can be attributed to the elevation of the female. With this displacement of the African American male and his role in the family, Black youths increasingly found themselves locked into a cycle of failure and crime.

To claim that African American men do not carry baggage—the legacy of slavery, segregation and cultural brainwashing—is tantamount to suggesting that there exists no legacy of the Holocaust in the lives of Jewish people. It is impossible to begin to chart the history of African American men in this country by starting with from the Post-Civil Rights Era in the 1970s. To do so is to commit irreparable damage to the character and integrity of those African American men who in spite of the baggage of slavery can lay claim to significant success in this country.

The Civil Rights Movement is best defined as the revolt of the African American male. It employed in that struggle the one institution that was owned by the Black community and controlled by the African American male, namely the Black church. The leadership of the Civil Rights Movement was Black and male.

The Civil Rights Movement demonstrated for the first time in the history of the Black community that black men were ready to stand up and declare that they would no longer be content to be excluded from mainstream America. The demand was to either include us as men on an equal basis with other men, kill us like dogs, or we will destroy the America we built with our free labor. It was in this struggle that black men gained appreciation for the color of their skin, the texture of their hair, the thickness of their lips and the content of their intellect and character.

Out of this struggle emerged a sense of Black nationalism in which black men were no longer ashamed of who and what they were. The untimely death of Dr. Martin Luther King Jr., in my view, permanently buried the African American male's fear of death at the hands of White male hate groups such as the KKK.

It was the disquieting and lingering legacy of slavery that gave birth to the Civil Rights Movement. The focus of segregation on the superiority of White men and the inferiority of black men became a tool used effectively to brainwash the black man into thinking that he was something less than a real man. Regardless of his chosen profession, vocation or character, he could not be an equal to White men.

I believe the success of the Civil Rights Movement which gave birth to a growing middle and upper-middle class Black community has not openly dealt with the baggage of slavery, segregation and cultural brainwashing present in African American men. In his confirmation hearing, Supreme Court Justice Clarence Thomas referred to the baggage of segregation. When he was courted by the Republican Party as a possible candidate for the office of president or vice president of the United States Of America General Colin Powell referred to the baggage of segregation.

The baggage of segregation is so heavy and volatile that a growing number of African Americans are turning away from the idea of an integrated America choosing to focus instead on a Black America that values its own even in a segregated context. They claim Black folks are tired of striving to be accepted by White people as equal with them. They no longer desire to be integrated as equal in substance, quality and substance with that which is White. This view is growing and gaining more consensus among Black folks today.

There is at the personal level in the lives of African American men this everpresent thing called cultural brainwashing. Cultural brain washing refers to that feeling deep down inside your innermost being that you and all that encompasses your being is in some way inferior to whatever is "White." Few men, if any, can testify to ever completely killing off this voice inside their spirit that rises to the surface and reminds them that they are Black and male thus do not quite fit in some positions, places and in the company of some significant people. "White makes right" reverberates in their conscious or subconscious mind.

Black men are programmed to remind themselves on a regular basis that they will forever remain unequal to White men no matter their credentials and accomplishment. Society in general places social signs in their paths to reinforce this notion that they are not on equal par with men of other races and especially White men.

O. J. Simpson made his way to the top of the economic and social ladder using his many talents to gain for himself significant wealth and worldwide popularity. Mr. Simpson in reality had the kind of lifestyle that suggested that he was one of the few black men to experience acculturation and significant assimilation into White America. For all practical purposes, he was White. However, when Mr. Simpson's wife was murdered he was arrested, tried and acquitted as a Black. The aftermath of the Simpson trial demonstrates in the clearest manner that regardless of the degree of success a black man may experience the baggage of segregation is never far away from the doorway of his life. O. J. Simpson could never have imagined that many of his closest Anglo friends viewed him not as a man on the same level with other men but as a black man not quite equal with other men.

It is important to make the point that cultural brainwashing has nothing at all to do with either truth or reality. It is strictly a "head thing" put there by years and years of programming that in essence directs one to think of himself as a black man, but more *black* than *man*. For the first time in a long time Mr. Simpson has had to learn to think of himself as a black man who had the delusion of having assimilated into the world of White men.

I mentioned that on the personal level black men carry baggage that contains the residual effects of four hundred years of slavery and segregation. This baggage is all wrapped up in a package of perpetual cultural brainwashing that contributes to the constant psychological and emotional struggle of African American men to find their place in contemporary America.

The second set of baggage the African American males carries with him is the baggage of previous relationship. There are at least six sources from which this set of baggage is derived. These sources include but are not limited to: the *family context* in which he was born and grew up, the *community* in which he lived as a child, the *educational system* in which he received his education, his *personal relational experiences* in dating, courtship, marriage, divorce, widowhood, *secrets from the past* and *new baggage.*

It is my contention that the personal negative baggage resulting from the legacy of slavery, segregation and cultural brainwashing is inherent in all African American males and that kind of baggage is common to all black men. What differs is the specific content of the baggage. For instance, the baggage from previous relationships, "Relational Baggage," is common to all African American men. Because no man is born into or grows up in a relational vacuum it can be concluded that every man has relational baggage. However, the contents of "Relational Baggage" unlike the content of personal baggage differs from one man to another even when they have the same parents and grow up in the same household.

It is important to emphasize that as it pertains to the baggage of previous relationships "Relational Baggage," every man has his own unique set of personal baggage containing the contextual experiences that have resulted from his particular relational experiences. These varied experiences are both positive and negative. To the extent that the relational context in which a man has lived is positive, to that extent he will be unfragmented in his relational skills. Conversely to the extent that the man has lived in a negative relational context to that extent he is likely to be fragmented in his relational skills.

Having spent more than three decades ministering to African American boys and men up close and personal, I observed yet another set of baggage that a number of men carry. In this baggage are "secrets from the past." These secrets include but are not limited to such things as sexual and physical abuse, physical and emotional neglect and battering, drug use, jail and prison time, to name a few.

There is a tendency on the part of some men to try and dismiss the presence of this set of baggage under the guise of Christian conversion. I understand full well the power of the gospel to change a man's heart and give him a new beginning. Yet I am convinced that unless and until a man is willing to face the skeletons in the closet of his private life with a view to coming to grips with the need to deal with these secrets from the past, he is not prepared to enter into a constructive lasting relationship.

Clarence was a handsome man and much to his delight women tended to favor him. However, there was something about Clarence that caused him to resist being hugged by a brother in Christ, and he was very insecure in his relationship with his wife. In time I learned that Clarence had a few secrets from his past that he had never shared with anyone, not even his wife. As a boy Clarence was sexually and physically abused by an older girl and an older boy with whom his single mother frequently left him.

One of the side effects of Clarence's secrets from his past was a tendency to keep people at a distance holding them in suspect. It seemed impossible to convince Clarence that you had a genuine interest in him. An innocent question about his past could send Clarence into a rage and cause him to avoid your presence for weeks. His wife never understood why he reacted this way; she simply learned to live with his emotional volatility.

I was visiting with a fellow preacher some years ago, and as we shared our experiences in the ministry the brother leaned over to me and in a voice that was close to a whisper said to me, "I need to tell you something that I have never told anyone."

"OK," I replied, "what is it?"

"Thirty years ago," he said, "when I was a young man, I killed a man and hid him in an alley. No one ever found out who killed that man, and I have never told anyone, not even my wife."

This man had spent a number of years in the Christian

ministry, more often than not spreading more discord than unity among the saints. All the time his secret baggage from his past weighed heavily on his mind and negatively impacted his relationships with his family and his church members.

James was in the process of dying from AIDS. I frequently visited with him over the months as he moved closer and closer to his death. Along the way I asked him how he had contracted this deadly virus. Knowing that James was a minister and married to a fine young wife with whom he had a lovely young son, I was ill prepared for James' answer. "I contracted the AIDS virus in a homosexual experience I had as a freshman on the college campus. Neither my parents, friends, nor my wife have any idea that I have been involved in bisexual activity."

In addition to the personal baggage, the relational baggage and the baggage of secrets from the past, the African American male has what I refer to as "new baggage." This new baggage includes but is not limited to such things as Black male identification, self-esteem, gender identity, expectations, communication and management.

The *personal baggage* of black men is rooted in the common historical experience of black men in America. *The relational baggage* is rooted in the relational context in which the man grew up as a boy and lives as a man. *The baggage of secrets from the past* is rooted in the negative experiences contained in the man's life map. *The new baggage* is rooted in the spiritual, social, domestic, economic and political deficits that permeates the environment of the Post-Civil Rights Era. This new baggage is for the most part the baggage of the sons of fathers who reaped the harvest of the Civil Rights Movement. This new baggage reflects the absence of in-resident fathers, poor parenting, the priority of materialism and a less relevant church, among other things in the socialization process of Black males on their way to adulthood.

I have been asked on a few occasions why it is that I tend to refer to myself as an African American Christian. I always respond by saying that I was born an African American male, I became a Christian by choice. The fact that I refer to myself as an African American Christian in no way subjects my faith to my race; it simply notes that the Lord Jesus revealed Himself to me in the context of my race and culture. The gospel of Jesus Christ that reached my mind and heart was made clear to me by God the Holy Spirit in my own racial and cultural context.

Today a growing number of young African American men seem to be uncomfortable with the idea of being identified as an African American man. They tend to think that the color of their skin and the texture of their hair does not really matter in contemporary America. A brief survey of men of every other race in America will show that these men identify themselves by their own race and culture. It appears as if only the African American male has bought into the idea that his race and culture do not matter.

In his "I Have a Dream" speech the late Dr. Martin Luther King Jr. envisioned a day in America in which people would be judged by the content of their character, not the color of their skin. That was more than thirty years ago and that day has not yet come for the African American male. In America race matters. Thus the African American male who does not have intact his Black male identification is in fact in search of himself.

In the new baggage of the African American male there is evidence of a lack of self-esteem. Many young black men simply do not feel good about themselves as men. These are not men who think White men are superior to them as did my generation. These are men who simply do not believe that they are good enough.

There is a growing consensus among young black men that there are no real distinguishable differences that exist between men and women in terms of roles and responsibilities. Thus a matrifocal family structure today in which the wife is the chief breadwinner is not viewed as unusual, nor does it feel uncomfortable to the young African American man. The average young husband today does not feel responsible for providing more than half the family income.

The disproportionate number of female-headed households in the African American community has contributed significantly to the feminization of Black males. Therefore, more than a few black men come to the marriage altar much more equipped to function as a keeper at home than as the primary provider and protector of the family in the market place. This lost of gender identity for the Black male is new baggage.

The baggage of unrealistic expectations is an attitude on the part of African American men that prompts them to think it is possible to have the best of everything without being educationally equipped to earn it. It is in this context that the African American "Buppies" have in their parenting grown children who are best described as a cut flower generation. The cut flower generation refers to children who can only survive at the social and economic level in which they grew up so long as they are sustained by their parents. Once separated from their parents their social and economic status seriously declines. The current generation of young African American men have little chance of exceeding the lifestyle of their parents; yet they expect to.

In the baggage of communication the African American male finds himself burdened with a negative image that he did not earn, does not understand and therefore lacks the ability to communicate to his audience who he really is and what he is feeling. I am of the opinion that profanity has become for a number of black men a means of public and private communication. This foul language may well be a reflection of a limited vocabulary, combined with the frustration of being constantly disregarded.

I must be clear here and distinguish between the black man's ability to rap and his ability to communicate. Rapping is a thing of culture and tends to be common among most black men especially as it pertains to wooingfemales. Communication on the other hand in the context of a relationship demands the inclusion of feelings and commitment. But for many black men sharing their feelings is more than they are willing to do.

Finally the African American male has the new baggage of self management. It is not at all unusual to find the parents of African American boys leaving the majority of the management duties to the young man. This freedom of choice includes his education, his morality, his time, his attitude, and his talents. This kind of freedom most often produces a boy who grows into a young man who has a false concept of what it means to manage oneself.

Developing and maintaining a relationship with black men means accepting them as they are with their baggage. It also means dealing in a positive and constructive manner with the baggage, each in its respective category. To this end, it is wise to focus on the positive baggage that the man has without disregarding the negative baggage.

To say to a man that his baggage is not important and should be set aside so he can move on with his life is to suggest to the man that he diminish his personal identity and disregard his history and experiences as an African American man. In addition it is impossible for anyone to deny the presence and the impact of their baggage in their lives and in the lives of those with whom they must live and serve.

To suggest that every African American man has baggage that is personal, relational, and contain secrets from the past and baggage that is new, is to imply that there are some current results of such baggage in the lives of black men. It is my contention that the baggage of the African American male in source and substance marks him as a man set apart from men of other races and cultures. The distinctiveness of the black man's baggage also sets him apart from other men in terms of his functional ability as a man in the social, economic, domestic context in which he lives.

At the top of the list in terms of the impact and results of the African American man's baggage in his life is the absence of a positive world view. I am often amazed as a professor to find in my classes of graduate and post-graduate students a genuine absence of vision, mission and a sense of destiny. Most students today come to seminary in search of a life mission, unlike students twenty years ago who came to Seminary because they had discovered their life mission and were seeking to be equipped to accomplish that mission.

When the media took to the streets of Pittsburgh, Pennsylvania during the annual NAACP meeting in July, 1997 to test the relevance of that great historical organization in the minds of today's generation, it was interesting to observe that most of the young men who were interviewed had no idea of what the organization was, nor did they know what the organization had done in the past. This generation of black men tends to live for the moment with little consideration for the struggles and accomplishments of yesterday. They tend to have even less concern and consideration for the possibilities of their tomorrows. This is a "what have you done for me lately," cut flower thinking, generation.

I frequently ask young black men what their plans for the future are as it pertains to family, friends, job, and the world. In most instances the response is silence. When I press for a response they often say they have not thought that far ahead.

This absence of a world view gives rise to the African American male's lack of a sense of permanence. I am not suggesting here that African American men are transients, moving constantly from one relationship and community to another. I am suggesting that they tend to avoid long term commitments of their time, talents and resources. This generation of men are more project oriented and they tend not to envision themselves remaining in the same job or community for a lifetime as did their fathers and grandfathers.

The troubling side to this lack of permanence in the minds of African American men is that they tend to treat relationships with the same project mindset as they do on their job. Thus a woman can find herself in a relationship with a man with her thinking in terms of lifetime commitment while he views their relational experience as a mere project.

The baggage of today's African American male is reflected in his fragmented thinking in the area of relationships. The fragmentation is most evident in his concept of commitment in terms of his role and responsibilities as a husband/father and his will to function as the primary provider in his family. There is also evidence of fragmentation in the young man's desire to have a middle and upper middle class lifestyle without due consideration of how he will afford such a lifestyle.

Finally the baggage of the African American male has produced in him a deep sense of powerlessness. He tends to think and act in ways that suggest that in the final analysis he really has little to contribute that will really make a difference.

CHAPTER 10

"SEX, MONEY, POWER" AND THE AFRICAN AMERICAN MAN

In ministering to African American men up close and personal as a pastor I discovered that most feel a strong sense of superiority over men of other races in the area of sexual performance. I frequently find it necessary to tell them that their studdish attitude towards sex and sexuality suggests that they have bought into the long standing stereotype of black men and sex. The stereotype suggests that black men are more generously endowed in their genitals than are men of other races and they are more sexually inclined than are other men. To put it another way, black men are perceived to be more interested in sex than they are in money and status. I have found that quite a few black men believe this to be the case.

Often older black men will suggest to the young Black man who has a dominant wife that he improve his performance in the bedroom as a means of gaining and maintaining control of his woman in the living room. A dominant woman is perceived by many black men as being in need of a sexually potent Black man. This attitude is not intended as a put down to Black women in any way; it is an affirmation of the superiority of Black male's sexuality.

I am convinced that there is no issue in the life of the average African American male that seems more important to him than his interest and his ability to perform sexually. So important is sex to black men that given the option few would want to live on if they find that they have become permanently sexually impotent.

It is interesting to reflect on how this preoccupation with sex in the lives of African American professional athletes and entertainers is frequently exploited by their managers. The fruit of this sexual exploitation is evident in the number of professional black men who excel in their professions earning millions of dollars but only have the memories of myriad of sexual encounters to retire on. Black high dollar professional men are treated more often than not as studs whose needs are defined in the narrowest terms: sex and expensive trinkets.

I am reminded here of one of the great African American football players of years past, whose sexual habits I was quite familiar with. One of his social habits was going to certain night spots and roping off a crowd of fifteen to twenty women and claiming them as his sex partners for the night. It is reported that this man would carry this crowd of women to his house and have sex with each of them during the night. Today he is retired, and unfortunately he has little more that the memories of those sexual episodes on which to live.

It was this stereotypical view of the sexual habits of black men that may well have contributed to the FBI's futile attempts to undermine the moral integrity of the late Dr. Martin Luther King Jr. during the Civil Rights Movement of the 1960s.

Even today when a Black man is accused of rape his defense is most difficult to arrange. Generally when a Black man is accused of rape he is assumed to be guilty unless and until he is able to present, with the aid of high-price lawyers, undeniable evidence of his innocence. This was the case in Dallas, Texas in 1996 when two prominent football players of a championship team were falsely accused of raping a young girl. Had there not been undeniable evidence to the contrary and the retraction of her story, no doubt the two black athletes would be spending time in prison today. Instead, due to their lawyers' work they collected a settlement from one of the local TV stations and will likely win their suit against the Dallas Police department.

There is a stereotypical link between African American manhood and sexuality that is deeply rooted in the minds of White men and women, and in the minds of black men as well. This led me to explore the possibility of a link between what black men receive in terms of pleasure and significance from sex, money and power.

There are at least five gratifying experiences that men derive from sexual intercourse:

1. Satisfaction of his sex drive;
2. Affirmation of both his libido and manhood;
3. The strengthening and enhancing of his felt love for his wife;
4. A reduction of tension in his body and in his home; and
5. Participation in life's most exciting and pleasurable experiences.[1]

A few years ago a pastor friend of mine invited a young black women to do a seminar with the men in his church. The seminar was on intimacy and sex in the context of Black male and female relationships. The young woman was known for her use of earthy street language and vocabulary in her seminars with men. She frequently used the "P & D" words in reference to the female and male sex organs. She also used very descriptive words and phrases to describe sexual intimacy and intercourse.

After the seminar which was held in the church sanctuary, one of the church staff came to see me to discuss what she described as vulgar language coming from the young woman behind the pulpit. In this staff member's mind such language should never be used in church.

I listened very carefully to this young woman and tried my best to understand her point of view. I agreed that the church is an unusual place to hear such words and phrases. Then I asked, "How was the attendance in the seminar?"

"Standing room only," she replied.

"You are telling me that hundreds of black men attended this seminar and listened to this woman use such earthy language about sex?"

"Yes," she replied. "They were there hanging on her every word."

It is my contention that when it comes to sex and sexuality black men have an attraction that is second to nothing else in their lives. Perhaps the female seminar leader's vocabulary was crude but the focus of her seminar was on target with black men. I am persuaded that most African American men spend a significant amount of time each day thinking about sex. I am not saying that black men are sexually active every day; I am simply saying that they do think about sex every day.

A White Christian counselor referred a young African

---

[1] Tim & Beverly LaHaye, *The Act Of Marriage* (Grand Rapids: Zondervan Publishing, 1976)

American couple to me having concluded that he could not help them for a number of reasons. The counselor in his conferences with this couple had labeled the husband as addicted to sex. When I inquired as to how the counselor came to such a conclusion the young man said it was because he told the counselor that he thought about sex frequently on a daily basis, and that he was always interested in pursuing sex with his wife. I told the young man that in my opinion his so-called sexual addiction was not unlike most African American men I know, many of whom were twice his age.

At this point the question that might arise is whether or not a difference exists between the sexual attitude of a saved African American man and an unsaved African American man. My contention is that in terms of sexual attitude there is little if any difference between the two. However, there is significant difference between the sexual practices of a saved man and an unsaved person.

Salvation does not eliminate the natural link in the minds of black men between their manhood and their sexuality; it does empower the man with the ability to control and manage his sex drive in sanctification and honor before the eyes of God. In fact one of the criticisms against the Black church is that it often preaches a gospel that if embraced strips the black man of his maleness. This is probably true because of the difference between a man's perception of his sexuality and his actual sexual practice. The Christian man holds marriage in high honor and, in the words of Proverbs 5:15, "drinks water from his own well and is satisfied always with the wife of his youth."

It is my contention that monogamy does not equal a diminished libido in any man, saved or loss. However, God in His wisdom uniquely designed women to respond to their husbands with corresponding desires and gratification.

As a pastor I have found lust to be a constant struggle for Christian men. But the church is not willing to dialogue with men about this spiritual struggle. Many church people falsely assume that marriage settles the problem of lust for the man. In more than a few instances I have found this not to be the case. The Christian man must be given a spiritual environment in which he can live and serve that does not encourage his lust, yet does not condemn him for his struggle. It should choose instead to model humility and confession of sin. No, lust does not mean that a single man is inherently immoral. It does mean that he is inherently fallen. Lust does not mean that the married man does not love his wife. It does mean that his maleness is flexing its hormonal muscles.

In the context of sex and sexuality the African American Christian man must often exclaim, "O wretched man that I am! Who can deliver me from this struggle?" (Rom. 7:24). The answer is of course the crucified and risen Christ. He alone is able to deliver holistically and constructively without displacing the man's manhood.

Few if any men find themselves in disagreement with the five sexual satisfying experiences mentioned before. Most men will even agree that they often struggle with sexual lust on a regular basis. However, when it comes to money and the satisfying experiences it provides for men there is serious disagreement on how similar experiences are regarding money and sex.

It is my contention that in terms of the pleasures of life the second most sought after experience in the lives of black men is the acquisition of money. "A feast is made for laughter, and wine makes life merry, but money is the answer for everything" (Ecc. 10:19). There are a large number of men who believe that money is the answer to all of life's problems; to them lack of money is comparable to the absence of life itself.

"For the love of money is a root of all kinds of evil. Some people, eager for money, have wandered from the faith and pierced themselves with many griefs" (1 Tim. 6:10). This verse regarding the love of money and the price to be paid by those who love it and eagerly seek after it is the same for those who love sex and eagerly seek after it.

The ministry is replete with men and women from the highest to the lowest levels of public view and influence who find themselves in serious moral trouble because of their love for money and sex.

"When tempted, no one should say, "God is tempting me.' For God cannot be tempted by evil, nor does he tempt anyone; but each one is tempted when, by his own evil desire, he is dragged away and enticed. Then, after desire has conceived, it gives birth to sin; and sin, when it is full-grown, gives birth to death" (James 1:13-15). This passage is often explained from the outlook of the dangers of sexual lust and so it should be. However, it also does justice to the text to expound it in the context of the dangers of the lust for money. These are days in which the love and the lust for money parallels the love and lust for sex.

Having ministered to several men who found themselves caught up in sexual immorality, I thought through the issue of what sex means to a man. Then I discovered that for many men money was as seductive as was sex. This led me to think through the possibility that for a number of men sex and money have the same essence.

There are five satisfying experiences that men derive from money:

1. Providing the same kind of erotic sensation as does sexual intercourse;
2. Attainment of a sense of power and independence that is to them the essence of manhood;
3. Empowerment in his relationships with his wife and children;
4. Reduction of feelings of frustration at home and at work; and
5. Participation in one of life's most exciting experiences.

When it comes to sex and money, the African American male is often most possessive and unforgiving. Black men lay claim to their money and are not easily separated from it. To steal a black man's money will most often incur his unrelenting wrath. The same is true with sex because in the mind of the African American male infidelity on the part of his wife is unforgivable and in many instances will incur his wrath. The wrath of black men is difficult to contain and thus often leads to serious destructive behavior and even violence.

I have also observed over the years that when the African American male for whatever reason loses his job and his money, his sex drive will seriously diminish even to the point of sexual impotence. This is because it is difficult for men to feel their manhood when they have no money.

This link between sex and money in the minds and attitude of black men has led me to conclude that any marriage that is consummated with the expectation of developing and growing into a lifetime of happy union must be built upon a solid foundation of money and sexual satisfaction. The pleasure that is derived from both makes a significant positive contribution to the marriage relationship in that it helps to keep the thrill of the relationship alive through changing times and changing circumstances.

The third piece in my triad of what means the most in the private lives of black men in terms of excitement, contentment and pleasure, is power. It is my contention that power for black men carries the same meaning as do sex and money.

The parable of the prodigal son in Luke 16 is about a young man who while living in his father's house as a son under the authority of his father had no sense of independence. He requested and received from his father his share of his father's estate. Having received his money he left home and made his way to a city and a country that was beyond the reach of his father's authority and influence. The money the young prodigal received from his father probably gave him a sense of power and independence.

Power in the context of African American men is about being empowered to decide and act on what he decides. It is about being independent as opposed to dependent on others in terms of the freedom to carry forth the desires of his own heart.

I recently asked a group of young black men who in their opinion were the three most powerful black men in America today. They listed Michael Jordan, Tiger Woods and Louis Farrakhan. This group of young male students were from Morehouse in Atlanta, Georgia, the University of Wisconsin at Milwaukee and a recent suburban high school graduate. These young men defined power as having bi-racial and cross-cultural influence on a national level combined with sufficient money to do as one pleases and national media power.

I found it interesting to note that these young men defined power as the ability to effect change socially, economically and politically. They also distinguished between positions of power and individuals with power. Thus according to this small group of young black men the average African American man in the community either has no power or has power but does not realize it.

When Michael Jordan tells the management of the Chicago Bull basketball team that he will only play if the current coach is retained and they retain the coach, that is power. However, I must admit that not many African American men have real power. Yet, power is the ambition of no small number of African American men.

In the past black men have evidenced a propensity towards

negotiating away their power in deference to the immediate self gratification of sexual satisfaction. This gratification often came wrapped in the package of Anglo females. The lucrative drug market in the Black community is evidence of the willingness of black men to trade in their power as men for money. However, today things are changing. There is a growing realization among young black men that sex and money without power is virtually worthless.

I contend therefore that there are five satisfying experiences men derive from power:

1. Satisfaction of his maleness by giving him an in-charge feeling;
2. Fulfillment of his manhood by giving him a sense of independence;
3. Enhancement of influence in his home and community;
4. Reduction of his frustration as a man by moving him from powerlessness to powerful; and
5. Equipping him with one of life's most exciting experiences.

The issue of money, sex and power is in my view linked together in the lives of men in general. However, in the context of the African American male experience it is seldom the case that we have the combination of all three. In more than a few instances black men are perceived to be content with sex as a means of pleasure, thus money and power are seldom added to their lot as necessary parts of what it is that is necessary for a man to find pleasure in a holistic manner.

I suggest that the church must give more consideration to ways of assisting black men in their pursuit of pleasure on the level with other men which includes sex, money and power. This empowerment of black men must of necessity begin with a relationship with God through Jesus Christ. For in the final analysis life with pleasure and authentic power is rooted in a man's faith in the resurrected Christ.

CHAPTER 11

"THE VILLAGE" AND THE AFRICAN AMERICAN MAN

The African American Village at large is a non-monolethic social and economically diverse yet organized community, engaged in a number of interrelated activities. These various and diverse activities are organized around and function through the common ground of race, culture, economics, politics and religion.

The Black Community Village is organized around an infrastructure of social institutions that function to meet the specific needs of the people in the Village These social institutions within the Black community parallel the social institutions in the Anglo community.

The African American Community in many instances is not unlike a separate colony populated by Black people and is most often controlled and manipulated by a White power structure that is external to the community itself. I am not suggesting that the Black community does not have power structures of its own. However, the internal power structure of the Village is not a creation of the people in the community; nor is it truly autonomous from the external White power structure.

A community consist of a variety of factors including, geographic territory, distribution of goods and services, the presence and influence of people, values systems, social and religious institutions, just to name a few. There is also within the concept of the Village the embodiment of power distribution which has to do with how the members of the community are organized at both the formal and informal level.

There is a sense in which the term *African American Village* refers not just to a particular geographical area of African American people living in a certain city in America but rather it is a reference to all African Americans in America regardless of their geographical location or social status. The perception of the term held by most people is that all Black people live in and share a common geographical location and a common value system and life-style.

However, African American people who share a common legacy and heritage of the North American experiences of slavery, racial segregation, discrimination and economic deprivation are quite diverse in their values, lifestyles, and religious beliefs today. Yet there remains a plethora of things that African American men, women, and children have need of that can only be obtained in the Village. This includes haircuts, hairstyling, soul food, and the Black church experience.

There is the reality of communities that are entirely inhabited by African American people. These communities have a much broader common ground than is found among those Blacks who live in integrated communities and are classified as middle-class Black professionals. Blacks who live in integrated predominantly White suburbs tend to be more acculturated towards the Anglo culture.

The local Black communities in this country today are often described as enclaves of poor people with low aspirations for achievement, high welfare recipient rates and high male unemployment. This stereotype needs to be overcome in the minds of people within and outside of the community if the Village is to be reclaimed.

For while it is true that desegregation opened the door for a number of Blacks to exit the Black community geographically, there remains a sizable number of middle class Blacks in the geographic Black community. In addition the failure of integration in public and private education has taught well the lesson that it is possible to have quality education and housing in an all Black context. In other words, public and private education are not necessarily better because they are integrated nor are they necessarily inferior because they are segregated.

As I have stated earlier, each local Black community has or needs five basic community-based and operated social and economic institutions in order to function effectively as a community. These include geographic territory, distribution of goods and services, the presence and influence of good role models, value systems, and social and religious institutions. In most instances the Black community either never had or has long since been stripped of most of these institutions, with the exception of religious institutions.

A few years ago I returned to my hometown of Lake Providence, Louisiana for a brief visit. It had been close to thirty years since I moved away from that little country town. As I drove through the community that I grew up in, I remembered with great fondness the people who lived along the roads and across the fields. These people were all like family, and everybody knew everybody's business and looked after each other's welfare.

The Village in those days was the place where you felt that you belonged. Everybody knew your name there. In the Village everybody celebrated the achievements of each individual in the community and conversely everybody shared in the failures and losses of people in the community.

In that rural southern community of yesterday, people shared their garden with each other and they shared their meat from the hog killings with the community. In the Village the children belonged to the community and were looked after by the community. It was a place where to be old meant to be respected and disrespect brought swift discipline. The Village was like that in those days.

As I drove through the old community for the first time in thirty years, it became evident to me that the village that was then is no more. Old people had died and the young people had moved away from the farms and left the south for the large cities. However, what struck me most was that the City of Lake Providence itself had died. In fact it had become recognized throughout America as the poorest city in the nation. The *Dallas Morning News* reported recently: "One of every two parish residents live in poverty, compared with one of seven nationwide. East Carroll also is plagued with corruption. A former police chief is in prison for fraud, and the longtime sheriff recently resigned after pleading guilty to charges of mail fraud and bribery."[1]

The evident death of my small hometown forced me to ask the question "Why did the City of Lake Providence in East

---

[1]   Diane Jennings, *Dallas Morning News* Sunday Paper, September 28,1997.

Carroll Parish die?" In a flash my mind returned to my present hometown, the city of Dallas, Texas, and it occurred to me that in Dallas many if not most of the Black communities are in a state of pathology and have the stench of death about them.

The pathology of the Village was likely caused by several historical events. First, the death of the village began with the southern migration. Second, the village was devastated by the impact of the welfare system. Thirdly, desegregation had a pathological effect on the life of the village.

Southern migration refers to the historical movement of rural southern African Americans from the southern cotton-growing states to the large metropolitan industrial cities in the North and Midwest. They were seeking a better way of life. The southern migration first took place in the Post-Civil War reconstruction period. It occurred again in the 1920s, 1940s and 1950s.

The sociological environment of the cities to which southern Blacks moved was a significant factor in shaping and molding the family structure of today's African American Village. In the rural south Blacks lived in a social and domestic context that is best described as intimate. In that environment relationships within the Village were strong and the extended family was a significant part of the family's support system. The Black church served as a major part of the social and economic infrastructure of the community.

However, when the southern Blacks moved north into the urban cities no such context existed to maintain strong intimate relationships between neighbors and the extended family ties. Moving to the north in search of better jobs and living conditions contributed further to the fragmentation of the African American people.

In an attempt to recreate the Village in the urban cities the southern immigrants transplanted their rural church structure and form of worship. Through the church they sought to reestablish the old rural pattern of personal relationships and internal community structure. They hoped to use the church in the urban context for the same purpose that it had in the rural south. That is they tried to create a sense of community in their new home and thereby strengthen the identity and economic base of the people in the community.

The slums and ghettos of today were originally urban communities inhabited for the most part by European immigrants. They served as communities of transition, and to this end the slum-based institutions (i.e., schools and welfare organization) were oriented to help European immigrants attain the tools necessary for mobility up and into mainstream America. They melted into the pot.

However, these same institutions failed to accomplish the same for the Black southern immigrants. Black people were not wanted in the pot. Instead institutions such as the welfare system functioned in a manner that kept the southern immigrant in his place in the slum environment. Thus African Americans were permanently trapped in urban slums which became chocolate villages of social and economic deprivation.

The welfare system that was a major part of President Lyndon B. Johnson's great society program delivered a shattering blow to the Black family structure and the Black community. The welfare system did much to all but entirely decimate the Village. It contributed to the disproportionate number of female headed families in the Black community. Thus it is responsible for much of the rampant violence in the Black community. It contributed to the development of the under-class in the Black community and it functions today as a part of America's means of managing the poor.

White females who controlled the welfare system and the distribution of the funds demanded that the Black female be in charge of the household. Welfare recipients were women who had children and no man in the house.

When the welfare caseworker visited the welfare recipient's house and a man was found in the bedroom, he had to dress and have one foot on the floor. Thus, if a man found himself out of work and unable to support his family, his wife could only get welfare assistance if he abandoned his family.

The Civil Rights Movement under the leadership of Dr. Martin Luther King Jr. also contributed to the demise of the Village. The focus of the Civil Rights Movement was the desegregation of all public facilities and our integration into the greater American society. Dr. King's dream was of an America in which people in general and Black people in particular would be judged based on the content of their character and not on the color of their skin.

It is interesting to note here that in the southern migration of Blacks to the northern urban communities, the African American male benefited least. Because of the color of his skin he was denied access to the job markets that were controlled by

Whites and other minorities. The public welfare system mandated that he be excluded from his family in order for his wife and children to receive public assistance. The Civil Rights Movement was led by black men and yet in many ways it inadvertently contributed less to him than it gained from him.

When Dr. Martin Luther King Jr. wrote his "I Have a Dream" speech at the Willard Hotel in Washington D.C. and delivered it at the Lincoln Monument thirty years ago, he envisioned this day of desegregation and federally enforced integration as one in which black men and White men would be accepted and treated as equals in the political, judicial, social and economic contexts of our country. Dr. King's dream was not that black men and White men would lose sight of their distinctive racial and cultural traits and traditions. He believed in integration, but he was not an acculturationalist. King dreamed of an America where race and culture were relevant only in a positive way.

Malcolm X, on the other hand, looked at America thirty years ago and saw this day of desegregation and legally enforced integration as a nightmare in which black men would be worse off than they were at that time. Malcolm was a segregationist, he believed that for the black man segregation was to be preferred in terms of economic, social and family benefits.

Unlike King Malcolm believed that race would always matter in a negative way in the minds of White Americans. Today there is increasing evidence that African American men are tired of trying to measure up to the expectations of White men only to discover that they are still not accepted as equals. The move today for a growing number of Black males is towards a segregated America in which black men set their own standards of excellence in their schools, professions and families without regard for the standards and expectations of White America.

The Black community of yesterday was a community that advocated education as the key to upward mobility. It celebrated Black achievement. It was a community of compassion. It exalted a standard of excellence. It had its own Black heroes. It produced great men and women.

Desegregation has contributed much as well to a number of African Americans in general. It has given access to higher education, better jobs and a growing Black middle class, just to mention a few of the positives. However, in many ways it has robbed the Village of the best and the brightest of its people. The best athletes are in White universities that can offer significantly more money and benefits than the predominantly Black colleges and universities. The brightest Black students are siphoned off to White universities as well, enticed with four-year scholarships. Black professionals live outside of the community. Genuine Black heroes are for the most part disregarded in the curriculum of integrated public schools. Black business establishments that abounded in the Village of yesterday are in serious decline. Black youths are without direction in their lives in terms of vocational choices and positive models.

I am reminded here of the context of slavery in which the whole of the Black race was under siege. In that context among the slave Blacks in the south and the free Blacks in the north, the idea emerged that the church was the key ingredient in developing corporate and individual identity and in creating community. Thus the heart of the drive of Black people in that oppressive context to create their own separate churches and denominations was a perception they had gleaned from their White oppressors that part of the American concept of humanness included the exercise of control of one's property. In the minds of those Blacks who knew well the agony and the limitations of oppression, to be human was to be free to do what one wanted with his or her own resources. Thus the organizing of Black congregations was for these pioneer men and women an assertion of their humanity. These men thought that being a man meant having control over some aspect of one's life, thus the efforts to be free of White control in their churches and denominations.

To ensure their freedom from White control in their churches and to some extent in their lives, the founders of the first separate Black churches and denominations included in their articles of incorporation stipulations which excluded Whites from official membership and control of church property. This action on the part of these pioneer Black church planters must not be perceived as overt racism on their part but as an assertion of their determination to create for themselves and their people a community Village where they were recognized as real men and respected as real men.

To reclaim the village we must think through the social and economic issues of our day and decide for ourselves that as a people we can have quality even in the context of Blackness. It may well be that recapturing the Village will require of black men a level of leadership that is unparalleled in this day but not unlike the leadership of black men of years past.

CHAPTER 12

THE MINISTRY OF THE HOLY SPIRIT AND THE AFRICAN AMERICAN MAN

I n his recent book *Adam! Where are you?* Jawanza Kunjufu lists twenty one reasons why most black men do not go to church. Kunjufu gives the following list:

> 1. Hypocrisy; 2. Ego/dictatorial; 3. Faith-submission-trust-forgiveness-snger at God; 4. Passivity; 5. Tithing; 6. Irrelevance; 7. Eurocentric; 8. Length of service; 9. Too emotional; 10. Sports; 11. Attire/dress code; 12. Classism/unemployment; 13. Education; 14. Sexuality and drugs; 15. Homosexuality; 16. Spirituality/worshiping alone/universalism; 17. Heaven; 18. Evangelism; 19. Lack of Christian role models; 20. Streets/peer pressure; and 21. Parental double standards forced when a child.[1]

The most significant thing about Kunjufu's list is not so much the content of the list but that the list came out of Kunjufu's dialogue with black men. It is high time for church leaders, both Black and White, to stop talking at and about black men and to begin talking with black men.

The Black church has a strong tradition of worship and praise that is unparalleled perhaps in the world in terms of its wholistic emphasis and soulful expression. The African American male owes a debt to the church for his intellectual, economic and domestic survival and development in North America given the history and legacy of slavery in this country and the impact of that history on black men in particular.

---

[1] Jawanza Kunjufu, *Adam! Where are you? Why Most Black Men Don't Go to Church* (1994), p. 55ff.

Those who worship in the Black church tradition are well aware of the richness of its spiritual emphasis and the indebtedness of black men to the Black church. However, the flip side of the Black church experience today is that it seems to have lost its effectiveness in reaching Black men with the gospel of Jesus Christ and influencing their lives for the good of the kingdom of God and the Village. There seems to be a general nonverbal consensus among Black pastors that implies that we are doing just fine with the "eight to one" Black female to Black male ratio in our churches.

The most significant institution in the lives of black men historically has been the Black church. No other institution has contributed as much to the identity and strength of black men as has the Black church. Yet the African American male is in comparison to the Black female basically unchurched and biblically illiterate. Even the black men who are members of the church seldom attend Bible studies and few are personally discipled.

In reaching black men for Christ it is necessary to understand that they demand more than religious rhetoric and religious hype. Black men require of those who would reach and lead them not only a transparent life to which they have unreserved access but also consistent sound Bible teaching. In this context, I believe that black men must have something more than religion, Islam, or others like it. The African American male must begin his pilgrimage to spiritual wholeness with an understanding of who Jesus Christ is and what it is that He has done, combined with an understanding of *the work and ministry of the Holy Spirit.*

The African American male must be taught in the clearest language possible the truth that Jesus is the only begotten Son of the living God. He must understand that Jesus died, was buried and rose from the dead. This basic knowledge about Jesus will begin the process of empowering the Black male to deal with the baggage of Black nationalism and the rhetoric of Non-Christian religions which suggest that Christianity is nothing more than a tool of White men used to control and oppress black men. In my view Christology must increasingly become the primary agent of the message and lesson of Christian education in the Black church.

In the context of discipling the African American male the second primary focus must be on the work and ministry of God the Holy Spirit. With a holistic knowledge of the role of the Holy Spirit in the spiritual life of the man the African American male will be able to recognize and distinguish for himself the Christ of Christianity. Thus the difference between mere religion, both Christian and non-Christian will become clear.

There are seven ministries of the Holy Spirit to which the African American male must be introduced and gain an understanding of:

1. *The convicting ministry of the Holy Spirit.* This is a ministry to the head and the heart of the man in his unsaved state. As the gospel is presented in whatever context over a long or short period of time, the Holy Spirit interprets the gospel message to the mind of the man with a view to persuading him that he is a sinner in need of salvation, Jesus Christ is God's standard of righteousness and by placing his faith in the crucified and resurrected Christ, he can obtain that righteousness and thereby have an everlasting relationship with God.

2. *The indwelling ministry of the Holy Spirit.* This ministry of the Holy Spirit happens the moment the sinner is persuaded to put his faith in God through the crucified and resurrected Christ. It is the indwelling Holy Spirit that provides the internal witness and external evidence of genuine conversion.

3. *The baptism of the Holy Spirit.* This ministry of the Holy Spirit happens the moment the sinner is brought to faith by the Holy Spirit. This is a positional truth, not one that the believer will feel, yet it is very real and secures the believer's relationship with God for eternity.

4. *The leading of the Holy Spirit.* This ministry of the Holy Spirit enables the believer to have a sense of the mind and will of God in everyday life. This ministry also provides the believer with security and daily affirmation that he is a son of God.

5. *The sealing of the Holy Spirit.* This ministry happens at the moment of salvation and gives the believer an eternally secure relationship with God through Christ.

6. *The grieving of the Holy Spirit.* This ministry of the Holy Spirit keeps the believer sensitive to the invasion of sin into his heart and life so that confession of sin will be an ongoing experience. In this ministry the believer is made to feel guilt when sin is committed.

7. *The gifts of the Holy Spirit.* This ministry of the Spirit equips and empowers the believer for effective service in the Body of Christ.

Understanding the ministry of God the Holy Spirit enables the African American male to understand that Christianity is in its very nature a supernatural relationship with the living God through Jesus Christ. It also equips him with biblical knowledge and a life experience that empowers him with the ability to distinguish Christianity from Non-Christian religions. such as Islam as well as all other empty experienced based cults and church membership.

It is my contention that evangelical Christianity proclaims a gospel to the African American male that demands far too little of him in terms of life change and commitment. In comparison to what is demanded of the African American male who became Muslims, Christianity is far too lax in its expectations of those who decide to join the church. This low expectation of men is in my view a primary contributing factor to the ineffectiveness of the black church in reaching black men.

The problem that a number of men have with church, in addition to the ones given by Kunjufu, is that those who become members of the church find themselves in a situation in which they lack the internal power with which to live out the commitments of their faith. To this end I suggest that it is the indwelling Holy Spirit to whom the Christian man must continually and repeatedly be encouraged to yield that is the power source for living a clean life in a dirty world.

PREACHING TO THE WIND

While driving down Martin Luther King Blvd. In South Dallas, I began to pay particular attention to the number of trucks that frequent the community, stocking and restocking the many liquor stores in the Village with various kind of alcoholic beverages.

It occurred to me as I thought about what I was observing that the many people, primarily black men who are the eager customers of those liquor stores, were in fact finding in the content of the liquor they were buying and drinking something that stimulated their spirit in a way to make them feel and experience some things in their present situations that they could not otherwise feel and experience. It was evident that they liked the experience the liquor provided for them. I subsequently learned that the beer that was delivered to the stores on Martin Luther King in the heart of the Village was much higher in alcohol content, packaged in larger containersand advertised more aggresively than was the same brand of beer delivered in the White community.

I have thought further about this evident human need demonstrated by the acquisition of liquor by these customers. The incorporation of another spirit into their body is required so that they can feel and act in ways that are not common to their natural behavior. I concluded based on the number of men who drink liquor on a regular basis, that there must be in most men a need to feel and experience a kind of spirit and energy that moves them beyond their limitations and inhibitions in any given situation.

I noticed for instance that men who were quite inhibited socially became quite the extrovert after consuming a few beers. Men who either felt they could not or were ashamed to dance "got down" and boogied when they began to feel the impact of the liquor they had imbibed. The man who lacked the courage to rap to a certain female would not hesitate to approach her under the influence of alcohol. It is evident to me that for a number of men alcohol is considered to be a necessary stimulation for their otherwise timid spirit.

I thought about what seems to be an evident general human need for a spirit to stimulate their own human spirit under its influence a man feels and acts out that which is foreign to his natural behavior. Then my mind moved from the many liquor stores on Martin Luther King Blvd. with their stock of liquid spirits and their loyal customers to the church building and our emphasis on the Holy Spirit.

There is a common link in terms of human spirit stimulation between what the man gets from the liquor store, namely, alcoholic beverages (spirits) and what a man gets from the church, namely, the Holy Spirit of God. The common link is that both the liquid spirit and the Holy Spirit have the power to stimulate and alter the inner spirit of the man who has either spirit within him. It is not possible to be under the influence of both alcohol and the Holy Spirit at the same time. One will rule out the felt need for the other.

I think it is true that men who drink liquor and take drugs to the point that they are controlled by them are in search of a means by which they can escape something, face up to something, feel a certain way, act out something, or say something that they are unable to say in strength of their natural human spirit. Men who drink liquor are expressing the fact that they have a felt need for something more than that which their own spirit possesses to get where they feel they need or want to be in terms of their feeling and behavior. To put it another way, the various circumstances and challenges in life most often causes men to seek out and take in that which stimulates their human spirit so they can handle situations one way or the other. Even for a number of men in the church, liquor is that spirit stimulator.

So it is with Christian men. The challenge to live holy and serve the Lord consistently creates a need in the lives of Christian men for a spirit energizer that moves them out and beyond the limitations and hang ups of their natural human spirit into an arena of feeling and acting in ways that are foreign to their natural spirit. For the Christian man that Spirit is none other than the Holy Spirit of God.

"Be not drunk with wine, wherein is excess" (Eph. 5:18, KJV). I take it that the text is saying that for the Christian man who is committed to being salt and light in this world for the living God, drunkenness is not the way to go. There is implied in the statement, "Be not drunk with wine wherein there is excess" the notion that Christianity is not a way of life that can be lived in the power of a man's own natural human spirit, thus even Christian men need to have their human spirit stimulated as a means of altering their natural attitude, human will and behavior. However, the option for the Christian man is not spirit stimulation with wine or liquor but, rather, spirit stimulation by way of the filling of the Holy Spirit.

The church serves as the source of spirit stimulation for the man who is born again just as the liquor store and drug dealer are the fount-of-plenty for the drunkard and drug user. The Holy Spirit provides the motivation for the spirit so that the Christian man is empowered to act in ways that are foreign to his natural human spirit. The saved man can no more stay away from the church in search of his spiritual stimulation than the drinker or drunkard can stay away from the liquor store in search of his alcoholic stimulation.

The text's focus is on control. A man has a choice of what he will allow to control him: alcohol or the Holy Spirit. Both will produce the same effect, namely, cause the man to act contrary to his nature. For the Christian man the only option as a source of stimulation is the Holy Spirit.

On the Day of Pentecost when the Holy Spirit came and filled the Apostles in the upper room in the city of Jerusalem, Peter and the other Apostles went out and began to preach Christ crucified and resurrected in the various languages of all the Jewish people who were there in the city of Jerusalem at that time. Those folks who knew who the Apostles were and heard them preaching in this religiously hostile environment thought they were drunk because of the boldness of their action and the courage with which they faced their audience.

Peter responded to this assumption about their being drunk and told the people that it was too early in the morning for them to be drunk. What they witnessed in the Apostles that day was due to the controlling power and influence of the Holy Spirit over their attitude and behavior. Thus when I make the comparison in our day between the attitude and actions of the man who is filled with alcohol and the man who is filled with the Spirit, I am in good company. The difference is in the cause behind the uncommon behavior and the nature of the behavior displayed.

The text attaches to drunkenness the statement "Wherein is excess." I take it that not only does alcohol cause the man who drinks it to act in ways that are contrary to his natural behavior but the nature of the behavior is characterized by debauchery. The story of the prodigal son in Luke 16 is an example of the meaning of the word *debauchery*. This young man, after demanding and receiving his share of his father's estate, went out and wasted both his life and his money. He lived a life of excessive indulgence in sensual pleasures, eating, drinking, etc. In contrast ,Acts 2 gives an example of what it means to be filled with the Spirit. It is a life of extraordinary behavior, yet controlled and in order.

The command to the Christian man is that he be "drunk" on (filled with the Spirit) the Holy Spirit. To be filled with the Spirit is to be controlled by the Holy Spirit in the same way that excessive wine drinking controls the one who imbibes.

The Holy Spirit's filling is not about being saved. It is a ministry of the Holy Spirit in the life of the saved person. The filling of the Spirit is all about the energizing of the human spirit and will of the man so that he is able to feel, think, and act in ways that are contrary to his natural human spirit.

The filling of the Spirit is all about the power to serve the Lord. It is not about making noise in church on Sunday. Spirit filled men are Christian men on a mission for Jesus. The mission is winning the lost to Christ by being salt and light for Christ in the context in which they live and work.

Beer commercials which fill the television portray a host of images that convey the message that beer whatever the brand, when consumed in ample quantities, will enable the young man and his woman to feel and act in ways that are more than a little bit exciting. Their sales pitch tells you that a day at the beach is not what it could be without a trunk full of cold beer at the man's disposal. Football and other sports are not as exciting to watch without liquor. Sex is not as intense in pleasure without the enhancement of potent beer. The alcoholic beverage industry is indeed a powerful, behavior-modifying multi-billion dollar industry.

I suggest that the church should emulate the liquor industry and advertise to the African American male that life is not all that it could be without the controlling influence of the Holy Spirit on our human spirit. A day in the life of a Christian can have eternal effects that transcend immediate self-gratification. Answers to problems are but a whispered prayer away. Sin no longer has dominion over one's behavior. Joy is intrinsic.

Men must be challenged to give up alcohol as a source of spirit stimulation, choosing instead to yield to the eternal attractiveness of the indwelling Holy Spirit. He (God the Holy Spirit) then controls their attitude and behavior.

The Spirit-filled life has two primary effects in the life of a man in terms of his behavior. First, it enables him to live his life wisely rather than foolishly. Second, it enables him to have and maintain a life of praise and worship of the living God. The Spirit-filled life is about living and serving the Lord which is consistent with God's original design for all men.

There are three internal and external signs of a Spirit-filled man: "Speaking to one another in psalms and hymns and spiritual songs, singing and making melody with your heart to the Lord; always giving thanks for all things in the name of our Lord Jesus Christ to God even the Father; and be subject to one another in the fear of Christ" (Eph. 5:19).

The command to be filled with the Spirit is to all Christians.

It is the believer's choice to obey or disobey this command. For every believer who elects to be filled with the Spirit, there is for them the experience of not being depressed no matter their circumstances in life.

The Spirit filled man is one who is "up" on life from within. The Spirit of God, when controlling the man's human spirit, elevates the mind of the man above his circumstances so that in spite of the situation the man is able to be encouraged and to encourage others to sing praises to the living Lord Jesus.

In this passage in the original language the command to be filled with the Spirit is in the present passive tense "πληρουσθε εν πνευματι." This means that in terms of the act of being filled with the Spirit no effort is required on the part of the believer. To be filled with the Spirit, the Christian man simply yields his mind and will to the power and influence of the indwelling Holy Spirit

The Spirit-filled man sings and makes melody in his heart to the Lord not as a means by which he is elevated to a certain spiritual level so that he can obtain the filling of the Spirit. No, the singing and making melody in his heart is an expression of his having been filled with the Spirit.

The second sign of a Spirit-filled man is an attitude of thankfulness to God for all circumstances of life which include the good, the bad, and the ugly, faced each day as an African American Christian man in today's society. The Spirit of God enables the Christian man to trust God to always do what is best for him. The Spirit of God causes the saved man to believe that whatever it is that God allows to come into his life, it is for his good, no matter how it appears at that moment. Thus there is a consistent attitude of gratitude.

Thirdly, the Spirit-filled man is characterized by a spirit of submissiveness. Stubbornness is not the way of life for the Spirit-filled man. Men who are controlled by the Holy Spirit are teachable. They are not "know-it-alls." They have no problem submitting to the will of others.

The filling of the Spirit is tied to the challenge of both living the Christian life and doing effective ministry in the context of an evil and perverted generation. It is the means by which a man is empowered to live a clean life in a dirty world. To the extent that the church recognizes the impossibility of meeting the challenges of living and serving the Lord effectively and consistently in our own strength, to that extent we will find ourselves willing to yield to the power of the Holy Spirit.

In his book *Adam! Where are you?* Kunjufu makes the following observation about the process through which men go as a means of becoming a member of the Islamic faith: The Nation of Islam does not immediately assume that a brother who expresses an interest in becoming a member of the Nation of Islam is capable on his own volition of following the principles of Islam. The brother is assigned a "Big Brother" who is in touch with him daily. There are formal single gender classes on how to be a Muslim. In Muslim worship services and educational experiences men and women are separated because they believe many males lack the discipline to acquire knowledge while in the presence of women. Classes explain Islam not only historically and scripturally but also in terms of day-to-day living. In Islam a man is taught that his position in the household in the head. He is taught to respect his wife and his children, to be the provider because all work is honorable, to respect his body as a temple and to abstain from eating pork, smoking cigarettes and consuming alcohol. He is also expected to give 10-20 hours per week to Nation activities, which could include doing work around the building, selling newspapers or being involved in special programs. Upon satisfactorily completing these activities the man becomes eligible for and receives further training and becomes a member of the FOI (Fruit Of Islam) which is the Nation's security force. The lessons continue.

It is my contention that the Evangelical preacher, unlike the ministers of the Nation of Islam, preaches a gospel message to African American men that demands far too little of them in terms of their time, resources and talents. This lack of demand is in my view a primary factor in the lack of success the church has in reaching black men.

The fact is that the Nation of Islam is having significant success in reaching black men today on the streets, on college campuses, in the inner city, in the suburbs and in the prisons. They are succeeding with a message that does not include Christ or the Holy Spirit. Thus I suggest that it is time for the church to change its timid and often passive posture so that it reflects the substance that it really has in terms of the demands of the gospel on the lives of those who embrace it.

In many ways the line of expectation and accountability for men in the church is so low and undemanding that it can be lived out in the strength of the man's natural strength. In all to many instances Christian men do not see any felt need for the power and influence of the Holy Spirit in their lives on a consistent basis if at all. Thus I contend that in reclaiming the Village there must be a radical change in what is preached and taught to black men. The message of the gospel must be followed up with strong lines of accountability and biblically based spiritual expectations.

PART 4

THE CHALLENGE IN DEVELOPING UNFRAGMENTED AFRICAN AMERICAN MEN

CHAPTER 13

THE AFRICAN AMERICAN MALE AND THE USE OF AUTHORITY IN THE HOME

B ob and Mary had been married for several years and had several children. Both worked outside the home and together they made a comfortable living. Bob was the kind of man who did not manage money well so every payday Mary went to Bob's job and collected his pay check.

But after listening to a series of sermons on the family in which the pastor laid particular emphasis on the man's responsibility to be the head of his family, Mary began feeling guilty for being the one who managed the money. And after thinking about it for a season, Mary made an appointment and came to the pastor to ask if she was doing the right thing as a Christian wife in managing the money in their household.

The young pastor told Mary that she really should not be managing the money for that was her husband's responsibility. "O.K.," Mary said to the pastor, "but if Bob does what he usually does and spends the rent money I am going to come to you for the money to pay the rent." The pastor agreed and went his way. Within two weeks Mary was back asking the pastor for the money to pay the rent. She had turned the management of money over to her husband, and Bob had spent the rent money just as she thought he would.

My pastor friend had made a mistake that is all too common among Evangelical preachers. His preaching and his recommendation to this sister was based on the conviction that he held regarding the biblical ideal of the role of the husband in the family. The biblical ideal is that in the family the husband is the head and as such has the responsibility and the authority to manage his family. The mistake that most biblicists make is in thinking that because God gives the headship of the family to the man and because men are structured by God to desire to function in the leadership role in the family, men are automatically equipped to marry at a young age and function as the head of his family.

In the evangelical community there is no small number of wives who have husbands who are trying to function as their head with only their adult maleness and their marriage license as the qualifying credentials for the job. To say the least being an adult male who feels the need for a wife does not in and of itself qualify a man to function as the head of a family.

The Nation of Islam in its training program teaches men lessons on headship in the family. They teach men respect for themselves and for women. The Black evangelical church in many ways does the same thing. Judging from what I have seen as a result of such teaching, most men are delighted to know that they are in charge of their family which means that they are the boss at home. This "I am the boss" attitude that husbands get from their mosques and their churches most often cast the wife into a role in which she is perceived as inferior to her husband and in time she finds herself being oppressed by her husband.

Having had the responsibility of counseling a multitude of couples in which the wife was physically beaten by the husband, I have found few cases in which the battering husband was simply a mean and hateful man. In most of the cases that I have dealt with over the years, the husband was frustrated by the unwillingness of the wife to submit to his dictatorial leadership as the head of the family. The words from the mouth of the husband most often begin with "I *told* her. . . and she . . ."

For a number of years, I spent a lot of my time teaching men what the Bible says about their responsibilities as a husband and father. In time I began to notice a big difference between the happiness of the men and the happiness of their wives and children. The men demonstrated an attitude of pride and superiority while his wife and children demonstrated attitudes of restraint and oppression.

At first I thought that the apparent unhappiness of the wives and children of these good men was due to the fact that their husbands were functioning as the head of the family and they being strong-willed black women were uncomfortable with that. To my surprise I discovered that such was not the problem.

The cause behind the unhappiness of the wives and children was the cold, calculated and often dictatorial attitude and leadership style of these husband-fathers in their homes. These men were diligent students of the Bible in their pursuit of a knowledge of the authority God had give them as the head of the family. However, once armed with this biblical knowledge these Christian men were genuine tyrants at home when their wives disagreed with them or acted in any way that did not meet their approval. These men understood headship to mean that they had the authority of God behind their liberty to limit the activities of their wives, while they functioned as unrestricted and unrestrained kings in their castles, their homes.

Such was the case with Jim. He collected both his and his wife's paychecks and gave his wife a meager budget on which to do all she had to do including buying groceries for the household. Jim, on the other hand, felt the liberty to buy anything he wanted whenever he wanted to, no matter the cost without even mentioning his decision to his wife. To Jim such was the nature of biblical headship.

In teaching men their biblical responsibilities as the head of their family it is necessary to include in that teaching the role of the Holy Spirit in empowering Christian men to function as compassionate, sensitive leaders in their home.

It is necessary to teach and model for African American Christian men obedience to the biblical command to live a Spirit-filled life in the context of the family. It is important to point out here that the Spirit-filled life can be had by any Christian man, no matter the level of his spiritual maturity. The essential ingredient in living the Spirit-filled life is salvation. Of course, spiritual maturity is always the goal.

It is the Spirit-filled husband who is able to love his wife as Christ loved the church. This love that the Spirit-filled husband has and demonstrates for his wife is beyond physical love. It is the kind of love that empowers the husband to invest himself in his wife so that she increasingly reflects his glory in her appearance, attitude and conduct.

It is good for the woman to look for this Spirit-filled love in the man during courtship for it is in that context that he begins his investment in her. While courting, the Spirit-filled man invests in the woman who will become his wife time, fellowship and the kind of love where he gives himself to her as one who only wants to please her. Courtship then leads to marriage.

Second, the Spirit-filled man invests in the woman by committing himself to her in engagement. Engagement sets the woman apart unto the man as his choice to become his wife. In this phase of the relationship, the Spirit-filled man invests in the emotional, spiritual and overall health and strength of the woman who will become his wife. Thirdly, the Spirit-filled man marries the woman and continues the investment, developing for himself a wife who will reflect his glory.

It is important to note here that the Spirit-filled man is not one who evidences an authoritative "I am in charge" attitude in his courtship and marriage. The Spirit-filled man is busy going about the business of demonstrating unconditional love in his relationship with his wife and children.

In the context of marriage, the Spirit-filled husband is empowered and equipped by the Holy Spirit with the Christian attitude that enables him not to rank himself higher than his wife spiritually, nor does he perceive himself to be superior to his wife intellectually, emotionally or physically. The Spirit-filled husband's attitude and behavior show a spirit of equality between himself and his wife. The wife feels and experiences not his authority as the head of the family but his love and commitment to serve her as his bride.

The attitude of equality that is evident in the home of the Spirit-filled man does not dismiss the idea that the man and his wife are very different in many ways. However, the differences that exist between them are the differences of design and gender, not differences of status and equality before God and each other.

It is the difference in biological and psychological design that exist between the man and the woman that enables them to function in ways that correspond to each other. The fact is the external male and female bodies are made to fit together and so are the internal design of the male and the female.

It has been my conviction and practice as a pastor for more than thirty years not to marry a Christian man to a non-Christian woman nor will I marry a Christian woman to a non-Christian man. I base my conviction and practice on 2 Corinthians 6:14. However, I have observed in many instances that a Christian man armed with biblical knowledge of his responsibility and role in the home and not filled with the Spirit is in many ways a far more abusive husband than a man who is a pure pagan.

The Christian man mistakenly believes that he has the right to exercise his authority as head of the family in such a way that everybody in the house jumps at his command. Thus he has sex on command from his wife. He has spending liberties that are exclusively his so that he purchases whatever he wants whenever he wants. He sets the budget and manages it all by himself. His wife and children have virtually no say in most things that concern them. The saved man who is not Spirit-filled is all too often nothing more than a tyrant at home.

The Spirit-filled husband understands and acts on the fact that gender differences between he and his wife are functional differences, not evidences of superior or inferior traits. They are gender-based functional differences that make it possible for each to correspond to the needs of the other.

The concept of a subordinate is only relevant in the Black male and female relationship in the context of the role and the function of the husband and his wife. In the marriage relationship God assigned the subordinate role to the wife in terms of function. This assigned role in no way implies that women are inferior to men. The distinctive role of men and women in the marriage relationship is related to function, not intellect or spiritual status before God.

The woman's assigned role in marriage is a matter of divine arrangement, not a matter of cultural socialization; nor is the role of women a matter of debate; it is a settled matter in the Christian home. The husband accepts his responsibility as head of his family and in the power of the Holy Spirit he manages himself well and he manages his wife as his equal in every way.

Scripture assigns the role of head of the family to the husband and assigns the wife to a role in the marriage in which she must live and function in subordination to her husband. This is true regardless of the husband's spiritual status. Thus every woman who decide to marry must of necessity choose wisely.

The wisdom in her choice must reflect her knowledge that the man she will marry will exercise authority over her. He will demand of her a spirit of subordination. To the extent that she is not inclined to yield to his authority she will likely find herself in a serious power struggle with her husband. The wife who finds herself in a power struggle with her husband risks being abused, neglected or divorced.

To be in a subordinate role for the Christian wife means

being under the managerial authority of the husband as his equal. However, not all Christian husbands embrace the idea of the wife thinking and acting as his equal. It is the Spirit-filled Christian husband who is given to thinking and treating his wife as his equal. The Spirit-filled Christian wife willfully functions in the subordinate role to her husband as a matter of spiritual responsibility before God. She is fully aware of the fact that her attitude of willful subordination to her husband is not in any way related to her intellect or strength as a mature woman. The Spirit-filled wife understands the fact that the subordinate role of the Christian wife in marriage cannot be avoided or disregarded, thus it is imperative that she choose her husband wisely.

This means spending much time in prayer and consultation with Christian friends before deciding to say yes to a marriage proposal. The Christian woman must only say yes to a marriage proposal when she is as confident as she possibly can be that she respects and will likely continue to grow in her respect and willingness to submit to the leadership of her husband.

I am reminded of the comments made by several young women who were students at several different universities. In response to the issue of the lack of available African American men for marriage, I noted that African American women outnumbered black men an average of five to one. These young women made the point that they would not marry a man who was not of the same social and economic class as they were. They felt that it would be difficult for them to respect and submit to a man who ranked beneath them in education and vocation.

In my view it is absolutely necessary for a wife to respect her husband if in fact she is going to submit herself to him as a wife. This respect must include not only his social class but more importantly it must include his spiritual integrity.

The Bible gives three reasons why the Christian wife is to function as the subordinate to her husband:

1. It is her spiritual responsibility;
2. God made man the head of the wife, which is understood not as a gender thing but as a divine arrangement; and
3. As the head of the wife the husband is to shepherd his wife with sacrificial love.

Based on the three dimensions of a husband-wife

relationship the wife is instructed to obey her husband in everything. The wife's assigned role places tremendous obligation on the husband before the Lord, the church and the community. The man abusing or neglecting this authority will ultimately end up under the disciplining hand of the living God.

Husbands who abuse and misuse the authority God has given them over their wives most often find themselves abusing the authority God has given them over their children. There was a time when wives were totally dependent upon their husbands for provisions. This is not the case today, in many instances. It is nonetheless true today that most husbands lay claim to their wives as their own private property as they have always done. It is out of this attitude of possessiveness and not the economic dependence of the wife that husbands today tend to abuse the authority they have with their wives.

The dependent nature of children is not just a matter of their childhood limitations; it is also a matter of their being perceived as the personal property of their parents. Thus, they do not have the authority to make demands or decisions. Children are one hundred percent dependent upon their parents for all of their needs, spiritually, emotionally and physically. In cases in which the parents refuse or are unwilling or unable to meet the total needs of the child/children they can become overwhelmed with defeat, lose heart, and become angry, bitter or rebellious.

Colossians 3:19 instructs the father not to provoke his children to wrath. Most Christian men no doubt accept this command from the Lord and seek to avoid provoking their children to wrath. Yet there are a large number of children in general and African American male children in particular who show an attitude of deep seated anger and wrath with corresponding behavior toward their father.

The source of much of the anger I have seen in black men originated in the context of their own homes in which they were provoked by their father. Thus I suggest that fathers must know and understand how to avoid provoking their children to wrath by their own abuse of authority.

The child who is the victim of abuse by his father is first and foremost an angry child and is in the process of becoming a young man in full blown rebellion against all authority. The angry young man is, to say the least, out of control.

Fathers who provoke their children to wrath are men who:

1. Rule their house with an iron fist;
2. Verbally and physically abuse their children and wife;
3. Dominate and demand;
4. Are impossible to satisfy in terms of their unrealistic expectations and demands;
5. Are emotionally detached from their wife and children;
6. Tend not to forgive offenses perceived or real; and
7. Possess low self-esteem.

When a son is in rebellion a common response by fathers is to put him out of the house under the label of tough love. This dismissal from the house is most often the final act after a period of verbal battering and sometimes physical battering of the young man. I suggest that in many instances the path to managing a son in rebellion begins with checking out the presence of authority in the home. First, this means determining if there is real authority in the home. Secondly, it must be determined who in the home has the authority. Is it the father, mother, or the children? Thirdly, if the father is not the authority figure, he must assume that responsibility. Fourth, the decision must be made as to how the authority in the home is to be applied.

In many instances fathers must be given counseling over an extended period of time. In due course they will get their heads together, assume proper responsibility as a father and learn how to use the authority. This means bringing the man to a point in his spiritual life that he not only understands his role as a father, but he also understands what it means to be a Spirit-filled father.

In the arena of male authority in the home, I often hear wives complain of having to provide sex on demand for their husband. Most men assume that sexual satisfaction is their right and is inherent in the concept of marriage. The basic idea being that it is the responsibility of the wife to avail herself to her husband for sex however frequent his libido may demand. For many men sexual satisfaction is understood to mean frequent sex on demand.

The problem of unfulfilled sexual desire on the part of the husband has several causes. Among the most frequently identified causes is the couple's lack of understanding of what sex means to each other. Men tend to think that sex means the same thing to their wife as it does to them. As I have mentioned earlier this is usually not the case although in some instances the meaning of sex to the wife parallels that of her husband.

Jasper and Sue were a happy couple and from all appearances they would remain happily married for a lifetime. However, this was not really the case. Sue was unhappy with Jasper's sexual interest and was not willing to settle for his low-level interest in sex.

As I met with Jasper and Sue, it became evident that Sue's interest in sex in terms of frequency far exceeded Jasper's. To cover his lack of interest Jasper involved himself in activities that kept him away from home most of the time. When he was home he was tired, otherwise involved or simply withdrawn.

In this marriage the wife's sexual interest seemed to parallel that of most men. Sue was the kind of woman whose sexual interest was more common among men. It was a serious struggle trying to motivate Jasper to give more attention to his wife in the area of intimacy. When all was said and done, the marriage between Jasper and Sue fell apart. It is my contention that the lack of sexual satisfaction in this case on the part of the wife contributed significantly to the demise of this marriage.

The problem of unfulfilled sexual desires in the context of marriage is also related to the premarital sexual experiences that each bring to the marriage. These premarital experiences include such things as sexual promiscuity, sexual abuse in the past, rape, impotence in the man, the negative impact of contraceptives, learned negative sexual attitudes, the negative impact of pornography, low self esteem, and poor health.

In more than a few marriages men were surprised by the discovery that marriage did not bring with it the anticipated total sexual satisfaction. As a means of attaining this desired satisfaction men tend to move to an attitude of sex on demand which does more to frustrate the situation than anything else.

To manage the problem of unfulfilled sexual desires the Spirit-filled husband should turn his attention to the Lord in prayer. He and his wife on their knees should pray that He lead them in developing the kind of companionship that will allow them to fully enter into this experience of sexual pleasure.

I have found it unwise for the Christian man and his wife to expose their sexual struggles to most counselors for a host of reasons, not the least of which is the potential for exploitation and the tendency of counselors to give unchristian advice to Christian couples. The better alternative is prayer and open communication combined with a healthy diet and exercise.

CHAPTER 14

CONFLICT RESOLUTION AND THE AFRICAN AMERICAN MALE

There is a lot written and otherwise communicated today about the angry African American male. The prevailing view is that black men are inherently violent prone. This notion of the violent black man is the birth child of the media, radio, TV and the printed page. The emergence of Urban Rap music and rappers like the late Biggie Smalls and the late Tupac Amaru Shakur with their violence-prone lyrics and lifestyle further affirmed in the minds of the larger society the belief that young violent black men are violent-prone.

Indeed violence dominates the African American Village today. It appears that there are more black men dying at the hands of black men today than there were in the heyday of the KKK. In view of the Black-on-Black crimes that are common in the Village and widely documented by many creditable sources inside and outside of the community, it is my contention that black men young and old need to be taught how to resolve conflicts in a constructive manner.

This need for lessons on constructive conflict resolution is not only evident from the Black on Black violence in the streets, it is equally evident in the context of many families. I recall with sadness the many times I have gone to the hospital and stood by the bedside of a wife who had been beaten by her husband over some minor or major disagreement.

Jack's wife finally informed him that she and the children were leaving him and that he would receive the divorce papers in a few days. When the divorce papers arrived, Jack became so enraged that he went to his wife's job, literally dragged her out of the office by the hair on her head, threw her into his car, drove to a deserted area, shot her several times and left her to die.

Jack's wife somehow survived the shooting, made her way to a major highway where a passing motorist stopped and took her to a hospital. She survived his rage and testified against him in court. Jack spent most of the rest of his life in prison for attempted murder.

Charles' wife had a habit of leaving him at least twice a year and remaining gone for about six weeks and then returning just as suddenly as she disappeared. It happened one day that she called home and told him that a man had forced her to get into his car and go with him to his house and would not let her leave. Enraged by the news, Charles rushed to the man's house to retrieve his wife.

Charles arrived at the man's house in a fit of anger. The man warned Charles not to attempt to come into his house. In his rage, Charles rushed towards the man's door, at which time the man shot him several times. When I arrived at the hospital emergency room where Charles had been rushed for treatment, the doctors informed me that he had died from several gunshots to his head. Charles and his wife had two young children who became victims of this tragic tangle of rage-filled relational state of pathology. Against the backdrop of similar experiences like this I, a pastor of more than thirty years in the African American community, set out to teach men how to deal with conflict in a constructive rather than a destructive manner.

When facing conflict, the issue the man must immediately decide is whether this is a situation in which his response will be to fight or to flee. When the decision is to stay and face the conflict men must be trained to *first* make every effort to **please or appease his opponent**. This response demands a level of selfless thinking and actions that are contrary to the natural tendency of most men, Christian or otherwise.

In the context of the family this means that the man acting as the head of the family *prioritizes the goals* of the family in the context of the *established value* system. This attitude empowers the husband-father with the necessary motivation to decide and act unselfishly. This usually means responding to the situation in a constructive manner, rather than reacting in a destructive way.

Secondly, in conflict resolution the Christian man must learn and develop the habit of making decisions a matter of **wisdom**.

Wisdom is the ability to distinguish between that which seems to be important but is not and that which seems to be unimportant but really is. This kind of wisdom comes from God and sometimes through the *spiritual giftedness* of fellow believers. It is wisdom that dictates to the man when he should fight and when the situation is such that he should flee.

Thirdly, the man who resolves conflict constructively learns well the art of **spiritual compromise** within the boundaries of his spiritual convictions. It is in the spirit of the will to compromise that a man evidences the will to meet his opponent half way. It is also the spirit of compromise that equips a man with the necessary positive attitude. The most difficult man to deal with in a conflict is one who must always have his way, no matter what the issue is. Men who refuse to compromise are men who have a tendency to abuse their authority.

Fourth, conflict resolution demands of the Christian man that he be adequately equipped with biblical knowledge with which he can **clearly define the biblical principles involved** in the issue over which conflict has arisen. This attitude is essential because it has the power to elevate the issue above the mundane to the level of the supernatural and biblical absolutes. This is a good time to consult with other mature believers about the situation or issue.

Fifth, among the more difficult habits for men to develop in the context of resolving conflicts is the habit of **praying with their opponent and then waiting for divine guidance** before deciding and acting on the issue. For most men their God-given authority as head of the wife empowers them to act in spite of the wife's disapproval. Learning to pray with the family about decisions when there is not disagreement will likely inspire the man to pray with his family when there is disagreement.

Sixth, the man who prays with his opponent about the issue at hand must learn to **expect to receive divine guidance** in and through the situation. This divine expectation infuses optimism into the environment of disagreement which keeps hope alive in the relationship. Destructive behavior in a relationship is often a reflection of hopeless desperation.

Seventh, conflict resolution means being willing to **tilt the decision towards the view of those who are most impacted by the decision.** So many times men are insensitive to the impact of their decisions on their wife and children. This insensitivity is evident in such decision as moving from one community or city to another, purchasing or not purchasing certain items for the house. It is good for husbands and fathers to strive to identify with those who are most affected by their attitudes and actions.

Finally, conflict resolutions demand the will to **study the issue** with those involved in the outcome. Men do well to learn how and when to say "I don't know" and then exercise the effort to find out more about the issue. First Corinthians 6:1ff is a good option at this point.

PREACHING TO THE WIND

The newspaper reported that four young African American men had been arrested for the murder of a local businessman. The incident had occurred nine months earlier in a suburb of the city of Dallas, Texas. According to the report, four young African American boys randomly chose a man they saw leaving his doctor's office. They carjacked his car, kidnapped him, took him to an isolated alley and for no apparent reason, killed him.

When I first heard the story I had no idea that I knew the parents of one of the young men. I learned later that these young men were simply riding around in one of their parents' car. They were bored, with nothing constructive to do, decided to go on a killing spree and did just that, taking a life. These were not young men who grew up poor. They had access to a quality education. They wore the best of clothes and drove their parents' new car. The missing ingredient in these boys' lives was not economics. The missing ingredient was an in-resident father.

The saddest thing about this entire affair is that all four of these African American young men were sons of African American mothers who thought they had done the best they could to bring them up right. Their mothers showed serious grief over what became of their sons.

Times are tough in our cities for people of all races, but it seems unduly tough for the African American family in general and the African American mother in particular. For the African American mother always seems to be the first one at the scene of a killing involving young African American males and the last one to leave the grave when there is a funeral. Young black men fourteen to twenty five years old are classified today as being high risk in terms of their potential for survival.

In this context of violence in the Village, the African American woman has emerged as the primary parent. Over half the children born in the African American community are born to women who have no in-resident husband. In addition, a growing number of our young teenage girls who have no intention of marrying are deciding to become teenage mothers for the sake of getting for themselves a sense of significance.

My conversations with a number of black women are most distressing and alarming. They seem to entertain the idea in their minds that the difficult time into which they were born and subsequently grew up, is justification for their not being able to become useful, productive parts of the Village in which they live.

Few women seem to have a sense of divine destiny about themselves in terms of why they were born in this time with all of its difficulties. The question is why did God decide to bring you "the African American woman" into the world at a time when being a Black adult female and mother in North America is so difficult? Why did God choose you to be a parent of an African American son in such a pathological social environment?

It is my contention that hard times and difficult circumstances are not excuses for giving up on life. God in His wisdom created you "the African American woman" and brought you into the world for just such a time as this.

In the Bible the Book of Esther focuses on a time in the history of the Jewish people when things were not going well for them. As a nation they had been taken captive and scattered about the civilized world of that day in various countries. In most of the countries in which the Jews lived they were hated and despised by the native folk. Such was their lot in that day.

Esther was born into that historical Jewish context of lost nationhood and destitute national, social, political and economic circumstances. In addition Esther's parents both died while she was still a child, making her an orphan.

Esther's dad had a brother who had a son named Mordecai. He was himself caught up in the captivity and oppression of the Jewish people of that day, but Mordecai was a godly man and as Esther's first cousin Mordecai took her in and raised her as his own daughter.

Even though Esther by divine providence was born into an oppressive social, economic and political context and soon became an orphan, God in His providence provided a surrogate parent for young Esther. In addition God gave Esther a comely face and a beautiful body. In the context of Esther's time it is her beautiful face and well built body that God used to position her to save her people from genocide.

While Esther's life circumstances were going from bad to worse in terms of her family and race, on the national scene the reigning king Ahasuerus and his beautiful queen Vashti were in the process of breaking up and getting a divorce. In that emerging national domestic scandal, God set the stage for Esther to be in position because of her beauty to save her people from total annihilation.

In the midst of her adversity, Esther was given by God the very attributes that she needed to become successful. God did not choose to give Esther parents who would live to raise her until she was an adult. Her parents died early. God did not give young Esther money with which to hire herself a nanny in place of her parents until she reached adulthood. He did not even give Esther a college education with which to compete with other young women of her generation on her way to success. To this young orphaned Jewess born into a context of national and personal difficulty, God gave the gift of an attractive face and a well-built body, and in this venue those virtues mattered most.

When the king decided to put away his queen Vashti and select a new queen, Esther's opportunity began to emerge. Mordecai knew that when it came to beauty which is what the king prized above all else, his cousin Esther had no equal in the kingdom.

African American women would do well to remind themselves that beauty of face and form are gifts from God and should be viewed and respected as such. I am of the opinion that far too few black women treat their bodies as a gift from God, a vessel to be used by Him to accomplish His will. The Bible says that our bodies are temples of God the Holy Spirit who lives in us, and we ought to glorify God with our bodies.

It seems as if today a growing number of black women on their way to the pinnacle of success have checked their femininity at the door of opportunity and taken on the aura of masculinity. I think it is important to say that it is still true that God has a place for African American women who are open to being used in high places. Her ability to use her knowledge of etiquette, graciousness, decorum and professionalism is an asset.

As Esther made her way up the ladder of success moving ever closer to becoming Queen to the king, she began to toy with the idea of forever keeping her Jewish nationality a secret. It was at this point that her cousin Mordecai reminded her that her rise to fame and fortune was not just a matter of her capitalizing on her beauty. He declared that God in His sovereign power had brought her to the kingdom for such a time as the one in which they lived.

It is good to be reminded that life as we live it from day to day is not a matter of luck, fate, destiny, or beauty. It is God Himself who establishes us in our day in order that He may use us to do His will. To African American women God says, *"For such a time as this you were brought to the kingdom."*

There was a time in our country when the local graveyard was filled with sons and daughters visiting the graves of their mothers on Mother's Day. It was possible to stand almost anywhere in the graveyard and watch sons cry for their mothers. Today things are different. Today the mothers of African American sons are filling the graveyards, visiting and crying over the grave sites of their lost sons.

For the African American woman these are difficult times to be a mother and yet it may well be a great time to be a black woman and mother in North America. For the providence of God still exists in these difficult times. The providence of God is innate in God's nature because of who He is. This divine virtue is rooted in God's sovereign power and thus His ability to make everything work out according to how He planned it.

In the context of the life of the young ethnic woman Esther who was born in a country that was not her own, grew up an orphan in a social and economic climate in which her people were under the threat of sudden annihilation, the providence of God moved her into the king's palace as queen. In this position young Queen Esther evidenced the faith and the courage to use her position of power to help the fate of her people.

These are days in which the African American woman is at the top of her game in many ways. Although the media focuses on those black women who are on welfare and having baby after baby as a means of increasing the amounts of their welfare checks, there are a number of Black women who are not on welfare and are not exploiting the system by means of prolific child bearing. For these black women this is their day.

The African American woman today holds the distinction of being the second highest wage earner in America, second only to White men. The Black woman is also in that group of women in America who are most satisfied with how they look and how they are built. African American mothers are given credit by their successful sons as being the "wind beneath their wings."

I believe that today's African American woman is more American than Scarlett O'Hara ever was in terms of her style, language, patriotism, courage and success. In this context of success and high achievement, let it be said to the African American woman "For if you remain silent at this time, relief and deliverance for the Jews (Black man) will arise from another place, but you and your father's house (Village) will perish. And who knows but that you have come to royal position for such a time as this?" (Esther 4:14).

This is not a time for Black women to be silent and indulge themselves in flattery of their beauty and success. These are days in which Black women in general, mothers and daughters in particular, must come to the aid of their sons, brothers and husbands with a relentless determination to lift them up toward the goal of equality and the zenith of success in this country.

CHAPTER 15

RECLAIMING THE VILLAGE

The idea of reclaiming the Village must begin with a primary focus on reaching the African American male with the gospel of Jesus Christ. Social, educational, economic and politically-based programs in and of themselves are woefully inadequate for the task. The evangelization of African American men requires a contextualized gospel message communicated in their language and relevant to their social, political and economic situation. The gospel must affirm the Black man as a man among men and be biblically and exegetically sound. In addition this preaching of the gospel must include Christian discipleship that is specifically designed for African American men many of whom are completely unchurched.

But what about the evident disdain many African American men have for the Black preacher and the Black church? Is it not illogical to think that the Black preacher and the Black church can affect the evangelization of black men. Not in their current state. To reach black men the Black preacher and the Black church must become more Black male user-friendly in leadership, program and style.

It is my contention that the White church and its clergy have essentially forfeited its right to minister in the Village to African American men. This forfeiture is due primarily to the alignment of the White evangelical church and clergy with the Republican Party which is perceived by the masses of black men to be anti-Black male. In addition, the history of the Village is filled with Eurocentric-based Christianity that promotes White male superiority and domination. Thus, among many black men Christianity Anglo style is seen as without spiritual integrity.

In response to the evident need to reclaim the Village, a number of White church denominations are targeting the inner cities as places to plant churches with a view to reclaiming the Village. These churches are most often short-lived not because the church planters are uncommitted to the mission but primarily because the focus of the churches is on women and children as opposed to men and boys. The New Testament model for evangelism and discipleship places the primary focus on men, not women and children. In addition the leadership for the Black community historically has come from the working and middle class Black communities, nc ; the inner city poor.

In recognition of the shortage of available African American men for marriage due to a variety of reasons such as drugs, AIDS and imprisonment, no one would suggest a magic spiritual formula such as the popular "name it and claim it" imperative as a means of reclaiming the Village. The better option is to focus on developing and implementing programs that will effectively mentor black men and boys from a bibliocentric and Afrocentric Christian perspective.

The mentoring of black men requires an African American male contextualized strategy because of the distinctive heritage and legacy that is in the social, economic, domestic, educational and political baggage of all African American men. This distinctive heritage and legacy include psychological brainwashing which is rooted in the historical stereotypes of black men as the wild savage, Black Sambo, the angry, violent Black man and the irresponsible functionally illiterate female-dominated Black man.

The biased historical stereotypes of black men cannot be disregarded any more than can the prior history of Jewish people and Native Americans. No other group of men in this country has the dubious distinction of being the descendants of a North American ethnicity conceived in the era of slavery except the black man. Thus those who effectively mentor black men must reject the idea that the history of the black man began in the Post-Civil Rights Era. I am reminded here of the words of the Apostle Paul "And to the Jews I became as a Jew, that I might win Jews; to those who are under the Law, as under the Law, though not being myself under the Law, that I might win those who are under the Law" (1 Cor. 9:20).

It is my contention that the ethnicity, culture, social and economic context combined with the historical experience of any people is relevant in any attempt at effective Christian evangelization. Thus the ministry to black men of necessity must be contextualized to fit both corporately and individually the African American male in his historical and contemporary spiritual, social, domestic, economic and political context.

We must not assume that identifying with the historical black experience is simply a matter of being of the same ethnicity and culture. Effective ministry to black men requires much more than black skin. The essence of identifying with black men is the ability to enter into their experience at the level of the head, heart and life perspectives. In other words, ministering to black men requires of the minister the ability to take biblical truth, wrap it in an Afrocentric theological package and serve it on the platter of liberation with the soothing drink of Black male masculinity.

To this end the effective minister to black men must be able to speak intelligently to the issue of the West African roots of African American men in the 1600's, with a view to providing *a balanced historical view of black men in America*. This means being able to set forth the historical facts that in the West African region from which the ancestors of today's African Americans were taken, the native African people of that day had their own organized religion, a strong tribal based government and a productive economy.

The focus of this discussion of 17th century West African history is to dispel the stereotypical idea that black men are the descendants of a distant wild and uncivilized subhuman species from the dark continent of Africa. The goal is to establish that black men like other men in this country came from noble human stock with intellect and skills with which to function effectively in a civilized society.

The ancestors of the modern day African American male who were brought to this country as slaves were primarily young men and boys. Few women were brought. Those young men and boys who survived the trans-Atlantic slave trip and the months of de-Africanization in the islands before they were finally brought to North America to work the cotton, tobacco and rice fields were physically the fittest of the fit. Any man that was not superior in physical stamina got sick and or just died and was discarded somewhere along the long horrid road to permanent enslavement in North America's closed system of institutionalized slavery.

There is little doubt that today's African American males

are descendants of the strongest of the strong and the fittest of the fit among the slave men of days past. This superior physical fitness is a primary contributing factor to the unwillingness of many black men to get regular physical check-up by doctors. They are descendants of men who seldom if ever got sick from anything.

Jawanza Kunjufu in his book *Adam Where Are You! Why Most Black Men Don't Go to Church* listed twenty-one responses that he got from conversations with black men. I am well aware that black men are seriously underrepresented in the Black church. Yet, I am of the opinion that the local Black church is still a viable option in reaching black men.

The increasing discussion among black men about the value and virtue of having all Black schools, communities, businesses and such suggest that increasingly black men are reasserting their commitment to Black nationalism. The growing consensus is that White men will never accept black men as their equal, no matter the credentials and accomplishments they acquire and bring to the social and economic table; thus they will stop trying to be accepted on the White men's terms.

The viability of the Black church in reaching black men is rooted in just such a consensus, namely, that Black culture is a viable and valuable culture on the level with other cultures. The black men will not abandon their culture in deference to being accepted by White men. The Black church is the mother and sustainer of Black culture.

Historically the Black church was the source from which black men in the context of slavery, segregation and political disenfranchisement, developed and maintained psychological liberation. In the Black church the Nigger, boy, Sambo and other degrading labels were shed and he who was a nobody became a significant somebody in the church. In other words the Black church gave black men a sense of identity as men who had value and skills like other men.

In the context of the Village, the Black church was the one and only institution that reflected the personhood of black men. It gave them opportunities to develop and practice leadership abilities. The Black church gave the Black man educational opportunities, so that their intellectual abilities could be developed and practiced. The local black church taught the black man how to manage his family to make it stable. In the church black men found economic opportunities that were not available to them in the larger community and finally the Black church provided a Village network through which black men could develop their businesses among their own people.

The positive historical influence of the Black church in the lives of black men must not be interpreted to mean that there are no barriers in the church's attempts to reach black men in the Village. One barrier the Black church must overcome is the black men's disdain for the Black preacher. This disdain that black men have for the Black preacher is inherent in the psychological brainwashing that has happened to black men. It is true that Black preachers are sometimes guilty of allowing their maleness to get in the way of their call to the ministry. It is also true that such occurrences are for the most part the exception and not the rule. The positive contributions of the Black preacher to the good of black men do not excuse them, but the good things do far outweigh the failures.

The negative attitudes of black men towards the Black preacher is perhaps more related to the assault of the media, entertainment and the majority race on the integrity of Black male leadership in general. In the South the White power structure traditionally killed off Black preachers as a means of controlling the Black community. When killing the Black preacher was not perceived to be the most advantageous means of negating the empowering influence of the Black church in the Black community, the larger community sought to kill his influence with claims of immorality and thievery.

The assault on the moral integrity of the late Dr. Martin Luther King Jr. by the FBI is a classic example of how America sought to protect White male superiority by planting seeds of distrust against the preacher in the minds of black men. The fact is the Black preacher emerges in the context of Black history as the most prominent and enduring figure the community ever produced. In the Village the Black preacher was often the man empowered to lead.

The second barrier to effectively reaching black men with the gospel of Jesus Christ is the legacy of Eurocentric theology. This theology tends to have an exegetical and expositional bias in favor of White male superiority. Its theological bias was the foundation upon which a number of White evangelical Bible colleges and seminaries based their decision not to admit African American men as students until recently. Eurocentric theology formed the foundation for the fundamentalist Christian institutions to support segregation and stand against the Civil Rights Movement. Today the Eurocentric theologians are heavily inclined towards a Republican conservative political, religious and social agenda that seems to have as its goal the reclaiming of America for Anglo male dominance. The unfortunate reality is that those African American men and women who are the most equipped biblically and theologically to reach black men are wed to the Eurocentric theological tradition and are thus ill equipped to effectively contextualize the gospel message to African American men.

The third barrier to reaching black men is the perception of the gospel as a message of passivity. Black men who in general tend to evidence a degree of aggressiveness in their self expression, sexuality, entertainment, worship, music, dance, athletics and overall lifestyles set themselves apart from other men in a positive way. Black men are less stoic emotionally than are European men. The gospel of Jesus Christ is generally preached to black men in words that cause it to be perceived as a message of restrictions, limitations, barriers and even oppression.

In a pastor's conference I once said that my son had both his ears pierced and wore earrings. In addition I said he also wore his brandname jeans low enough for his Calvin Klein drawers to be seen. Several pastors in that session reacted very negatively to my evident affirmation of my son's style of dress.

In response to those pastors' negative reaction, I said, "You evidently think that the fact that my son wears his pants low enough to show his shorts, his morality is as low as is his pants." Then I continued to show how my son wears his pants to reflect his African American male style; it in no way suggests that he has low morals. The fact is he is nineteen years old and still a virgin. His morals are strong; his style is contemporary.

The effective evangelization of black men requires a message that is relevant to the African American male context and liberating in its focus in terms of Black culture, spirit and lifestyle. This emphasis on preaching a liberating gospel as opposed to a gospel that is stoic, restrictive or passive in no way suggests that the content of the gospel is to be changed. It is the application of the gospel that must be adapted to the African American male context.

The fourth barrier that must be removed in order to minister effectively to black men through the local church is the dominance of black women in the church. The dominance of black women in the local Black church in many ways reflect a feminine bias in the message and ministry of the Black church. Many pastors evidence a lifestyle that suggests that they are physically weak and timid. The messages preached are all too often a message of the condemnation of the black male and an affirmation of the black female as she is.

In general, most churches have few roles for men in leadership, other than as pastor. Many Black churches have memberships numbering into the thousands with church facilities that cost millions of dollars and yet the pastor is the only man with any authority in the ministry. All too often in many Black churches the women are the ones who make the ministry work.

The effective pastor in the arena of Black male ministry is one who is himself a man among men in his physical fitness, discipline, lifestyle and overall self management. Second, he is a man who surrounds himself with men who are his equals in every way and even his superior in many. The effective pastor is a man with a vision and a burden for real men; yet he does not exclude women from leadership in the ministry.

In addition to removing the barriers that stand between African American men and the Black church that prohibits effective ministry to them, there is also the issue of the current state of black men in America. Keeping in mind that the goal is effective discipleship of black men, recall the unique legacy of black men in America and how that unique legacy of slavery, the residual affects of segregation and cultural brainwashing has contributed to the current fragmentation of black men.

Ellis Cose in his book *The Rage of a Privileged Class: Why Are Middle-Class Blacks Angry? Why Should America Care?* writes:

> In some respects, the answer to "Why are these people so angry?" is not at all simple. For one thing, none are angry all the time. A few deny their anger even though they show it. And while all African Americans, in one way or another, have spent their lives coping with racial demons, the impact has not been identical. Some have been beaten into an almost numb submission, into accepting that they will never reach the goals they once thought possible. Others have refused to accept that being black means being treated as a lesser human being, and they respond to each insult with furious indignation. A number wonder whether given the blessings they have received, they have any right to be angry

at all.[1]

To support his contention that middle class blacks are angry, Cose presents what he calls sketches that give a sense of why some middle class blacks are angry. He puts that anger in the context of the hopes, fears and insecurities that come with being human irrespective of race. The sketches include a Trade Association Vice President, a partner in a law firm, a journalist, a law professor and others. The underlying point is that black men are angry regardless of their social and economic status.

I contend that effective evangelization of black men must deal with their anger in a constructive manner. It cannot be disregarded nor can it be dismissed or hidden under the banner of racial reconciliation. Dealing with the anger of black men means dealing with the structures in our society both secular and sacred that provoke rage in black men.

In his book *Race Matters* Carnel West writes:

> To engage in a serious discussion of race in America, we must begin not with the problem of black people but with the flaws of American society—flaws rooted in historic inequalities and long-standing cultural stereotypes. How we set up the terms for discussing racial issues shapes our perception and response to these issues. As long as black people are viewed as a "them" the burden falls on black people to do all the "cultural" and "moral" work necessary for healthy race relations. The implication is that only certain Americans can define what it means to be American—and the rest must simply "fit in"
> The emergence of strong black-nationalist sentiments among blacks, especially among young people is a revolt against this sense of having to "fit in"...[2]

The second thing to be noted about the current state of black men is the economical oppression of the working class. This oppression is evident in the relationship between the economiccally disadvantaged and urban demographics. On average African American men earn less than 75 cents to every dollar earned by White men. This percentage difference in the per dollar income between black men and White men suggests that in America the wage system is biased in favor of White men. In addition the jobs that tend to offer higher pay, security and benefits for the whole family tend to be located in communities that are great distances from the African American community. Thus to the extent that either public transportation or the man's

---

[1]   Ellis Cose, *The Rage of a Privileged Class: Why Are Middle-Class Blacks Angry? Why Should America Care?* (Harper Collins Publishers), p. 13 .

[2]   Carnel West, *Race Matters* (Beacon Press, 1993), p. 3.

own private transportation is available to that extent he is either able or unable to access those companies that offer such jobs.

The social environment today is such that it tends to characterize the African American male stereotypically as violent prone regardless of his social or economic status. Carl T. Rowan in his book *The Coming Race War In America* writes:

> In 1995 we saw on several fronts the opening salvos of the race war that some refuse to believe possible. The O.J. Simpson trial unleashed racial passions deeper than any in America since the Civil War over slavery. It pitted not blacks against whites, but husbands against wives, sons against fathers. Here was a murder that couldn't possibly merit a national orgy of hatred and anger, compared with thousands of other murders that took place in the U.S. in 1994. But the sole issue of race—of a black celebrity allegedly killing his long-abused white wife and her white friend—grabbed Americans by their throats, their gonads, what was left of their brains, and immersed them in spasms of anger and hatred. The jury verdict provoked Americans to abandon the "presumption of innocence" to attack the jury system to acquiesce in barring the larger "public"- via TV cameras—from courtrooms, and to declare in effect that Simpson was a convict who could not be rich from selling his story the way almost everyone else associated with the case was doing.[3]

The fact is in contemporary America, African American men are stamped with the label of being violent prone and no amount of wealth or success can remove that stigma. This is a difficult label with which to live with as an African American male.

Finally the African American male today is increasingly positive towards Non-Christian religions. This growing positive attitude and spiritual commitment of black men today is reflective of the less than user friendly reputation of the Black church among black men. It is also reflective of the bad press that Black preachers receive in the media, entertainment industry, literature, etc.

What does it mean to disciple/mentor black men in the context of the eve of the twenty first century? I am speaking here of effectively discipling/mentoring black men. I use the word "effectively" to make a distinction between the many who minister to black men and those who genuinely make a spiritual difference in the lives of the men to whom they minister. I am making the same ministry distinction here that was made between the many Non-Jewish ministers who preached to the Gentiles in the days of the

[3]   Carl T. Rowan, *The Coming Race War in America* (CTR Production, 1996), p. 41.

Apostle Paul and the effective ministry of the Apostle Paul to the Gentiles.

The goal of an effective discipleship ministry to black men is to develop holistically each man in the group to his maximum potential in Jesus Christ. The heart of such a goal is a strategy of evangelism that has at its core *evangelism and discipleship*. There are a multitude of programs today that focus on the African American male. For the most part the majority of the programs are designed to aid the black man economically. The idea seems to be that to the extent that black men are able to make a living for themselves and their families to that extent they will become productive citizens. The truth is men who have jobs are more likely to be better husbands and fathers. In addition there is no end to the number of self-help books written to aid men in improving their lot economically, socially, etc. In the main these are good books and seem to be making a positive difference in black men across this country.

However, it is my contention that such programs do not meet the standards of what it means to effectively mentor black men. The primary deficiency in most programs focused on black men today is in the area of their spiritual life. There is a spiritual vacuum in the lives of black men that has not and cannot be filled with any degree of success byr non-Christian religions.

Thus those whose aim is to bring about permanent change in black men, while at the same time filling the spiritual vacuum in their lives, must proclaim the gospel of Jesus Christ without apology or compromise via the word and personal modeling. These men understand the fact that the African American male does not make a distinction between the message of the gospel and the messenger of the gospel as it relates to truth and relevance. Those men and women who do not or cannot live what they preach to black men need not apply for the mission of reaching black men.

I have suggested earlier that there is a relationship between a man's will to work and his walk with God. I have also suggested that one of the primary contributing factors to the success of the Nation of Islam in reaching black men is their ability to turn men into productive workers. Men who are members of the Nation of Islam are inclined to work regardless of the nature of the job, so long as it is constructive and productive. In general it cannot be said that Christianity promotes as a part of its indoctrination the will and the skill to work. In fact in many instances it seems as if the church is a haven for the unemployed.

Effective discipleship of black men must not only advocate the will and the skill to work. Of equal importance in discipling black men is sharpening the economic base in the Village. There is no institution in the Black community that is more equipped to promote economic development than the Black church. This promotion of economic development must include in its scope not only the Black community but also the White community.

This means investing in summer jobs for black youth. It means developing before and after school programs for Black children. It also means networking with churches, businesses and other groups in and outside the community with a view to sensitizing them to the economic needs of black men. Any attempt to reach black men today with the gospel of Jesus Christ must include job training, preparation for interviews, continuing education/training, counseling in maintaining current employment and obtaining advancement on the job. I have found it impossible to develop men in the faith without the man having a job in which he could express himself.

The discipling of black men includes teaching them family values. Teaching family values to black men requires an up close and personal exposure to family life God's style. There is a very real possibility that the men in a discipleship group have seldom if ever seen a man who loved his wife and children as much as he loved himself, a man who worked to provide for his wife and children and who sought to protect them from destructive forces in the community. This vacuum in the lives of many black men cannot be filled with theory and rhetoric; it must be explained by way of an actual family who is a model of what the Bible teaches.

Teaching family values means helping the men in a group develop a life vision that has at its core the mission the Lord Jesus Christ has for him as a single man or for him and his family if he is married. Developing a life vision takes the man into his past life map and works him through the potential path of his future life map. The goal is to aid the man in coming to grips with his new life in Christ in a holistic manner.

It is difficult to say, yet it must be said, that family values that focus on marriage as a permanent monogamous relationship between a man and his wife for a lifetime with their own children in their home can hardly be done by men who themselves are a contradiction of that very principle. This is not to suggest that the ministry can only be done by those who have a perfect marriage. There are no perfect marriages. It is to suggest that any effective ministry to black men by the Black church will require a modeling of the message.

For those who react to this true but hard statement regarding the moral prerequisites for mentoring black men in the area of family values, I must remind you that the Nation of Islam and other Non-Christian religions are far more effective than the Black church in reaching black men. It must be acknowledged that a portion of their success and our failure is due to the moral inequalities of the Black church and her leaders.

Finally discipling black men means teaching them communication skills. There is significant truth in the observation that black men are much better at initiating relationships than they are at developing and maintaining them. A primary contributing factor to the inability of black men to develop and maintain relationships especially in the context of his family is his underdeveloped communication skills. Communication skills are useful for their employment and not just for social enrichment. I have found it impossible to develop men in the faith without the man having a job in which he could express himself. Positive communication skills are more than a little bit important in a man's ability to secure and maintain a good job.

A primary contributing factor to the inability of black men to communicate is often their limited vocabulary and their misplaced anger. Invariably the wife and children of black men are objects of expressions of frustration and anger that is not really directed toward them but is related to other relationships and people in their lives.

The effective mentor teaches the man how to develop a vocabulary that says what he wants to say in a positive way. I should mention that often along the way, the mentor must tolerate, while being careful not to affirm, foul language and crude street slang. In the process the protégé by spending time with his mentor will learn by personal example how to express himself in a constructive manner without profanity. As it pertains to the anger felt by black men the effective mentor provides opportunity for venting in a constructive manner in a constructive environment.

It is my contention that reaching black men is a mission

which involves men reaching men with the gospel of Jesus Christ. The goal of the mission is to develop men holistically to their maximum potential. The strategy of such a goal is to build strong black men who are whole and complete in Christ Jesus. The focus here is on developing an effective approach to discipling/mentoring African American men as a means of reclaiming the Village. The effective minister among black men begins right where he is with the men that are around him. It does not really matter where one is, nor does it matter what the status or class of the men are who are around you. What matters most is that these men are viewed as God's opportunity for the discipler to build into their lives.

In the context of discipling black men the idea of social, economic and political homogeneity is essentially irrelevant. In general black men are not inclined to dismiss each other because of social class differences. However, they are very sensitive to any suggestion or implication that certain men are above them because of how they dress, what they drive or how they talk. Thus the mentor of black men must have the kind of spirit that travels well up and down the social ladder of class and status.

The second thing the mentor of black men must do is alter the church program as deemed necessary in order to facilitate the strategy. This alteration might include the order of services, dress in services, preaching style, small group meetings and transparent modeling of the ministry and the message.

"Come, follow me," Jesus said, "and I will make you fishers of men" (Matt. 4:19). These words of Jesus to His disciples is both the heart and the foundation that motivates the effective mentor and is the foundation upon which the whole mentoring process is built. It is not possible to mentor black men without having and demonstrating a genuine heart for them as men equal with you and at the same time perceived to be at a level to wish they can aspire. In other words black men tend to follow men who they perceive to be a cut above them in terms of their morals, discipline, commitment and general holiness.

The effective mentor of men must be prepared and willing to focus on the protégé's personal life in terms of his character and general attitude. The character of the man has to do with how sound he is in the area of his integrity. Character embodies such things as morality, honesty, truthfulness, integrity, genuineness. The character of a man influences everything he thinks and does. The effective mentor spends times listening and observing the protégé in the area of his character with a view to commending strengths and leading him to reorganize in areas that must be changed.

I have two adult daughters both of whom are married. I can recall many a young man who made their way into the fold of my mentorship for the expressed purpose of trying to get close to my daughters. Fortunately, I had the insight to see the flaws in the character of a number of them. I have had multitudes of experiences as a seminary professor in which a student sought to endear themselves to me as a means of obtaining scholarships, grades or some other special treatment. In most if not all of these instances, the problem they had was rooted in their character.

I recommended Ted to a church planting ministry because he had demonstrated as a student that he was an excellent exegete and expositor of the biblical text. In fact when Ted graduated he was voted the best expository preacher in the class.

The church planting organization to which I recommended Ted hired him based on my recommendation and the positive interviews they had with him. When Ted arrived in the city in which he was to plant his church he met with the local committee to discuss strategies for proceeding.

As Ted met with the local steering committee, he increasingly turned his focus away from the mission of planting the church to the matter of his salary which had already been settled with the church planting organization. Within the course of a few days, Ted had revealed himself to the local committee as a young man with a character flaw. He sought to manipulate the local committee to disregard the financial commitment they had made with the church planting organization and deal exclusively with him.

Ted illustrates the fact that seminary training, special gifts, and even mentoring in and of themselves do not necessarily deal with the character of the protégé. The single most effective means of dealing with the character of the protégé is by climbing into his personal life and digging your way to his character. Then it is necessary to deal with whatever you find.

The character of the protégé is most often but not always reflected in his attitude. Feigned actions may well camouflage a multitude of character flaws. Thus the mentor must be willing to invest the time necessary to expose the protégé to different situations, environments and circumstances with a view to moving beyond the surface attitude to the real disposition of the man.

To meet Ernest was to like him. There was no end to his willingness to be of assistance to anyone in need. He was heavily involved in the church and always available to open and close the buildings.

However, in time it became increasingly evident that there was something different about the attitude that we saw in church and small group meetings and the attitude his wife and children lived with at home. In time I learned that Ernest could actually slap his wife in the face and by the time he turned around he would have a pleasant smile on his face and speak with a voice that was warm and compassionate.

The effective mentor must make every effort to discern the attitude of the protégé so that he can determine for himself that what he sees is what others live with. It is not possible to challenge with a view to changing an attitude that the mentor is not aware exists.

The mentor must inquire into the professional life of the protégé. The public and private life of the protégé are fair game for the mentor. Thus how a man spend his time professionally in the job market as well as his personal habits must be open to the mentor.

It is not easy to access the private lives of African American men and so those who are privileged to be given access must treat such permission as a genuine privilege. This means managing well confidentiality, knowledge of his weaknesses, areas of vulnerability, fear, and limitations. To mishandle any one of these areas is to forfeit the right of access.

The mentor must be personable yet demanding. It is important to note here that a number of men who evidence a desire to mentor black men have yet to understand that African American men tend to be personable. They prefer to deal up close and personal with those whom they trust. Black men are suspicious of touchy male types, preferring to deal with men who remember their names and can speak their language.

In this context the mentor does well to develop an open door policy in terms of the access his protégé have to him. An open door policy means that he is always available for a quick hello or a brief word of success, struggle or failure. Black men most often prefer not to be left waiting to see their mentor. Open access is a sign of their importance and an affirmation of their personal significance.

It is my contention that the mentoring of black men requires of the mentor that he give unconditional access to his protégé. Yet his time with the protégé must always be structured in a way that promotes mutual respect and personal fellowship. In other words, in the minds of black men the fact that you care is far more important than what you say. Caring means that you are there for him when he needs you to be there.

In the context of giving the protégé unconditional access to him, the mentor must demand of his protégé accountability. This accountability must be firm and consistent, yet sprinkled with flexibility so that the relationship between the mentor and his protégé is not strained, but stable and strong.

The absence of accountability between mentor and protégé will most often spoil the relationship in time. The scope of the areas of accountability includes morality, personal habits, integrity, spiritual development, family, job and other relationships. In the area of accountability the focus is not just a matter of performance but also attitude, diligence, quality, etc.

I well remember the day when Tim came into my office looking a bit guilty but not at all willing to admit that he had done anything wrong. Tim was a seminary student and had developed a relationship with a young woman in the church and they were talking of getting married.

It happened one night that Tim and his fiancee got involved in heavy petting and in the process they decided that it would be alright for Tim to lay on top of her, so they did that. Then they decided that it was OK for them to strip down to their underwear and lay again in the same position. They did that too. In time Tim and his girlfriend were lying skin to skin but they were not actually having intercourse.

When Tim came to see me it was because the young woman had felt guilty about the experience and told a fellow believer. When I confronted Tim about the situation he was not at all pleased that I felt the liberty to inquire into his personal life. He was even less pleased with the idea that I held him accountable for his behavior. You see Tim was the kind of young minister who demanded everything of others while demanding far less of himself. In our relationship Tim's access to me was unconditional with a strong strand of accountability built in.

The effective minister among African American men must demonstrate the will and the willingness to face the challenges of the mentoring process. Inherent in the challenge of reaching black men is the willingness to invest the necessary time and interest to develop the kind of relationship with the men to whom you minister that is both felt and perceived by them as a loving relationship. It is the love that flows between the mentor and the protégé that provides the environment in which truth can be spoken.

Mentoring requires a relational context in which truth can be spoken and received in a way that contributes to the holistic spiritual growth of the protégé. The goal of mentoring is to develop men who are committed to following the Lord Jesus Christ. The goal is not to develop men who are only committed to following you. The protégé must grow up in Christ as His disciples, not the mentor's disciples.

In the process of mentoring the mentor must demonstrate the will to inquire into the sensitive areas of the protégé's life. This means invading and exploring the protégé's *morality, marriage, money and ministry.*

In a recent interview with a prospective seminary student I asked the young man if he were married. To which he quickly responded, "No, I am not." Then I asked his age. "I am thirty years old," he replied and he added, "I have never been married."

Then I asked, "How do you manage your sex drive and please do not tell me that you do not have sexual desires."

The young man was stunned by my question and for a while he did not answer. Then he replied, "Not well."

"What do you mean?" I inquired.

"Well," he said, "I am sexually active but I try to keep it to a minimum."

"How do you square your infrequent practice of immorality with what you preach?" I asked.

"I cannot," he replied.

As I finished the interview with this young man I said to him, "I think you would make a good seminary student. You might even prove to be a brilliant student. However, if you really wish to receive my affirmation you must first learn to manage your sex drive with sanctification and honor for such is the will of God for you." It is my contention that few things say as much about a man in terms of his character and his potential for building lasting relationships and doing effective ministry as does the man's morality.

The relationship a man has with his wife provides a window into his character. Thus the mentor must inquire into the quality of the relationship a man has with his wife and children. I am reminded here of a young man with whom I spoke regarding his desire to do doctoral work at the seminary. In the discussion, I suggested to him that he must be careful not to place such high priority on obtaining his doctorate that he sacrificed his relationship with his wife and children.

This young man in a few years found himself in divorce court. He lost his wife and children. The strange thing about this situation was the positive testimony given of him by the members of the White church he attended and served. These White Christians raved about this young man and thought his wife was an awful woman. I met with the wife of this student and discovered that he had been a very poor husband to his wife in the areas of provision, access and positive involvement in their lives. The wife had for years been the primary wage earner. This man was seriously under-motivated.

The reason his fellow White Christians loved him was because they did not know him as a husband and as a father. Their admiration for him was strictly academic. This same man demonstrated the second area of sensitivity that must be inquired into. That is the area of money. This young postgraduate student was unwilling to work for a living. He seemed to have been of the opinion that he was entitled to money that others earned.

Deficiencies in the areas of morality, marriage and money most often suggest that the character of the man is flawed. The mentor must understand that unless and until he is able to work in these sensitive areas of his protégé's life, he is likely not to be effective. Thus I suggest that in facing the challenge of inquiring into the sensitive areas of the life of the protégé, the mentor must demonstrate the will to confront when necessary.

The effective mentor of black men must demonstrate the will and the willingness to **challenge negative attitude, habits and hang ups that may be a part of the protégé's life-style.** It has been my experience to find no small number of men involved often to the point of addiction with pornography. This involvement tends to develop in the man a host of negatives, including lust, masturbation and often immorality. Thus the mentor must challenge these attitudes and habits with a view to affecting change in the man.

In more than a few cases the involvement of men in pornography is the fruit of the kind of entertainment they are exposed to and in which they participate. Thus the entertainment of the protégé is an area to which the mentor must concern himself. I am reminded of a young couple who called me to see if I thought it was OK for them to watch a pornographic movie with another Christian couple as a means of enhancing their sex life. It can be said of a number of Christian men that X-rated movies are high on their list of entertainment.

The personal habits of the protégé must not escape the attention of the mentor. It is not uncommon for fine Christian men to drink sociably and even use drugs as a means of entertainment of relaxation. These are negative habits that must be challenged by the mentor with a view to affecting change.

High on the list of that which must be challenged in the life of the protégé by the mentor are the hang-ups that are in the baggage of the protégé. These hang-ups include superstitions, nudity, being hugged by another man, etc.

In the context of effective ministry among black men one will soon discover that forgiveness is not among the attitudes and actions frequently practiced. It is most difficult for most black men to forgive those who hurt them deeply. This unwillingness to forgive offenses against them means that it is difficult for black men to believe that their offenses are easily forgiven by the Lord. In the main the offending black man will often as an act of repentance do something special for the one he has offended and retain in his mind the offense he has committed against that person.

Jasper and William were good friends and they both were married. It happened along the way that Jasper and William's wife Sue became lovers. These two Christian families often went out together and enjoyed themselves. Neither William nor Jasper's wife had any idea that their mates were lovers.

It happened one day that Jasper called William's house and without her knowing it William listened in on the conversation between his wife and Jasper. When Jasper finished talking to William's wife it was clear to William that his wife and his friend were cheating. Hurt and angered by what he had learned about his wife and friend, William went to Jasper's house and found him home alone. William talked his friend Jasper into letting him handcuff him to a chair and then he proceeded to beat him literally into a pulp.

In time Jasper recovered from the severe beating he received from his friend but both their families ended in divorce and they were never friends again. Jasper was sorry for what he had done to his friend William, but felt he could never have forgiven him.

The one thing above all else that black men find unforgivable is infidelity. Sexual immorality on the part of the wife of an African American man is the unpardonable sin. Yes, he does expect his wife to forgive him of his infidelity but he will not forgive her and most often he will not remain married to her.

The mentor of African American men must face the challenge of teaching his protégé how to manage failure constructively. In the lives of black men failure in any one area tends to infer failure in all other areas of the man's life. Thus the mentor must strive to aid the protégé in first putting the failure in perspective and then while giving compassionate yet stern attention to the man's fragile self-esteem, nurture him back to self confidence and courage.

After fifteen years Bill lost his job and for the first time in his young life he found himself unable to find employment. In spite of Bill's college credentials and his years of experience in his professional field his inability to get a job in time began to eat away at his self-confidence. As his mentor, I realized that above all else Bill needed a job.

As a means of helping Bill manage the loss of his job and his inability to find new employment, I met with him for prayer and fellowship every week. In addition, I worked with his wife in finding ways to boost his male ego. I also found it necessary to give Bill a job in the ministry not so much because he needed the money but because he needed meaningful work.

The effective mentor of black men must understand the role of integrity in the mentoring process. Ephesians 6:14 instructs the believer to stand firm with the belt of truth buckled around the waist, with the breastplate of righteousness in place. The breastplate of the Roman soldier of years past was designed to cover both the front and the back of the soldier.

I am reminded here of Proverbs 4:23 where we are told to watch over our heart, for out of it flows the issues of life. I am also reminded of the words of Jesus that "where your treasure is there your heart will be also" (Matt. 6:21). Jeremiah 17:9 says, "The heart is the most deceitful thing there is and desperately wicked. No one can really know how bad it is!" It is out of the heart that the mouth speaks. I take it that in living and serving the Lord, being involved as we are in a life and death struggle with the powers of evil in this evil day, we must dress up with the kind of spiritual armor that protects our heart from the schemes of the Evil one.

In the mentoring process the mentor must realize that it is not just a matter of being shielded from the assault of the enemy, the heart must be kept from exposing itself to the schemes of the Devil. I am saying that the heart of the believer is not all loyal to the cause of Christ and thus it must be protected from the schemes of the Devil that will induce it to commit treason against the kingdom of heaven.

This piece of heart protecting equipment is called "the breastplate of righteousness." I take it that the focus is on the content of this breastplate, namely righteousness. The breastplate of righteousness is designed to protect the heart of the believer from the deceitful schemes of the Devil.

It is the role of spiritual integrity to establish in the protégé a life pattern of consistency so that attitudes, performance, honesty and morality are predictable. The virtue of consistency is best caught from the mentor by the protégé by way of the transparent attitude, motivation and behavior of the mentor.

In the context of being transparent the mentor does well to avoid flaunting his strengths. Mentors who flaunt their strengths not only give the impression of being arrogant and proud, but they tend to attract men to their discipleship group who are proud and arrogant and thus in time prove to be poor examples of godliness.

Of equal importance for the mentor of black men is his avoidance of concealing or flaunting his weaknesses. It is most often the case that black men will interpret a mentor who conceals his weakness as a hypocrite and reject him outright later. He will view the mentor who flaunts his weakness as insecure and unstable and thus not worthy of trust.

In the context of strengths and weaknesses the mentor of black men must strive to gain and maintain the respect of the men who he mentors. He must work at becoming both their friend and their hero. He cannot help them if he gives the impression that he is in the same barrel and at the same level in the barrel as they are. Black men are inclined to follow strong Black leaders.

I am not suggesting that the mentor of black men fake it; for indeed, he must be for real. He cannot risk being a phony for he will be tested and found out. In the context of being tested by black men I am reminded of the early years of my ministry. At the time I was in my early twenties and even though I was married, the men could not believe that my moral convictions were all that I said that they were. So they set me up by sending a very beautiful woman in for counseling. In short order this young woman supposedly had fallen madly in love with me. I quickly referred her to someone else for counseling.

Even today as a man nearly sixty years old I find men watching me to see if I am watching the butt, bust and legs of women as they pass by. Men watch my eyes and they pay close attention to the women who hug me and whose embrace I return. The mentor of black men must understand the bottomline. They are not easily convinced that you will not play given half a chance.

It is important that the mentor of men be open about his struggles, failures, setbacks and successes. However the openness should always reflect the reality of God's involvement in the struggle as sustainer and deliverer. Mentors must avoid giving the impression that the Christian life is one long struggle with few victories. Mentors must be overcomers and their struggles should reflect that attitude.

It is my contention that men who mentor men must be men who model manhood God's style. Mentoring men requires more than aspiration; it requires genuine spiritual preparation for the task. To this end the mentor of black men must be willing to fully invest themselves in their protégé's life. "We loved you so much that we were delighted to share with you not only the gospel of God but our lives as well, because you had become so dear to us" (1 Thess. 2:8). In the religious context of the idolatrous Thessalonians a primary tool of evangelism and discipleship for the Apostle Paul and his missionary team was their will to invest themselves in the people with the kind of love and tenderness that a mother shows for her infant child. I take it that in discipling the mentor must not only love what he does but he must love people. For you see the very foundation upon which modeling in mentoring is built is genuine love for people.

I recall walking along the beach of the Mediterranean Sea in Tel Aviv, Israel among some of the most beautiful women I had ever seen. In addition to being very beautiful the women on that beach on that day for the most part wore see-through bikini swimwear. My wife was not with me on that trip; as a matter of fact, she was back in the States pregnant with our youngest child.

In that seductive moral context, it was not so much my testimony that restrained my lust as I am sure I could have concealed any indiscretions on that beach half a world away from my abode and place of ministry. What I could not escape and the thing that truly restrained my thoughts, attitude and behavior was my love for my wife, even though she was half a world away. I loved her so much that any thought of infidelity was inconceivable.

So it must be with men who mentor men. Their love for the protégé must be so strong that they are restrained from doing even those things that have the appearance of evil for the sake of avoiding being a hindrance to them.

"Do not be anxious about anything, but in everything, by prayer and petition, with thanksgiving, present your requests to God" (Phil. 4:6). In addition to modeling love and commitment to and for the protégé, the mentor of men must model a life of dependent trust in the living Lord Jesus Christ.

The mentor of men must be willing to risk everything as a model of faith and dependence upon God. This does not means acting foolishly; it simply means that faith is never visible unless and until all is at risk. The mentor who hides behind the shield of conservatism in hope that he will not be exposed as one who has little faith, will not likely develop strong men. Thus the mentor of men must model faith and trust in God.

"Therefore I urge you to imitate me" (1 Cor. 4:16). A popular basketball player was heard to say on TV when questioned about his being a model for other young aspiring athletes to say, "I am not nobody's model." Such an attitude is not at all possible for the mentor of men. It is my contention that in mentoring men with a view to developing strong mature Christian men in the Village only those who can live it can do it (1 Cor. 2:1).

APPENDIX A

I n his book *We Have Been Believers,* James H. Evens Jr. gives an excellent analysis of the late Dr. Benjamin Mays' historic work *The Negro's God.* Dr. Mays had examined in depth the idea of God in the African American experience. Mays sought to show how the idea of God is related to the social situation in which African-Americans found themselves. In this work, he analyzed "Mass" and "Classic" literature of African Americans, the former term referring to sermons, spirituals, and Sunday School literature, while the latter term refer to formal addresses, treaties, poetry, and fiction. Mays examined this literature during three distinct chronological periods: 1760-1865, the Civil War period to 1914, and 1914-1937. He concludes from his study that there were three basic attitudes toward God present among African-Americans. The first was God as *compensatory,* referring to those ideas of God that promised divine recompense for earthly suffering; the second was God as *a support for social adjustment,* referring to those ideas of God that served as "apologia" for the liberation struggle; and the third was the notion that God was *no longer a useful instrument"*in the African-American quest for justice and freedom.

Evans considers Mays' work important insofar as it shows that notions of God among black folk are in some ways grounded in their experiences. His work is certainly important and must be granted considerable thought by those who would reflect on the significance of God for black existence, particularly black male existence. It must be remembered too that May's work is also significant for the black female's existence.

It is important, however, to qualify Mays' work. Mays suggests that the relationship between ideas/notions of God and the social experiential location of the one who has those ideas/notions is unidirectional. That is to say Mays seems to suggest that the social-experiential reality is more fundamentally theologically determinative than any other considerations. Though I cannot fully address this assumption now, I do believe it to be problematic.

The importance of May's work lies in the fact that he shows that black folk have tended to apply a sociological interpretive scheme to religion, Christianity in particular. In this respect, the embodied theology was probably more in keeping with the covenantal reality of Jesus Christ as biblically witnessed to through most Eurocentric systematic theological articulations. Appropriation of May's work would do well to be both theological and pastoral. It is possible to interpret black existence in America as the quest to recover true community in light of their experience in America that regarded blacks as three-fifths human. A theological appropriation must articulate a Christological account to be truly human and not merely assume that it is self evident what that means. Social quests for liberation are all determinative in this regard. This is my primary critique of Mays.

He assumes the correctness of the black search for identity to be rooted ultimately in a theistical Christological account of the human. A pastoral appropriation of Mays' work requires modification of the individualistic emphasis of most evangelical sermonizing if it is to be truly liberative black evangelical preaching.

It is the third period of Mays' study and the idea of God that emerged in that period that I find most interesting and relevant to the focus on "Reclaiming the Village" of the African American Community today. Again I quote James Evans:

> In the third period in the classical literature, from 1914 to 1937, the central problematic is relating the idea of God to the need for self acceptance for black people. The need for cultural integrity and the Washingtonian plea for economic self-reliance called into question the role of an all-powerful God whose sovereign presence blunted and devalued any human achievement on the part of African-Americans. Thus for some people it became necessary to reject the traditional idea of God in order to accept themselves as full, free and competent human beings.[1]

Any study of African American history will confirm the study of Dr. Mays that the social, economic, political and family context of African American people was always interwoven in their God-focused belief system. The African American concept of God historically was never separate and apart from the context in which they lived. The very heart and soul of Black theology is this historical fact of black church history.

[1] James H. Evans Jr., *We Have Been Believers: An African American Systematic Theology* (Minneapolis, MN: Fortress Press, 1992), pp. 58, 61.

During the period 1914–1937, the quest for freedom and equality for African Americans was stronger than ever before. The demand for autonomy and cultural integrity was an unwavering quest for African Americans. State's Rights was on the rise and segregation was the law in the South. White supremacy and mob rule was the prevailing reality. In that context, according to Mays, for a number of Black people the traditional beliefs about God was no longer relevant because it seemed to put God on the side of the White oppressors and thus curtailed any affirmation of Black achievement.

There is in my view a similar social, political, economic and religious situation in which African Americans live today. States Rights are on the rise. Social programs are being abandoned and, in the minds of a number of black men there seems to be a dichotomy between the traditional ideas and beliefs about God and their quest for access and equality. In the minds of a number of young African American males the God of the Bible is pro-European and anti-Afrocentric.

The problem that a number of black men increasingly have with Christianity today is that is seems often to affirm inequality and injustice in favor of White men. It is often the expressed perception of Black men that the Christian's God is in conflict with their quest for wholeness. There is also the perception that the Christian God, unlike the Muslim god, is in accord with the masters of the oppressive context in which they live. Thus for a number of black men in order to become genuinely liberated and move towards real equality and access in American society they must abandon the traditional ideas of God. For the upper middle class Black males this means embracing the new age theological idea of god and for the less affluent it means embracing the god of the Nation of Islam.

The value of Dr. Mays' work is in his focus on the relationship between the context in which African Americans live and their ideas of God. This experience-based faith is with us to this very day. Thus in speaking to the issue of developing unfragmented men as a primary means of "Reclaiming The Village," serious consideration must be given to the marriage in the minds of African American men between their idea of God and their experience as black men in America. To the extent that the traditional view of God emerges as irrelevant or in conflict with their struggle to obviate their life situation to that extent black men will find themselves in search of a god who is relevant to their situation.

In the history of evangelical Christianity it must be noted that with few if any exceptions Black Christian leaders who did not affirm the status quo of social, political and economic life situations of Black people in America were labeled as non-Christian. Men who were civil rights leaders such as Dr. Martin Luther King Jr. and Rev. Jesse Jackson were easily classified as Non-Christian by evangelical Christians. Political activists such as County Commissioner John Wiley Price in Dallas, Texas, are regarded as unsaved by the Dallas evangelical community in spite of the fact that Mr. Price is a committed member of a local church and is seriously involved in the ministry of his church.

I have sought to make the argument that as a means of "Reclaiming the Village" there is a need to develop unfragmented men. I have suggested that God has given in the Bible a pattern for developing whole men. The pattern for developing unfragmented men can be accomplished by means of a process that is also biblically based, but not without the will to face certain challenges inherent in the process.

In this mission of "Reclaiming the Village" the Black church emerges as the primary tool. In responding to the inherited mandate to lead in "Reclaiming the Village" the Black church must of necessity become more user-friendly to the African American male. To this end the Black evangelical church must rethink the scope and the focus of its message and ministry. James Harris writes:

> Modern conservative evangelicalism emphasizes the moral value of maintaining and perpetuating the status quo rather than demanding that extant cultural, social and political practices and institutions be transformed. The sermons, writings and other forms of propaganda advocated by evangelicals have major political implications for those who subsist at the bottom of the social and economic pecking order, and whose lives require the transformation of the social system and its rules. The modern evangelical movement seeks to obviate the Civil Rights movement and its philosophy of liberation and social change. However, this current practice does not coincide with the gospel message and its example of freedom and liberation for the individual and society.[2]

Historically the periods of significant growth in black church membership has been those times when the church was extensively and significantly involved in the struggles of the people. Thus I suggest that to the extent that the church again

---

[2] James H. Harris, *Pastoral Theology: A Black Church Perspective* (Minneapolis, MN: Fortress Press, 1991), pp. 8-9.

involves itself in a significant way in the struggles of the modern day African American male with a view to reaching him as a means of "Reclaiming the Village," to that extent the church will be an effective tool in "Reclaiming the Village."

To suggest that the evangelical church must rethink the focus and scope of the ministry is not to suggest that the substance of the message be changed. The transformation of the "Village" must begin in the heart of the African American man. Spiritual transformation involves being born again by means of faith in the death, burial and resurrection of Christ, in the positional reality of being baptized into the body of Christ and the experience of having undeniable assurance that Jesus Christ has come to live in your heart.

It is my contention that the process of developing unfragmented men as a means of "Reclaiming the Village" begins with the evangelization and discipleship of African American men. This focus on African American men as a means of transforming the "Village" is a significant change from the current focus and emphasis of evangelism in today. The church today tends to aim its evangelistic efforts at the women and children in the Village. I am not suggesting that women and children be neglected or disregarded in contemporary evangelism; I am simply suggesting that the biblical model for transforming communities begin with spiritually transformed men.

The church that is an effective tool in the mission of reclaiming the "Village" must be a church with a liberation ministry focus.

> Liberation churches are cognizant of the major concerns affecting the African American community. Most national surveys document that the major problems are crime, unemployment, drugs, teen pregnancy, education, self-hatred, single parenting and healthy. Liberation churches are addressing these issues and to many men want to make the church monolithic and do not acknowledge that there are some churches patrolling the streets and providing employment ministries, drug counseling, classes on teen sexuality, tutoring, test-taking skills and scholarship for college. They offer self-esteem and cultural program to reduce and eliminate self-hatred and workshops on nutrition and provide free medical examinations.[3]

In the mission of "Reclaiming the Village" the goal is to develop unfragmented men. The primary tool in this mission is

---

[3] Jawanza Kunjufu, *Adam, Where Are You!: Why Most Men Don't Go To Church?* (1994), p. 84.

the Black church, the central message in the mission is the gospel of Jesus Christ. The primary focus in the mission is the family.

It was Daniel P. Moynihan who suggested that the family structure of lower class Blacks was highly unstable and in many urban centers approaching complete breakdown. This report was written during the Nixon administration in the 1960's. According to Moynihan, the Black family was in a state of pathology. Listed among the causes of this pathology was slavery, reconstruction, urbanization, unemployment and poverty and the wage system.

My response to the Moynihan Report at the time was very negative like most of my associates. However, in the years that have come and gone since that report I have often wondered what it was that Mr. Moynihan knew that empowered him to speak prophetically to the future of the Black family in America.

In the past thirty years, the Black family has evidenced serious signs of pathology in terms of its structure. It is my contention that the pathology of the Black family became the pathology of the "Village." In this context it is interesting to note that during the time when the Black family has been in decline the Black church has experienced profound economic growth, evidenced by the building programs of churches even in the poorest communities. It seems that during the times that both the family and the community are in decline, the church in the community stands strong economically.

It is my contention that the mission of reclaiming the "Village" must focus on rebuilding the infrastructure of the family. The idea is that since the decline of the family led to the decline in the community as the church stood idle, it seems logical that rebuilding the family will recapture the community.

In reality the mission of "Reclaiming the Village" requires the involvement of a strong evangelical church that is equipped to project a ministry of liberation. This ministry must have a sound message that is Christocentric in focus and contextualized to fit the life situation of the African American Community.

y Dad:

As a child you walked around
  In muddy boots or shoes,
Hunting in the woods or
  Listening to Muddy Waters sing the blues.
From dusk to dawn you wore those muddy shoes,
  Because at that time
Which shoes to wear wasn't an option for you.

So a lot of people didn't want
  Your dirty old dust raggedy muddy shoes.
As a child
  You played, worked, ran and cried
In those muddy shoes,
  Not knowing what the future had in store for you.

I can visualize your big head and little body
  Slouching around East Carroll Parish
In those muddy shoes,
  Wondering about what God had in store for you.

Now as a man
  Your once muddy shoes have a lustrous shine;
And your life now compared to your life in the past
  Is more than fine.
Now you work instead of hunt
  And listen to Shirley Caesar instead of the blues.
Now no matter what time it is
  You can choose your shoes;
And now a lot of people would love to wear
    Your "Muddy Shoes."

— Eddie B. Lane II

Books by the author in
The African American Christian Family Series,
**available from Black Family Press*:*

The African American Christian Family:
Strenghtening the Bonds that Tie (1994)

The African American Christian Single:
Maintaining a Clean Life in a Dirty World (1995)

The African American Christian Family:
Building Lasting Relationships (1996)

The African American Christian Parent:
Parenting in the Context of a Spiritual Deficit (1997)

The African American Christian Man:
Reclaiming the Village (1998)